CONSTRUCTING GIRLHOOD THROUGH THE PERIODICAL PRESS, 1850–1915

Ashgate Studies in Childhood, 1700 to the Present

Series Editor: Claudia Nelson, Texas A&M University, USA

This series recognizes and supports innovative work on the child and on literature for children and adolescents that informs teaching and engages with current and emerging debates in the field. Proposals are welcome for interdisciplinary and comparative studies by humanities scholars working in a variety of fields, including literature; book history, periodicals history, and print culture and the sociology of texts; theater, film, musicology, and performance studies; history, including the history of education; gender studies; art history and visual culture; cultural studies; and religion.

Topics might include, among other possibilities, how concepts and representations of the child have changed in response to adult concerns; postcolonial and transnational perspectives; "domestic imperialism" and the acculturation of the young within and across class and ethnic lines; the commercialization of childhood and children's bodies; views of young people as consumers and/or originators of culture; the child and religious discourse; children's and adolescents' self-representations; and adults' recollections of childhood.

Also in the series

The Idea of Nature in Disney Animation
From Snow White *to* WALL-E
David Whitley

Genre, Reception, and Adaptation in the "Twilight" Series
Edited by Anne Morey

The Orphan in Eighteenth-Century Law and Literature
Estate, Blood, and Body
Cheryl L. Nixon

History and the Construction of the Child in Early British Children's Literature
Jackie C. Horne

Heroism in the Harry Potter Series
Edited by Katrin Berndt and Lena Steveker

Constructing Girlhood through the Periodical Press, 1850–1915

KRISTINE MORUZI
University of Alberta, Canada

Routledge
Taylor & Francis Group

LONDON AND NEW YORK

First published 2012 by Ashgate Publishing

2 Park Square, Milton Park, Abingdon, Oxon OX14 4RN
711 Third Avenue, New York, NY 10017, USA

Routledge is an imprint of the Taylor & Francis Group, an informa business

First issued in paperback 2016

British Library Cataloguing in Publication Data
Moruzi, Kristine.
   Constructing girlhood through the periodical press, 1850–1915. – (Ashgate studies in childhood, 1700 to the present)
   1. Youths' periodicals – Great Britain – History – 19th century. 2. Youths' periodicals – Great Britain – History – 20th century. 3. Girls – Conduct of life – Periodicals. 4. Journalism – Social aspects – Great Britain – History – 19th century. 5. Journalism – Social aspects – Great Britain – History – 20th century. 6. Girls – Great Britain – Social conditions – 19th century – Sources. 7. Girls – Great Britain – Social conditions – 20th century – Sources.
   I. Title II. Series
   070.4'8327'0941'09034-dc23

Library of Congress Cataloging-in-Publication Data
Moruzi, Kristine.
   Constructing girlhood through the periodical press, 1850–1915 / by Kristine Moruzi.
      pages cm. — (Ashgate studies in childhood, 1700 to the present)
   Includes bibliographical references and index.
   ISBN 978-1-4094-2266-2 (hardcover)
   1. Children's periodicals, English—History. 2. Youth's periodicals—Great Britain—History. 3. Girls—Books and reading—Great Britain—History. 4. Young women—Books and reading—Great Britain—History. 5. Girls—Great Britain—Social life and customs—19th century. 6. Young women—Great Britain—Social life and customs—19th century. 7. Girls—Great Britain—Social life and customs—20th century. 8. Young women—Great Britain—Social life and customs—20th century. I. Title.
   PN5124.J8M67 2012
   052.0835'2—dc23

                                                                              2012003108

ISBN: 978-1-4094-2266-2 (hbk)
ISBN: 978-1-138-27084-8 (pbk)

To Kate and Sarah,
my girls of the period,

and to Mike,
who made it possible

Contents

Contents

List of Figures

Acknowledgements

While I was in Cambridge conducting research for this project, a local newspaper reported on the reprinting of *Girl's Empire*, a British magazine for girls published between 1902 and 1904. The serendipity of this discovery highlighted my own belief that nineteenth-century girls' magazines are interesting not only for their intrinsic value as artifacts of nineteenth-century girls' culture but also because our own ideas about girls in the twenty-first century remain unstable. Then, as now, issues of marriage, motherhood, and employment framed debates about girls' roles and responsibilities.

I want to thank Grace Moore for her ongoing support throughout my research. My debt to her—for her expertise, patience, and enthusiasm—is immense. Ken Gelder and Peter Otto provided support and encouragement at different points during the research, and Clara Tuite graciously agreed to read the manuscript on very short notice. Sally Mitchell, Emma Liggins, Susan Hamilton, Cecily Devereux, and Linda Hughes all provided immensely useful suggestions that have made this book better than it otherwise would have been. Andrew King, Laurel Brake, and Judith Johnston responded generously to my email queries and directed my research in helpful ways.

I want to thank both the University of Melbourne and the Social Sciences and Humanities Research Council of Canada for their financial support, without which it would have been difficult to conduct the research necessary for this book. Librarians at the British Library, Cambridge University Library, Girton Archive, Monash University Library, the State Library of Victoria, and the University of Melbourne Library provided timely assistance.

I am extremely grateful for the network of friends and colleagues that developed during the course of the solitary work of researching and writing. Claire Thomas, Sue Pyke, and Libby Angel were consistently enthusiastic about my research. Our shared interests in nineteenth-century literature and culture became the source of numerous conversations that regularly prompted me to refine my thinking. Michelle Smith continues to be a welcome colleague and scholar of Victorian girlhood, and I look forward to many more opportunities to share ideas about girls' culture. Through more long-distance phone minutes than I care to tally, Emma Pink provided wisdom, laughter, and encouragement on subjects ranging from academia to parenting. George and Anne Marie Moruzi provided welcome support that enabled a lengthy research trip. Jim and Gerry Sharp have always encouraged me to do what I love, and this book is testament to that faith. My wonderful girls, Kate and Sarah, kept me smiling as they reminded me to enjoy life. Last, but definitely not least, this adventure would never have been possible without Mike's love and support.

Chapter 1
Introduction:
Girls of the Period

Pronouncements about the "girl of the period" were common in the British periodical press in the second half of the nineteenth century and into the early twentieth century. Detractors declared that she was too fast, too modern, too independent, too casual, and too fashionable. She failed to respect the authority of her parents, and she neglected her family and community responsibilities. She was, altogether, less virtuous than girls of the past. In contrast, her advocates defended her as being stronger, healthier, and better educated. She was equally as pure as her mother and her grandmother had been.

The accounts appearing in the press inevitably attempted to depict a universalized, generally middle-class, girlhood, as though there existed a single pervasive model of femininity to which all girls could and should be held accountable. In Eliza Lynn Linton's provocative 1868 *Saturday Review* article, "The Girl of the Period," she contrasts the "fair young English girl" of the past, "who could be trusted alone if need be, because of the innate purity and dignity of her nature," with the Girl of the Period, who "dyes her hair and paints her face" and whose only object in life is "plenty of fun and luxury" (356). In comments such as these, the form and behaviour of contemporary girls are generalized in order to compare them, often critically, to an imagined, nostalgic view of girls of the past.

Linton articulates only two possible positions for the contemporary girl. She is either the embodiment of the virtuous womanly ideal of the past or the prostitute of the present. Linton's critique of the Girl of the Period, while obviously intended to provoke a response, suggests a deep anxiety about the control that girls are assuming over their own lives. Rather than living according to a feminine ideal of domesticity and subordination to patriarchal structures, modern girls are choosing to exercise, at least to a limited extent, their own power and are articulating a more complex reality of girlhood that is comprised of multiple models of femininity, most of which incorporate ideals of purity, virtue, and morality. The prevalence of these discussions in the mainstream press and in girls' periodicals not only reflect the challenges faced by both adults and girls of adapting to the shifting economic, political, social and cultural landscape in Britain, but also the importance placed upon defining girls and the experience of middle-class girlhood.

Although the depictions of girlhood appearing in girls' magazines sometimes fall victim to a similar nostalgia for the past, they nonetheless provide an alternative view of middle-class girls that attends much more closely to the specificities of their lives, thereby offering a less universalized and much more detailed perspective on girlhood between 1850 and 1915. Designed to appeal to girl readers, these magazines had to offer a product that more closely reflected the realities of girls' lives even though much of the magazines' contents were composed of romantic fiction. To attract and maintain a dedicated readership, each girls' magazine had to define a specific model of femininity that would be sufficiently unique to differentiate it from its competitors while also appealing to a broad audience. Girls' magazines consequently reflect the ways in which girls could be distinctly defined beyond the universalizing tendencies elsewhere in the press.

By studying periodicals purchased and read by girls, it becomes possible to draw conclusions about the types of girls appearing in their pages, and the extent to which the girls themselves were involved in refining the models of femininity that were offered to them. Moreover, by examining complete runs, changes in ideals of girlhood become more evident. Some periodicals were more successful than others in creating a product that attracted a loyal readership. In these magazines, attempts to address the real changes to girls' lives and prospects are discussed alongside articles representing traditional ideologies of feminine decorum and modesty. These magazines endorse feminine ideals of purity and domesticity even as they simultaneously attempt to expand or shift these ideals to provide girls with better opportunities for education and employment. Choice becomes an important concept as girls are presented with improved information about jobs, colleges, and husbands, yet marriage remains a critical concern even when the girls' magazines ostensibly assert that remaining single is an acceptable alternative.

Different aspects of nineteenth- and early twentieth-century girlhood, including religion, modernity, health, education, marriage, and heroism are emphasized in girls' periodicals. In some ways, this differentiation represents a savvy marketing strategy. By appealing to a unique model of girlhood, each magazine hoped to define and thereby attract a dedicated group of readers. More importantly, however, it shows how editors, advertisers, contributors, and readers themselves attempted to disrupt the model of universalized middle-class girlhood elsewhere in the press by providing specific examples of girls' agency through fictional action, letters to the editor, true stories of girls' successes, and articles designed to inform girls about possible educational and employment opportunities. Individually, each girls' magazine shows unique, even if overlapping, models of girlhood. Together, these periodicals demonstrate that there was not a universal model of young femininity. Instead the period is marked by different kinds of girls and different models of girlhood that attempted to address and adapt to the radically shifting terrain regarding girls' future roles as wives, mothers, and workers while also capitalizing on the rapid increase in books and magazines available to middle-class girl readers.

Every era is made up of many girls of the period, and consequently there can be no quintessential "Victorian" or "Edwardian" girlhood. The universalizing of late nineteenth- and early twentieth-century girlhood represents an attempt to contain girls whose very modernity is perceived as threatening to the fabric of imperial and national identity, especially when set alongside *fin-de-siècle* fears of degeneration and decay. While girls' periodicals show that girls can be guided towards certain behaviours and away from others, they also reflect an anxiety about the extent to which girls are becoming difficult to contain within traditional norms that privilege female self-sacrifice over freedom and independence.

Changing Nature of Girlhood

During the early decades of the nineteenth century, the middle-class woman was increasingly positioned as the moral and spiritual center of the home, and she became, as Coventry Patmore describes, "The Angel of the House."[1] As the century progressed, however, girls began to resist the inactivity that this ideal imposed upon them. They desired better education—like that offered to their brothers—and more opportunities to develop themselves and their skills. Susan Gorsky argues that "[e]xploring the role of women during the nineteenth century means considering the evolution of feminism" (1), including not simply the determination to alter laws discriminating against women but also the reconsideration of traditionally-held values and beliefs about women's roles in society. The "Woman Question" was fiercely debated throughout the second half of the century as women began agitating for political and legal rights, especially after the 1832 Reform Bill explicitly excluded women from political citizenship. The employment possibilities available to women were poorly paid, which became problematic as "surplus" women remained unmarried and had to support themselves. The standard education in dancing, painting, and embroidery was increasingly perceived as stultifying and unsatisfactory. Girls' education was often haphazard, offered by poorly trained governesses, if at all, and without any standard curriculum. The advent of formalized schooling in the 1850s and the establishment of colleges for women in the 1860s marked the beginning of a shift in attitudes towards girls' capacity for learning, as well as the growing belief that girls needed to be better educated if they were to fulfil their future roles as wives and mothers, an idea initiated by Mary Wollstonecraft with the publication of *Thoughts on the Education of Daughters* (1787) and *Vindication of the Rights of Woman* (1792).

Girls tried to escape the drawing room by employing a Christian ethic of charity towards others. Charity was, of course, an important facet of constructions of femininity during this period. In *Disciplines of Virtue: Girls' Culture in the Eighteenth and Nineteenth Centuries* (1995), Lynne Vallone explains that "charity work and almsgiving had traditionally been considered part of women's domestic duty" (16). Moreover, women were "especially suited to perform charitable works as an extension of the domestic ideology that kept her arts in the home" (17). The charitable ideal forms an explicit portion of the children's periodical *Aunt Judy's Magazine*, for example, where editor Margaret Gatty encouraged children to sponsor "Aunt Judy's Cot" at the Great Ormond Street Children's Hospital. In addition to monetary charity, which readers eagerly supported, the middle-class charitable ideal operating in children's magazines encouraged children, and especially girls, to consider establishing and teaching at local Sunday Schools— as Ethel May does in Charlotte Yonge's *The Daisy Chain*, a domestic novel

---

[1]   Patmore published his four-poem series between 1854 and 1863. It is often referred to by the title of the first two poems, "The Angel in the House."

popular with girl readers—and to consider district visiting as a suitable unpaid occupation.[2] At the same time, women's rights activists like the Langham Place group mobilized to improve the situation of women. Active between 1857 and 1866, its members included Barbara Leigh Smith, Elizabeth Rayner Parkes, Emily Faithfull, Matilda Hays, Maria Rye, Jessie Boucherett, and Adelaide Procter.[3] The group sought to improve the work opportunities for women by employing female compositors for their feminist magazine, *Victoria Magazine* (1863–1880), and by establishing a Society for the Promotion of Employment for Women. Members of the group regularly published articles about the skills and training required for potential jobs. By the end of the century, middle-class women were increasingly employed as typists, clerks, journalists, writers, editors, teachers, nurses, doctors, and many other occupations.

Improved employment opportunities were accompanied by a lengthy, multi-pronged campaign to improve women's legal rights. From the 1850s until well into the twentieth century, efforts were ongoing to obtain voting rights for women on the same terms as men. This campaign culminated in the granting of women's suffrage in 1928, with limited suffrage granted in 1918. Other significant reforms were introduced earlier, such as the 1869 Municipal Franchise Act, which allowed female taxpayers to vote in municipal elections. From 1871, women were eligible for election to local school boards. In addition, the Married Women's Property Acts of 1870 and 1882 granted married women the right to acquire, hold, and dispose of their own property, and the age of consent was raised to 16 in 1885.[4] Similarly, the repeal of the Contagious Diseases Acts in 1886 was also seen as a great accomplishment for women of all classes because it helped to eliminate the sexual inequality between men and women and provided a political platform for women.

By 1880, middle-class girls seemingly had access to a much wider variety of educational and employment opportunities. Yet, as Sally Mitchell explains, the freedoms offered to these "new girls" were "provisional" (3) because although they "suggested new ways of being, new modes of behavior, and new attitudes that were not yet acceptable for adult women" (3), the lived experiences of girls during this time were not significantly different from those of girls earlier in the century. Girls continued to be contained within the domestic, in the homes of their fathers and later their husbands. Yet the texts available to them were beginning to explore exciting new possibilities for education, employment, and marriage.

---

[2]   By the end of the century, however, district visiting was seen as an occupation requiring specific skills and training.

[3]   The group took its name from the office of the *English Woman's Journal*, launched in 1858 and located at 19 Langham Place, London.

[4]   In the first four chapters of *English Feminism: 1780–1980* (1997), Barbara Caine provides an excellent overview of the women's movement in the nineteenth century.

Girls' Reading

The didactic tradition of children's literature emerged in the late eighteenth century, where children were guided towards appropriate Christian behaviour. Children's writers like Anna Letitia Barbauld, Sarah Trimmer, Hannah More, and Maria Edgeworth developed the tradition of the moral tale in the 1780s and '90s, which continued to flourish well into the 1800s.[5] This didactic tradition sits alongside the publication and popularization of fairy tales by the Grimm brothers and Hans Christian Anderson, introducing elements of fantasy into the reading of adults and children alike. Yet before 1850, children's books and magazines were predominantly religious in orientation. Two of the earliest children's magazines, both beginning in 1824, were religious periodicals.[6] These magazines were aimed at both boys and girls and were designed to guide them towards appropriate Christian behaviours.

Only after 1850 did the commercial possibilities of children's periodicals become viable, in part because of reductions in the newspaper duty (4d.), the advertising tax (3s. 6d.), and the paper tax. The gradual elimination of these taxes between 1855 and 1863 produced a revitalized periodical press that became an important contributor to the enhanced literacy, and especially children's literacy, of the second half of the nineteenth century as children came to be seen as a new target market for books and magazines, and as publishers increasingly sought to produce less expensive, higher quality popular reading material for children. As Julia Briggs and Dennis Butts explain, "The contribution of the periodical publishing to the growth of children's literature in this period cannot be overemphasized" (163). For most children, the primary point of access to fiction was through the periodical press, largely because weekly and monthly magazines were more affordable than books.

By the end of the century, not only was the market for children's books and periodicals much larger, but it was also increasingly gendered as girls and boys were directed towards texts written specifically for them. For example, the rise of domestic fiction for girls, such as Charlotte Yonge's *The Daisy Chain*, is concomitant with the rise in boys' adventure fiction by writers like Frederick Marryat and W.H.G. Kingston. Gendered magazines also became more prevalent, beginning with the *Boy's Own Magazine* (1855–74), the *Boy's Journal* (1863–71), *Boys of England* (1866–99), and the *Boy's Own Paper* (1879–1967). Girls' magazines were slower to appear but were well established by the 1880s and 1890s.

---

[5] For an excellent overview of the early history of children's literature, see Peter Hunt's *Children's Literature: An Illustrated History* (1995), especially chapters three and four. See also Mary Thwaite's *From Primer to Pleasure in Reading*, second edition (1972) and Mary Jackson's *Engines of Instruction, Mischief, and Magic: Children's Literature in England from Its Beginnings to 1839* (1989).

[6] One of the earliest Sunday School Magazines was the *Child's Companion; or, Sunday Scholar's Reward* (1824–1923) and the Anglican equivalent was the *Children's Friend* (1824–1929).

In addition to magazines intended specifically for them, girls also took advantage of magazines aimed at their brothers and their mothers. Edward J. Salmon's 1886 survey of girls' reading suggests that girls were reading a wide range of material—whether it was intended for them or not—from the *Girl's Own Paper* and the *Boy's Own Paper* to *Punch* and *Cassell's Family Magazine*.[7] Their favourite authors, according to the survey, ranged from the highbrow George Eliot to the sensation novelists like Mrs. Henry Wood and adventure fiction writers like W.H.G. Kingston.[8] This survey is not without its problems, of course. Salmon explains how Charles Welsh "collected from various schools" replies to 13 questions designed to elicit information "from the young themselves" about the literature they read. The responses, "some two or three thousand," are "thanks to the courtesy" of the "chiefs" of various boys' and girls' schools ("What Girls Read" 527). The summary of the survey provides no information about which schools were surveyed, and Salmon himself finds some of the results "curious" (528). He notes that "[h]ardly one of the recognized writers for girls is mentioned, and ... I cannot help thinking that the list far from adequately represents what girls read" (528). The popularity of Dickens and Scott is likely owing to their frequent presence in school or home libraries (rather than because girls had actually read their books) and perhaps because girls felt they needed to vote for writers who were known and respected. Nonetheless, unless the survey "is to be entirely discredited, it must open the eyes of parents to the real needs of our girls" (529). The survey provides a starting point for studies of girls' reading, even if that reading was a result of books purchased by parents and friends as presents. Salmon concludes that "[i]f girls were to choose their own books, ... they would make a choice for themselves very different from that which their elders make for them" (529). The implications of girls selecting their own reading are vital to this examination of the periodical press since magazines offer much more flexibility and choice over reading material.

That these diverse reading choices merited discussion and concern in girls' periodicals is a reflection of the critical anxiety caused by, as Jennifer Phegley explains, "the mass production and mass marketing of print culture ... and the consolidation of middle-class power that gave women the leisure time to devote themselves to reading" (1). Like their mothers, middle-class girls had access to an unheralded quantity of reading material. The range of material, and the leisure time afforded by their middle-class existence, meant that girls' reading could no longer be controlled to the extent that it had been in the past. Furthermore, "the gender of the reader ... is not as fixed and stable as we might expect, even in the case of journals carrying unequivocally gendered titles" (Fraser, Green, and Johnston 64).

---

[7]   The *Girl's Own Paper* is the clear favourite with 315 votes, followed by the *Boy's Own Paper* (88). *Cassell's Family Magazine* receives 35 votes, and *Punch* receives 24 votes.

[8]   Charles Dickens comes in first with 355 votes, followed by Sir Walter Scott (248), Charles Kingsley (103), and Charlotte Yonge (100). Mrs. Henry Wood receives 58 votes, and George Eliot receives 50 votes. W.H.G. Kingston appears much lower on the list with 19 votes.

Although girls were likely reading their mothers' magazines and were thus guided towards domestic behaviours like cooking, sewing, and household management, they were also reading material intended for their brothers, which featured a much broader range of activities and adventure.

Unsurprisingly, many of the periodicals aimed at girls are interested in guiding girls towards what they considered "acceptable" texts for young women, and these works were often highly didactic, aimed at instructing girls in their future roles as wives and mothers. As Kate Flint has explained, the study of the "woman reader" is important not just for her potency as a cultural icon but also because it "illuminates important networks of ideas about the presumed interrelations of mind, body, and culture" (11). Like the "woman reader," the "girl reader" is a site of conflict and contestation.

Girls' Periodicals between 1850 and 1915

Girls' periodicals between 1850 and 1915 reflect the shifting nature of girlhood during this period. Appearing either weekly or monthly (and occasionally both), and with prices typically ranging from 1d. to 6d., these periodicals represent an attempt by publishers and editors to define and attract a dedicated readership while also remaining open to new readers. Each issue of a girls' periodical typically includes an ongoing serialized story as well as regular features such as an editor's column, a correspondence section, and essay competitions. These elements are designed to appeal to the existing readership. At the same time, the editor sought to provide easily accessible content that did not depend on former knowledge of the periodical, such as new serialized fiction as well as shorter fictional pieces, poems, puzzles, and articles providing information about employment or educational opportunities. Although some of the earliest girls' magazines contain no illustrations, almost all of those appearing later in the century took pride in the number and quality of their visual content. These illustrations provided girls, for the first time, with images of themselves engaged in a variety of different activities designed to encourage them to be healthy, active, and educated.

The earliest girls' periodical was the 1838 *Young Ladies' Magazine of Theology, History, Philosophy, and General Knowledge.* Kirsten Drotner argues that its short run indicates its "prematureness" (118) in targeting the "'young ladies' of the upper and upper-middle classes" who "had not developed as a separate magazine audience but still contented themselves with memoirs, novels, sermons, or household periodicals" for their reading. A much more successful girls' periodical is the High Anglican *Monthly Packet of Evening Readings for Younger Members of the Church of England* (1851–98), edited by Charlotte Yonge until 1893. Its content, much of which was religious, indicates a readership of girls preparing for Confirmation although the removal of "Younger" from its title in 1866 suggests the core readership may have been aging.

The 1860s marked a significant shift in girls' periodicals as commercial publishers began to realize that there was money to be made from girl readers.

The *English Girls' Journal, and Ladies' Magazine: A Weekly Illustrated Book for Every Dwelling* (1863–64), priced at one penny, was followed by the *Young Ladies of Great Britain* (1869–71), with both magazines focusing on fashion. Samuel Beeton, already well known for his *Englishwoman's Domestic Magazine* (1852–90), launched the weekly *Young Englishwoman* in 1864. Including black and white and later colour engravings, the magazine contained fiction, music, poetry, recipes, fashion, and household management tips. It continued as *Sylvia's Home Journal* in 1878 and then became *Sylvia's Journal* in 1892 until ceasing publication in 1894; these latter two titles distance themselves from the distinctly youthful audience suggested by the "Young Englishwoman."

The 1860s also saw the emergence of magazines aimed at both boys and girls, and at a broader range of children. *The Chatterbox* (1866–1953) is the longest running of these "compound" magazines, which Drotner describes as "catering to the whole of the large Victorian nursery" (118). The protagonists in much of the fiction tend to be younger than those appearing in girls' magazines, although these magazines do occasionally contain older, teen protagonists, such as Marjorie and Eleanor in Juliana Ewing's *Six to Sixteen*, which originally appeared in *Aunt Judy's Magazine* (1866–85). *Kind Words for Boys and Girls* (1866–79) continued as *Young England* until 1937. *Good Words for the Young* (1868–72) was edited by George Macdonald between 1869 and 1872, then becoming *Good Things for the Young of All Ages* until ceasing publication in 1877.

Although not strictly a girls' periodical, the appearance of the *Girl of the Period Miscellany* in 1869 coincided with, and indeed exacerbated discussions of, the growing debate about women's roles. According to Drotner, the *Miscellany* "prefigured a new magazine trend" that "emphasized sensible instruction rather than uplifting moralism or extravagant directions and displayed self-reliant young heroines" (119). While girls' magazines appearing after 1869 are typically more reflective of the realities of girls' lives, the comic potential of the *Miscellany* highlights the question of women's rights and freedoms to its primarily male audience.

Routledge's monthly *Every Girl's Magazine* (1878–87), edited by Alicia Leith, marks the first "modern" magazine for girls, in the sense that it was intended to be entertaining and informative, but not overly religious or didactic, while also decreasing the emphasis on homemaking. *Atalanta* (1888–97) succeeded it, becoming more focused on encouraging girls to pursue secondary, and possibly post-secondary, education. The weekly *Girl's Own Paper* (1880–1908) first appeared in 1880 and soon became immensely popular. In 1908, it became the *Girl's Own Paper and Mother's Magazine*, again signalling a shifting demographic. Also during this period were monthly middle-class girls' magazines like *A.1.* (1888–90), edited by Jane Menzies, the *Girl's Realm* (1898–1915), edited by Alice Corkran, and the *Girl's Empire* (1902–1904). Proto-feminist magazines like the *Young Woman* (1892–1915), containing few illustrations, were aimed at a slightly older readership and contained polemical articles on the importance of a single sexual standard for both men and women.

Because girlhood can be, and was, seen as a transitional state between childhood and adulthood, defining the "girl" is both a challenge and a contradiction. Anita Harris has discussed the difficulties of defining a girl, noting that "any book that focuses on an age- and gender-based category as its subject of inquiry immediately runs into the problem of implying a natural, fixed state of being for that category" (191). Developmentally, girlhood could be considered to end when a girl began menstruating. The age of sexual consent for girls in Victorian England was raised from 13 to 16 only after W.T. Stead's series of controversial newspaper articles on child prostitution were published in the *Pall Mall Gazette* in 1885. Legally, a girl became an adult at the age of 21, at which point she could dispose of her own property, yet she lost those rights when she married. Widows and spinsters who were householders were given municipal suffrage in 1869 and were able to vote for, and become members of, school boards in 1870. Yet it was not until 1918 that women over the age of 30 were given parliamentary franchise, with universal franchise granted only in 1928. In practical terms, a girl in Victorian England often remained a "girl" until she married. "Girl" was a useful signifier of marital status since it suggested a female who was not yet contained within the domestic space of marriage and maternity.

The contradictory definitions of girlhood in girls' periodicals and in British society more broadly make it difficult to clearly identify the target readership of girls' periodicals between 1850 and 1915. Harris has noted that "membership in the girl category [extends] out at both ends" (191). Based on an analysis of the contents of magazines that explicitly identify their target readership as girls, the ideal girl reader is likely between 15 and 25. Stories with protagonists younger than 15 are typically found in self-identified "children's" magazines, rather than girls' periodicals. Similarly, few of the protagonists in the fiction found in girls' periodicals are married with children. Instead, the vast majority of the fiction is comprised of girls in their late teens and early twenties. At the same time, however, girls' magazines were regularly faced with an aging readership and were constantly trying to obtain new, younger girls as readers as its older readers moved on to other—presumably women's—magazines.

Moreover, although the target readership of girls' periodicals ranges in age from early teens to mid-twenties, the multiplicity of forms and content found in these periodicals sometimes implies readers on either side of this range, and the target readership occasionally shifts over time. After 1910, the increasing number of *Girl's Realm* stories containing protagonists in their early teens suggests a younger readership than in its earliest years. In general, the girls in these magazines were not always clearly or consistently defined, in part because definitions of girlhood were already ambiguous. In addition, a magazine's interests were not necessarily best served by defining its readership too narrowly since that could limit the number of potential buyers. Alternatively, of course, improved sales sometimes resulted from advertising to and attracting a clearly defined readership. The rapidity with which magazines appeared, and then disappeared, further reinforces the sense that "the category of girl is constantly shifting" (Harris 191). If girlhood were less changeable, it would have been easier to identify an ideal girl reader and keep her interest in a particular magazine. Moreover, editors and contributors to girls' magazines were often faced with the difficulties of keeping pace with a rapidly evolving girls' culture marked by distinct generational differences.

Many of the girls' magazines published between 1850 and 1915 with "girl" in the title identified in the *Waterloo Directory of English Newspapers and Periodicals: 1800–1900* had runs of a year or less, such as *School Girls* (1894–95) and *Girls* (1893). These short runs presumably indicate a small readership and unhealthy circulation numbers, although the circulation required to keep a magazine in business also varied widely. The *Monthly Packet*'s relatively scant circulation of 1500–2000 suggests that financial motives were less crucial to the publishers than the content of the magazine, an idea I explore further in the next chapter. In contrast, the *Young Woman* had a much more robust circulation of 50,000 and the *Girl's Own Paper* was the most impressive with 250,000.

Girls' periodicals between 1850 and 1915 are composed of an enormous variety of material, from serialized fiction and short stories to editorials, illustrations, correspondence, advertising, essay competitions, and articles on topics like literature, natural science, history, geography, education, and employment. Almost all girls' periodicals depended heavily on serialized fiction and short stories, which could occupy over half of a given number. Writers of girls' fiction, such as E. Nesbit, Rosa Nouchette Carey, Evelyn Everett-Green, Isabelle Fyvie Mayo, Isabella Varley Banks, and L.T. Meade, often contributed to multiple periodicals.

Barbara Onslow's *Women of the Press in Nineteenth-Century Britain* (2000) provides an important contribution to the study of women and nineteenth-century journalism. She highlights the pivotal role of women in the periodical press and the ways in which their contributions varied. She explains how "women, with limited access to finance and little encouragement to engage in business, found it difficult to enter the realms of publishing and editing at national and provincial daily newspaper level. Thus male editorial predominance in the high-profile sectors of the press has clouded women's editorial work elsewhere" (1). The world of girls' periodicals was an arena less fraught with this discrimination. Women like Charlotte Yonge, Alice Corkran, L.T. Meade, Alicia Leith, Jane Menzies, and Flora Klickmann edited successful girls' periodicals, and women were frequent contributors. More in-depth examination of contributors' lists is needed, yet even a preliminary analysis demonstrates how writers, especially women, wrote for a variety of girls' periodicals and clearly had a network of publications to which they contributed.

Largely because books were so expensive, periodicals formed a large portion of girls' reading material. In addition, because their favourite authors were likely to contribute to more than one magazine, girls would read a variety of magazines. While the network of publications read by girls is difficult to determine, some evidence exists within the magazines themselves. Girls were clearly reading more than one magazine as well as actively seeking recommendations for further reading. Charlotte Yonge, for example, remarks in 1871 that "[m]ost of the readers of *The Monthly Packet* are readers also of Aunt Judy's Magazine" ("Cumberland Street Children's Hospital" 92). Many magazines included a review feature recommending other books and magazines that were felt to be of interest to readers. The reading culture of the period was created and reinforced through the periodical press. Not only did the editors want girls to read their magazines, they wanted to promote the reading of other books and magazines as well.

In general, the periodicals contain fiction that is more conservative than the informational articles, which tend to present opportunities that extend beyond traditional definitions of the feminine ideal. Even fictional girls who resist these conservative depictions of femininity are eventually contained within marriage and the domestic sphere. Sally Mitchell writes that girls in the liminal space between childhood and adulthood are given "permission to behave in ways that might not be appropriate for a woman" (25). Moreover, as Sarah Bilston remarks, "Writers who supported such traditionalist ideals were prepared to represent *girls* yearning for self-actualization and self-determination when they were unwilling to depict *women* exhibiting these desires" (7). By concluding their fiction within the tropes of marriage and domesticity, writers were able to extend certain freedoms to these girls of an "awkward age" (Bilston 1) without fearing for the implications of this freedom.

Although many girls' periodicals include progressive stories depicting female protagonists engaging positively and productively with the issues of the day, the relative conservatism of most of the fiction is striking. Much serialized girls' fiction is written by novelists who were already well known, and who presumably had a reputation for a certain kind and quality of writing. Editors were interested in publishing popular writers since this would contribute to the magazine's reputation and would hopefully attract new readers or encourage casual readers to subscribe. One reason for the regular recurrence of certain authors is the editor's need to establish and maintain a pipeline of publishable material. Onslow notes that "[r]ejected manuscripts were not necessarily without merit nor even inappropriate, but 'in common fairness' regulars could not be 'elbowed aside by casual contributions'" (109). This obviously contributed to a publishing environment where regular contributors were given preference, thereby preventing new, possibly more radical, fiction from appearing.

However, the heterogeneity of other contributors means that opposing viewpoints are frequently the norm and could be explicitly positioned to be provocative. I explore this in more detail in my discussion of the *Girl's Realm*, to which both suffrage activist Christabel Pankhurst and anti-suffrage activist Ethel Harrison contributed position papers. The correspondence sections in the *Monthly Packet* and *Atalanta* similarly support this idea, with girl readers frequently taking opposing positions regarding girls' roles and responsibilities. A strong editorial presence sometimes helps to provide thematic and ideological cohesiveness, but defining the "genre" of girls' periodicals is complicated by the sheer range of content. Often the feature that most obviously defines a girl's periodical is the editorial "tone," such as that found in Charlotte Yonge's *Monthly Packet* and

Alice Corkran's *Girl's Realm*, and by certain features that characterize the house style, such as *Atalanta*'s "Scholarship and Reading Union" and the "Notices to Correspondents" in the *Girl's Own Paper*. Developing and maintaining a "house style" that "tries to construct ... a set of standards which it tries to represent as normal and which most nearly represent how that journal wishes to present itself to the pubic" (Fraser, Green, and Johnston 79) was one of the many challenges faced by editors in the nineteenth century. Despite the multifaceted nature of the periodical, its success depended on attracting and maintaining a regular readership through recurring features and a design that helped readers to recognize the product.

An important aspect of a periodical's house style comes from the types of girls appearing in its pages, and how these girls reflect the shifts in women's roles and responsibilities throughout the Victorian and Edwardian eras. The dominant models of girlhood appearing in middle-class girls' periodicals address issues of religion, health, education, marriage, heroism, and modernity. Not every type of girl appears in every magazine, of course, but these themes appear, in various guises, in most periodicals. At times, certain issues dominate while others recede to the background. The idea of modernity, for example, ebbs and flows in a magazine with a lengthy run like the *Monthly Packet*, with flurries of articles and correspondence in the late 1860s and early 1870s coinciding with discussions of the Girl of the Period in the general press, and again in the late 1880s and early 1890s to coincide with the rise of the New Woman. Articles depicting healthy girls and educated girls often appear alongside one another in the 1880s and 1890s, when girls' education and its consequences for health became important topics of conversation. Many types of girls could, and did, appear in each magazine, sometimes in direct opposition to each other. Articles about the educated girl, for example, often appear alongside fictional stories of romance and marriage at a time when the desire for education conflicted with the requirements of married life. These models of girlhood were often depicted unquestioningly, and girl readers were left to draw their own conclusions about their viability. Their significance lies in the extent to which these opposing representations—in the same issue of a magazine, across its run, and in different periodicals—provide spaces in which girls were exposed to different models of girlhood and could begin to choose models of femininity that most closely reflected their lives and interests, or in which it was possible to refine these definitions of femininity.

Regardless of their political persuasions, girls' magazines almost uniformly followed trends in the general press by increasingly including articles that discussed the training and demands of newly available occupations for women, although the fiction that appeared alongside such articles often represented employment only as an economic necessity. The tensions between the ideal of feminine domesticity and the new realities of women's lives are reflected in girls' magazines of the period and demonstrate how difficult it could be to reconcile these opposing forces. At the same time, however, these tensions also demonstrate how relevance and topicality were understood to be crucial to a magazine's success. A magazine might present itself as a reader's "friend," yet this typically commercial enterprise was concerned with covering relevant trends and stories that pertained to definitions of girlhood in the second half of the century.

In *The New Woman: Fiction and Feminism at the Fin de Siècle* (1997), Sally Ledger argues that there was not just one "New Woman" at the *fin de siècle*. In reality, the New Woman had multiple identities in that she was, variously, "a feminist activist, a social reformer, a popular novelist, a suffragette playwright, a woman poet" (Ledger 1). Similarly, many different girls were being reflected and refined in, and to some extent produced by, girls' periodicals. There was not just one middle-class girl, not even one "new girl" of the *fin de siècle*. Taking account of these different girls in their myriad forms is critical if we are to avoid conceptualizing the girl as homogenous. The girls that appear in these magazines reflect a wide range of perspectives. From urban to rural, from religious to secular, from needing paid employment to living a life of leisure, the magazines demonstrate the complexities of negotiating definitions of girlhood during this period, with different girls appearing alongside one another, often quite explicitly, within the pages of their magazines.

Different models of girlhood frequently appeared alongside each other in the correspondence sections of girls' periodicals. In response to a question posed by the editor or another correspondent, girls contributed a variety of different perspectives on topics including education, employment, home duties, and modernity. These correspondence sections and essay competitions are designed to encourage readers to engage with the ideas of the magazine and with the "imagined community" (to use Benedict Anderson's phrase) of likeminded readers. Yet these perspectives sometimes explicitly reject ideas set forth by the editor or transform them into something more palatable for the girl readers themselves, thereby disrupting the magazine's promise of "false unity," where it appears to present "a unified policy, or set of beliefs, as if the journal itself were a single author" (Brake and Codell 1). These "encounters" (Brake and Codell 2) in the periodical press allow the imagined reader to become real and enable a dialogue—to a certain extent— between the reader and the editor. Their frequency in the pages of girls' magazines demonstrates the degree to which girls were engaged with the ideas and ideologies embodied in their magazines. Although the responses to readers' queries were often designed to guide girls' behaviour towards certain acceptable norms, the multiple voices within a given number allow for resistance and redefinition.

Yet whether the correspondence in girls' magazines was written by "real" girls or contributed by magazine staff is a vexed question. Richard Altick writes that "[o]ne suspects that many of the queries [in the family papers], especially the ones which today would be addressed to reference librarians, were concocted in the editorial office" (*English Common Reader* 360). While that may be the case, many of the queries were undoubtedly genuine and "provide an instructive panorama of the humble Victorian reader's everyday perplexities" (Altick *English* 360–61). The volume of correspondence in a magazine like the *Girl's Own Paper*, the popularity of essay competitions in *Atalanta*, and the impressive support for

"Aunt Judy's Cot" in *Aunt Judy's Magazine* emphasize that readers were evidently contributing to "their" magazines in a myriad of forms. While some queries may have been, and undoubtedly were, strategically inserted to garner attention and be provocative, the magazine's interests were clearly being served by printing responses to readers' inquiries. This would encourage girls' identification with the magazine and promote the purchase of subsequent numbers to read the responses to their queries.

Theorizing Girls' Periodicals

The nature and ideology of girlhood in the periodical press is subject to constant negotiation and redefinition. In *A Magazine of Her Own? Domesticity and Desire in the Woman's Magazine 1800–1914* (1996), Margaret Beetham writes that "femininity is always represented in [women's] magazines as fractured, not least because it is simultaneously assumed as given and as still to be achieved" (1). The "traditional" view of femininity is curiously disconnected from the more radical opportunities that are also present in the pages of girls' magazines, often owing to the commercial challenges of the medium. At the same time, however, blaming the polarized contents in these magazines on the market negates the complex relationships that were constantly being negotiated as the realities of everyday life shifted for girls in Victorian and Edwardian England. As Lyn Pykett has written, in tracing the history of periodical studies:

> Periodicals can no longer be regarded in any simply reflective way as "evidence" (either primary or secondary), as transparent records which give access to, and provide the means of recovering, the culture which they "mirror." Far from being a mirror of Victorian culture, the periodicals have come to be seen as a central component of that culture ... and they can only be read and understood as part of that culture and society, and in the context of other knowledges about them. ("Reading" 102)

Girls' periodicals are clearly reflecting the discourses appearing elsewhere in the press about women's roles. At the same time, however, they are also articulating multiple models of femininity in their pages that must be examined alongside each other and situated within the social, cultural, economic, and political frameworks of the period. The periodical press occupies a central role in the construction and dissemination of ideas of girlhood because at least some of these magazines, like the *Girl's Own Paper* for example, were so pervasive that they reflect—and construct—one or more dominant discourses of girlhood by presenting multiple types of girls in their pages. Moreover, even less popular magazines, such as the *Monthly Packet*, nonetheless represent important correctives to any universal conception of Victorian or Edwardian girlhood. Yet even as multiple models of girls are presented, common trends in these girls' periodicals demonstrate how traditional ideas of femininity can be, and often are, juxtaposed with new expectations about work, education, and duty.

Defining the periodical "genre" is complicated not only by the range of content, but also by the influence and control of the editor, the type and variety of contributors, and the opportunities offered to readers to contribute to correspondence sections and essay contests. Often differences in magazine style and content and attitudinal shifts become obvious only over a period of years. By examining individual issues in relation to a magazine's entire run, opposing viewpoints and unusual content become more obvious. Furthermore, as Margaret Beetham notes, "Most readers will not only construct their own order, they will select and read only some of the text. The periodical, therefore, is a form which openly offers readers the chance to construct their own texts" ("Open and Closed" 98). Each girl's reading experience differs based on how she encounters a given issue of a magazine, whether as a single issue or part of a bound (often annual) volume, whether she turns directly to the next instalment of her favourite serialized story, whether she flips to the correspondence at the end to see if her question or response has been printed. Moreover, in returning to the periodical a day, a week, or months later, she may choose to read some or all of it in a different order, experiencing that issue or volume in an entirely different manner.

Jacqueline Rose posits the "impossibility of children's fiction," arguing that its impossibility is based on uneven power relations between the adults who write for children and the children who read that writing. Rose argues that writing for children is intended "to secure the child who is outside the book, the one who does not come so easily within its grasp" (2). Children's fiction must, therefore, always have a "message" since it is, and must always be, intended to influence the real, live readers of the text. At the same time, however, the periodical as a genre offers a unique opportunity for its readers directly to resist, or at least refine, the didacticism of the text. Importantly, many different "texts" are present in a given issue of a periodical. The periodical opens up places for resistance in the spaces between the articles, within the correspondence sections (although a degree of editorial control remains through the selection of correspondence), and in the autonomy a reader can exercise in selecting whether to read an article and in what order she chooses to read those articles.

Girls' Studies

Recent developments in girls' studies also influence this book. Pamela J. Bettis and Natalie G. Adams remind us that "girlhood is a construction made and remade through the material realities and discursive practices of the society" and thus "ideal girlhood is constantly being rewritten" (9). Certainly nineteenth- and early twentieth-century girls' periodicals reflect this rewriting of girlhood. The religious girl in the early days of the *Monthly Packet* is very different from the modern girl of the *Girl's Realm*, yet amidst this change there remains a degree of continuity. The girl of the present is being newly defined, yet she retains some aspects of the girl of the past. The importance of purity and virtue to the editors and contributors of the magazines, and to the girls themselves, provides a degree of stability to the changing nature of girlhood during this period. Indeed, these qualities may well inflect our understanding of girlhood today.

Mary Celeste Kearney explains in *Girls Make Media* (2006) that "if we hope to comprehend fully how the contemporary field of girls' media production has developed, we cannot study it apart from the larger history of girls' cultural practices and the various social factors that have both influenced its formation as well as complicated its development" (21). The girls that appear in Victorian periodicals are also being constructed in relation to their antecedents. The many references to grandmothers and great-grandmothers show how girls of every era reflect, yet also redefine, ideals of the past. Catherine Driscoll similarly suggests that the modern adolescence of girls "is not, as it is sometimes constructed, a clear break from Victorian discourses on girlhood but, rather, a way of mapping shifts across a range of discourses" (6–7). In a period where the term "adolescence" had not yet been formally introduced, girls' periodicals nonetheless grapple with changing expectations of an adolescent girl who was old enough to think about her role in her family, her position and influence in her community, and her function in society. Although the types of girls appearing in girls' periodicals during the Edwardian period are seemingly quite different from those girls appearing in the mid-nineteenth century, many of the issues about education, employment, and marriage are eerily reminiscent of these earlier times.

Valerie Walkerdine explains in "Girlhood Through the Looking Glass" that girlhood is "constituted in and through the discursive practices that make up the social world" (15). One of the predominant discursive practices in the nineteenth century was the periodical press, especially by the century's end, when the magazine culture was typified by a "vast welter of slighter and more ephemeral monthlies" (Fraser, Green, and Johnston 3). The success of this investigation of girls' periodicals is based upon a close analysis of the discursive practices operating on girls in their magazines, while also demonstrating the ways in which girls created their own spaces within the periodicals to refine these discourses.

Methodology

In this study, I focus specifically on middle-class girls' periodicals, with the exception of the *Girl of the Period Miscellany*, published between 1850 and 1915. I have chosen to limit my subject to middle-class girls for two reasons. First, as Deborah Gorham has shown, the changing attitudes towards girlhood were most contentious in middle-class households, because the middle classes were most strongly committed to the notion that "woman" was the center of the domestic realm.[9] For the working classes, enshrining women within the private sphere was a luxury they could ill afford. Working-class women were of necessity working to

---

[9]   In *The Victorian Girl and the Feminine Ideal* (1982), Gorham describes how "[t]he cult of domesticity" relieved tensions between the moral values of Christianity and the values of capitalism "[b]y locating Christian values in the home" (4).

help support their families and had little need to lament their confinement to the domestic. My second reason concerns the practicalities of access to nineteenth-century magazines. The ephemeral nature of magazines, and especially children's magazines, means that they were intended to be read, shared with friends, and passed on. Middle-class magazines were usually monthly publications, which meant that they were longer and typically printed on higher quality paper than those published each week.[10] By their nature, they were more likely to have been collected and preserved than their cheaper weekly competitors. Correspondents in the *Monthly Packet*, for example, occasionally wish to trade one or more years of the *Packet* for different years, or other periodicals, suggesting a collecting culture. These middle-class magazines are therefore more likely to be preserved in library collections around the world today. In contrast, the holdings of working-class children's periodicals are much more limited. Recent digitization projects have expanded the access to some children's periodicals, yet these projects are similarly dependent on the preservation of this ephemeral print culture.

Trying to define the progress and evolution of girlhood in the periodical press in the second half of the nineteenth century and into the twentieth century is not without its own unique challenges. The approach I have adopted here investigates six periodicals, the *Monthly Packet*, the *Girl of the Period Miscellany*, the *Girl's Own Paper*, *Atalanta*, the *Young Woman*, and the *Girl's Realm*, to determine how each attempted to define and refine constructions of girlhood through its pages while also responding to contemporary debate and changes in the education and employment available to women. A wide range of girls appear in the pages of these magazines, which typically contain articles about health, education, employment, and modernity, and encourage girls to adopt particular ideas or behaviours designed to guide them toward that magazine's model of girlhood. Yet, in each magazine, a dominant model of girlhood emerges. She rarely stands alone; she often appears alongside contradictory models, and she frequently changes over the years of the magazine's run.

The periodicals I have selected best represent the shifting nature of middle-class girlhood between 1850 and 1915. I discuss them in chronological order, based on the start date of publication, and I conclude just after the advent of World War I because 1915 marks the end of two of the periodicals under examination here and because the war caused yet another shift in perceptions of girlhood. The length of each magazine's run varies from as long as 76 years, in the case of the *Girl's Own Paper*, to as little as nine months for the *Girl of the Period Miscellany*. Their religious and political orientations vary significantly, from the High Anglican orthodoxy of the *Monthly Packet* to the evangelism of the *Girl's Own Paper* and the proto-feminism of the *Young Woman*. What they all do, however, is demonstrate the complexities of girlhood and show how girls were struggling to

---

[10] The fact that the *Girl's Own Paper* was published both as a weekly and a monthly magazine suggests that it was attempting to cross these class boundaries and to appeal to both working- and middle-class girls.

express themselves as useful, productive members of British society. These girls are not necessarily the "ideal" or "intended" readers that the magazines hopes to attract, but instead represent a model of girlhood to which girls will be attracted.

I could, of course, have selected many other periodicals. Given my argument that there were many "girls of the period," it was important to choose magazines with distinct house styles and with distinct views on girlhood. Yet, just as there are many different middle-class girls in Victorian and Edwardian England, there are also shades of different girls within each periodical. While I focus on the particular girl dominant in the pages of the given magazine, I also show the extent to which this girl exists alongside other types of girls. Although the religious girl depicted in the *Monthly Packet*, for example, is determined to uphold her faith, questions of education and employment are also frequently addressed. The bachelor girl of the *Young Woman* is placed alongside girls who are keen to marry. Each periodical is a fruitful site for discussion because of the complex and often contradictory girls who are simultaneously present within its pages.

In Chapter 2, "The Religious Girl: Girlhood in the *Monthly Packet* (1851–99)," I demonstrate the ways in which the *Monthly Packet* initially employed and reinforced the depiction of the High Anglican religious girl in order to contain girls within the home, and how the final years of the *Packet* were beset by challenges to this version of girlhood. Under the strong editorial influence of Charlotte Yonge until the last decade of its run, the *Monthly Packet* was primarily interested in guiding its girl readers (and later their mothers as well) towards a religious life. Yet the girl readers resisted some of the more conservative domestic ideologies endorsed within the magazine and began agitating for more and better opportunities to lead useful lives. Thus the *Monthly Packet* remained constrained by mid-Victorian religious ideals even as it attempted to remodel the girlhood in its pages to reflect the changing realities for girls at the *fin de siècle*.

Chapter 3, "The Latest Sensation: The Girlhood and the *Girl of the Period Miscellany* (1869)," capitalizes on the provocative "Girl of the Period" to respond to issues raised by the Woman Question through humour and satire. For its comic tone, its short run, and its primarily male audience, the *Girl of the Period Miscellany* differs substantially from the other periodicals considered here. Its importance lies in how it highlights the ambiguous definitions of girlhood in the late 1860s and early 1870s, where the "girl of the period" is a label to be applied to both girls and women who seek participation in the public sphere and demand better education, rights, and legal protection. The "girl" in the *Miscellany* is a visual figure, enabled through the magazine's extensive illustrations, which facilitates the production of illustrated girls' magazines in the 1880s and '90s.

The fourth chapter, "The Healthy Girl: Fitness and Beauty in the *Girl's Own Paper* (1880–1907)," addresses the longest-running periodical for girls, although for the sake of coherence I conclude my investigation in 1907, after which Flora Klickmann became editor, eliminated the weekly issue, and renamed the magazine. This evangelical periodical, published under the auspices of the Religious Tract Society, reflects the late nineteenth-century concern with girls' health and demonstrates how a healthy body, along with the appropriate domestic knowledge and skills, is an important aspect of a girl's future role as wife and mother.

In the fifth chapter, "The Educated Girl: *Atalanta* (1887–98) and the Debate on Education," I discuss this magazine in relation to the importance of changes in girls' education that began with Emily Davies' work in the 1860s to establish a facility for the higher education of women. *Atalanta* positioned itself as a supporter of this movement, yet it appears to have been somewhat uneasy about these changes to how and why girls were educated. Its fictional stories endorsing traditional messages of marriage and motherhood are set alongside articles that provided information about higher education, daily life at a college, and how to choose the best college. Although the magazine explicitly supports improvements in education for girls, it also wishes its girl readers to remain appropriately feminine, and the tensions between these two competing perspectives can be difficult to reconcile.

In Chapter 6, "The Marrying Girl: Social Purity and Marriage in the *Young Woman* (1892–1915)," I explore the *Young Woman*'s extensive discussions of moral and sexual purity for both men and women, the importance of having reliable information on prospective husbands, and the role of marriage. These articles appear alongside frequent discussions of the feminine "ideal," endorsing purity, morality, and charity. Against the background of eugenicist and Darwinian rhetoric, I argue that the *Young Woman* constructs its image of the marrying girl, at a time when the ideals of sexual innocence and purity were increasingly invested in the female body, in order to encourage her to make the best possible decision about her future husband and the father of her children.

Only in Chapter 7, "The Modern Girl: Heroic Adventures in the *Girl's Realm* (1898–1915)," do I discuss a magazine that was published almost exclusively during the Edwardian era, although both the *Young Woman* and the *Girl's Own Paper* continued into this period as well. The *Girl's Realm* differs from these other magazines in its presentation of the girl as a distinctly modern figure and its evocation of the unique possibilities of girlhood when liberated from the domestic. Its modern girl is capable of great acts of heroism and bravery, and the *Girl's Realm* uses contemporary events such as the Boer War, the women's suffrage campaign, and the rise of girls' adventure fiction to position the girl as a hero both at home and abroad who maintains her femininity. The "girl's realm" is thus extended to include areas beyond the traditional domestic space and the twentieth-century girl is depicted as confidently entering these new realms.

In Chapter 8, "Conclusion," I emphasize the narrative of female agency that develops in the girls' periodical press between 1850 and 1915. I also highlight the importance of this print culture in the definition and refinement of femininity and girlhood during this period of rapid change. The girls who appear in these periodicals are intriguingly multifaceted and subject to fierce discussion and debate, both within these magazines themselves and elsewhere in the press.

Underpinning discussions of girlhood in the late nineteenth and early twentieth centuries is a Christian ethos that was often used to bolster a feminine ideal of virtue and submission. Until well into the twentieth century, religion continued to occupy a central role in British girlhood, yet this role remains difficult to quantify. As Joseph Altholz observes, "The faith of the Victorians was much and powerfully reinforced by their religious press" (142). In girls' magazines, the role of religious faith is often an implicit aspect of a girl's life, particularly in the fiction and the poetry. In an overtly religious magazine like the *Monthly Packet*, however, religion is presented as an important part of daily life. In the next chapter, I will show how religious girlhood in the *Monthly Packet* came under increasing stress from the onslaught of change and how, during its lengthy run, the magazine had difficulty adapting to the changing realities of a girl's life.

Chapter 2

The Religious Girl:
Girlhood in the *Monthly Packet* (1851–99)

The religious girl depicted in the pages of the *Monthly Packet of Evening Readings for Younger Members of the Church of England* is guided towards a feminine ideal of duty to her family and God, service to the community, and charity towards others less fortunate than herself. Under the strong editorial control of Charlotte Yonge, from its earliest days the magazine entwines religion and femininity as it directs girls towards moral and spiritual purity and respect for the traditional male hierarchies of church and family. The *Packet* was founded in 1851 in the immediate aftermath of the controversy surrounding Tractarianism, and its depiction of girlhood reflects this religious ideology. During its lengthy run of almost 50 years, the changing conditions of girlhood and the decline in popularity of High Anglicanism meant that the magazine needed to adapt its ideal of religious girlhood. The challenges of adapting the religious girl to meet new circumstances are evident in the correspondence published in the magazine. The girl readers are actively engaged in refining the image of the religious girl, and their interjections demonstrate a reality of girlhood increasingly at odds with the some of the more conservative aspects of the magazine's religious ideal. In its final decade, attempts were made to realign its feminine ideal of duty, charity, and sacrifice by removing Yonge as the editor and including content to reflect the new realities of girls' lives. However, the powerful influence of Yonge—both as a novelist and as the editor of the *Packet*—and her ideal were virtually impossible to separate from the magazine, and these attempts were ultimately unsuccessful. The 1890s marked a concerted attempt in the *Packet* to contain Yonge's influence and reconfigure her religious feminine ideal to satisfy its *fin-de-siècle* readership, but the magazine ceased publication in 1899.

The *Monthly Packet* appeared after two decades of religious and political turmoil. The 1830s and '40s saw the rise of the Evangelical and Oxford Movements, both of which were attempts to reform institutional religion after decades of abuse.[1] Key members of the Oxford Movement included John Keble, Edward Pusey, and John Henry Newman. Between 1833 and 1841, these men and others wrote and published a series of 90 tracts (from which the name "Tractarian" derives), each of which argued for a religious principle that was felt to be important to the

---

[1]   C. Brad Faught's *The Oxford Movement: A Thematic History of the Tractarians and Their Times* (2003) provides a comprehensive analysis of the Movement. See Chapter VI, "Religion Movements and Crises" in Richard Altick's *Victorian People and Ideas* (1973) for a summary of the Oxford Movement and the crises of faith during the nineteenth century.

Church of England. These principles included an emphasis on the importance of the Sacraments of Baptism, Confirmation, and Communion; frequent, preferably daily, church-going; and the call for church-building, missionary work, and Sunday school teaching. In 1845, however, Newman converted to Catholicism, a move that shocked and troubled the Tractarians, especially when others followed his conversion.

The *Monthly Packet* first appeared in this increasingly complex religious environment. As William Gibson notes, "the Church of England's monopoly had been eroded into the status of one denomination among many. By 1850 even the most conservative churchmen acknowledged that the Church operated in a pluralistic society and religious behaviour was becoming, by definition, voluntary behaviour" (171). The *Packet* was started at the suggestion of Mary Anne Dyson, an invalid, and her brother, the Rev. Charles Dyson, who wished to position it as an alternative to the *Churchman's Companion*, a High Church magazine viewed with disfavour among some church members for its increasingly political views.[2] The Dysons invited Yonge, a long-time friend and already a recognized author, to edit the magazine, which was to be published by Mozley and Son, a well-known religious publisher. The magazine was a "collaborative venture, emerging at a time of great tension," and its objective "was to secure the loyalties of the next generation of Tractarians, by ensuring that their early associations were entwined with Church of England doctrine of the purest kind" (Yonge *Letters* 64).

In the pages of the *Monthly Packet*, religion provides the guiding principles towards which all feminine behaviour should be directed. Moreover, the influence of religion on constructions of femininity in the religious periodical press cannot be underestimated. Sue Morgan writes that "nineteenth-century religious teaching exercised considerable authority in defining the ideological parameters of femininity and masculinity through the mass reception of sermons, educational tracts and prescriptive literature, and much ecclesiastical ink was poured forth on delineating modes of behaviour appropriate to either sex" ("Women, Religion and Feminism" 1). As the editor, Yonge was instrumental in defining the religious girl presented in the *Packet*. She wrote substantial portions of the content, especially in the early years, and her fiction frequently appeared in its pages. The serialization of more than 27 of her novels, which often took two or more years to complete, as well as regular features like the "Cameos of English History," the "Conversations on the Catechism," and advice on books and reading, make her voice powerful and pervasive in the magazine.

The *Packet*'s commitment to a moral code of duty, sacrifice, and charity is closely connected to Yonge, both as an author and as editor of the *Monthly*

---

[2]   In *The Letters of Charlotte Mary Yonge (1823–1901)*, editors Charlotte Mitchell, Ellen Jordan, and Helen Schinske describe the Tractarian network of family and friends that surrounded Yonge, including the Dysons, the Moberleys, the Kebles, and the Coleridges. They also examine the close relationship between Yonge and Mary Anne, whom Charlotte nicknamed her (slave) "Driver" (12).

Packet. As Jack Zipes explains, in these roles Yonge "played a crucial role in constructing the reading of middle- and upper-class girls through two generations" (2147). Even late in the century and despite Yonge's declining popularity, the wholesome, religious nature of Yonge's writing was well understood. The degree and nature of her influence is suggested in Ethel Turner's children's novel, *Seven Little Australians* (1894), when 16-year-old Meg is led astray by reading unsuitable novels and the latest magazines. The narrator observes that Meg was "surprised at the new world into which they took her; for Charlotte Yonge and Louisa Alcott and Miss Wetherell had hitherto formed her simple and wholesome fare" (53).[3] Amy Cruse demonstrates in *The Victorians and Their Books* (1935) that Yonge's influence was felt by more than simply middle-class girls. William Morris and Dante Gabriel Rossetti loved *The Heir of Redclyffe* (1853). Tennyson was so absorbed by the story of delayed confirmation in *The Young Step-Mother* (1861) that he stayed up late to read it. Even Charles Kingsley, an opponent of Tractarianism, liked her writing. He advised Yonge not to "mind what *The Times* or anyone else says; the book [*Heartsease* (1854)] is wise and human as well as Christian, and will surely become a standard book for aye and a day" (Cruse 57). Yonge was well aware of her influence on others. In her response to an offer from Macmillan to edit a series of books, she feared she would not have sufficient editorial control and felt she must decline "in thorough fairness to those who take my name as a pledge for the strict line of distinctly Anglican orthodoxy" (Nowell-Smith 88).

The *Monthly Packet*

Each issue of the *Monthly Packet* in its early years generally includes a "Cameo" from history (such as the May 1851 "Last Days of Saxon Prosperity), a "Conversation on the Catechism," a variety of fiction, either part of a serial or standalone, and nonfiction excerpted from another source. The nonfiction was often religious history, such as "Missions of the Fourth Century" and "The Hospital de Lagaray," both in March 1851. Natural history was also of interest to Yonge, so she included articles like "Our Featured Neighbours" and "Nocturnal Life of Animals in the Primeval Forest" from *Humboldt's Aspects of Nature*. The February 1851 number, for example, includes 5 pages on "Missions of the Fourth Century," 10 pages on "Conversations on the Catechism," 12 pages of "Cameos from English History," and a combined 32 pages of fiction. Because these early contributions are unsigned, ascertaining the precise volume of Yonge's contributions is difficult, but her name can be unequivocally be attributed to over half of the issue's contents. The anonymity of the contributors gradually gives way to clearly identified authors, especially after the explicit identification of Yonge

---

[3]   Louisa Alcott was, of course, best known for *Little Women*, first published in 1868. Elizabeth Wetherell was the pseudonym of Susan Warner, who published *The Wide, Wide World* in America in 1850.

as editor in 1881.[4] In addition to Yonge, contributors included other staunch High Anglicans like novelist and educator Elizabeth Missing Sewell, historian and educator Emily Taylor, and later Yonge's protégé Christabel Coleridge.

Early issues were 64 pages long—although by 1860 they were 112 pages and stayed in this range until the magazine's end—and contained a number of fairly lengthy articles, none of which were illustrated. The magazine, in fact, never contained illustrations, marking it as more literary, and less ephemeral, than illustrated girls' periodicals appearing later in the century. Its single columns, size, and length are features more suggestive of books than periodicals. Initially priced at 6d. per issue, the price rose to 8d. in 1857 and then 1s. in 1866, which is also when the title of the magazine was changed to remove "Younger." Yonge edited the magazine alone until declining readership prompted Yonge to accept her friend and protégé Christabel Coleridge as co-editor in 1891. Publisher Arthur D. Innes forced Yonge to resign except as a contributor in 1894, and he and Coleridge acted as co-editors until the final issue in 1899.

The magazine often included poetry in its pages, much of which was religious. Joanna Baillie's "The Kitten" occupies four pages in the January 1852 number and is followed by a two-page poem "Christmas Angels" by Elizabeth P. Roberts.[5] Yonge's fiction frequently includes poetic epigraphs. *The Daisy Chain*, for example, includes lines from *Lyra Innocentium*, Wordsworth, Cowper, Longfellow, Southey, Chaucer, Tennyson, and Keble's *Christian Year*, to name but a few. Yonge incorporation of poetry into her prose writing is hardly surprising given the influence in her life of poet John Keble, the Oxford Professor of Poetry (1831–41). Yonge frequently did not distinguish between prose and poetry. As Elizabeth Jay remarks, Yonge's work on the *Packet* reflects "the hybrid nature of many contemporary magazines and periodicals, and her lifelong habit of seeing the two as so intimately related that it came naturally to her to further Tractarian poetics through the medium of prose fiction" (43).[6]

---

[4]   Until 1881, the magazine identifies the editor as "the author of *The Heir of Redclyffe*." For most readers, and particularly those of the *Packet*, this would have been sufficient to identify Yonge as the editor. For further details about contributors, see Charlotte Mitchell's "Charlotte M. Yonge's Bank Account: A Rich New Source of Information on Her Work and Her Life," especially pages 389–91.

[5]   The correspondence between Roberts and Yonge is examined by June Sturrock in "Establishing Identity: Editorial Correspondence from the Early Years of *The Monthly Packet*."

[6]   In Yonge's September 1892 article for the "Work and Workers" series on authorship, she makes little distinction as to the writer's genre.

Defining Religious Girlhood

From its inception, the *Monthly Packet* clearly identifies both its target readership and its goal of guiding girls towards a feminine religious ideal.[7] In the "Introductory Letter" in January 1851, Yonge makes it clear that the goal of the publication is to help "young girls, or maidens, or young ladies, whichever you like to be called" (i), form their characters. Aimed at girls between the ages of 15 and 25, the magazine

> is meant to be in some degree a help to those who are thus forming it; not as a guide, since that is the part of deeper and graver books, but as a companion in times of recreation, which may help you to perceive how to bring your religious principles to bear upon your daily life, may show you the examples, both good and evil, of historical persons, and may tell you of the workings of God's providence both here and in other lands. (i–ii)

The desire to help girls understand how to incorporate religion into their daily lives is a consistent theme in the publication. Alethea Hayter notes that "the extent to which these doctrines and practices permeate the smallest details of [Yonge's] novels can only be appreciated when they are compared to the widespread, though not universal, laxities of the pre-Tractarian Church of England" (17). The Church is Yonge's "constant subject. Rather than preach its doctrines directly, she prefers to illustrate them in life" (Bemis 125).[8] Adopting a Tractarian position of reserve, Yonge does not preach like the Evangelicals but instead presents Church practices and religious piety as part of daily life.

In the first "Conversation on the Catechism"—a series designed to prepare readers for Confirmation—the theme of sacrifice and charity for the religious girl is embodied by Miss Mary Ormesden. She gives great joy when, after the death of her father, she decides to continue living in the village in order to "be kind to the sick, to read to the old people who had once seen her grow up among them, and to teach at school the children of those who had once been her first class" (Yonge "Conversations" 14). Within the *Packet*, religious girls such as Ormesden understand and accept their responsibilities to family, church, and community, where they occupy important roles and will always have a home.[9] Miss Ormesden

---

[7]   Brad Faught explains that Yonge's "main audience consisted of upper-class and upper-middle-class young women who were given fictional models of ideal Christian women whose first duty was to God and the Church" (113).

[8]   Virginia Bemis argues that Yonge occupies a theological role in the *Monthly Packet* because her articles, in contrast to her fiction, "are directed toward those who ought to work at understanding [religious doctrine], particularly candidates for confirmation" (126).

[9]   This idea is eagerly received by her readers. In September 1854, after an inquiry about when the "Conversations on the Catechism" will be available for purchase in book form, Yonge responds that "the Conversations on the Catechism are so far from their conclusion that it is impossible to say when they can be published separately" ("Notice to Correspondents" 240).The three-volume edition of *Conversations on the Catechism* eventually appeared between 1859 and 1863.

guides her young friends through a series of "Conversations on the Catechism," which are written as conversations and designed to both entertain and instruct on religious principles. References to and quotations from hymns, like the St. Matthew's Day hymn in Keble's *Christian Year*, are also included.

In addition to her responsibility to her community, a girl must understand the importance of her familial role. Talia Schaffer observes that "Yonge's novels provide some of the most vivid (and heartrending) accounts of intellectual girlhood in Victorian England—the struggle to keep up with brothers' education, the desperate need for meaningful work, the frustration at the accumulation of petty but exhausting tasks—and yet Yonge insists that her characters learn to love their hampered lives" ("Mysterious" 245). Yonge's "The Daisy Chain" is one of the best examples of this aspect of the religious girl, the first half of which was serialized in the *Monthly Packet* between July 1853 and December 1855. The story centers on Dr. May and his 11 children in the aftermath of a carriage accident that kills Mrs. May and paralyses the eldest daughter, Margaret. The intelligent, enthusiastic, imperfect Ethel May struggles with the domestic expectations placed upon her. She wants to keep up with her brother Norman in his studies of Greek and Latin while also establishing and running a school for the local Cocksmoor children and raising money to eventually build a church.[10] When these pursuits interfere with her duties at home, and with her ability to keep herself neat and organized, her sister Margaret shows her that she has been doing too much and suggests that she give up studying the classics. When Ethel resists, Margaret asks: "And for that would you give up being a useful, steady daughter and sister at home? The sort of woman that dear mamma wished to make you, and a comfort to papa" (41). Of all the tasks before her, she is expected to forego her intellectual pursuits because family and community responsibilities must be privileged over such intellectual interests.

In stories such as this, Yonge hoped to entertain her readers while also instructing them, rather than preaching to them. Virginia Bemis notes that Yonge's "favored mode of teaching was the parable rather than the sermon. Through a story, one could see how doctrine was lived out, in a way that would allow readers to apply such lessons to their own lives" (124). In "The Daisy Chain," for example, the reader is indirectly encouraged to sympathize with Ethel's struggles to meet the feminine ideal embodied by Margaret and to acknowledge that Ethel must sacrifice her intellectual needs to safeguard the home against domestic disorder and religious doubt. The consequence of failing to meet one's domestic responsibilities is shown in Flora May, Ethel's older sister, whose ambitious preoccupation with her husband's political career causes her to neglect her maternal duties and leads

---

[10]   Leslee Thorne-Murphy writes that "Yonge refuses to use one of her age's most successful strategies to justify women's involvement in philanthropic endeavor; she will not portray a 'natural' domestic expertise legitimating Ethel's charity. Instead, Yonge's more complex and elusive approach to philanthropy creates an individual endeavor grounded in social reality" (884).

to the death of her child. In her portrayal of Ethel, Yonge is sympathetic to the struggles of the young girl to meet the demands of the ideal. She demonstrates "her awareness of the day-to-day frustrations of young females with the cultural and gendered influences on their lives, while doing her best to reconcile her young readers to their situation and encouraging them by depicting fulfilling channels for their energies" (Brown 102). Yonge is not oblivious to the dreams and desires of a young girl, and much of the story is dedicated to understanding how Ethel comes to accept her role within the household and be satisfied with the duties that role entails. Ethel even sacrifices the possibility of romance and eventual marriage, deciding that her role in the home is too important.

The poetry in the *Packet* continues to reinforce the ideology of conservative religious girlhood. The poem "Edburgha," republished from the *Englishman's Magazine* in April 1851, tells of merchants who return with riches from India and the Orient for their king. The king invites his seven children, including his favourite Edburgha, to select "some gorgeous thing" (l. 34), but Edburgha is "content" (l. 43) with her illuminated missal-book. She rejects the power and influence of the "world" (l. 55) and chooses the "better part" (l. 58) of religion. The poem concludes with a shift in the point of view, encouraging the reader to use Edburgha as a model and to see other readers as part of a community of girls who are striving to choose the path of religion: "We are as thou wert then—be thou/Our bright and blest example now" (l. 59–60). The girl reader is intended to reject the greed and materialism of the modern world and find happiness in her religious life.

Given the extent to which religious girlhood in the *Packet* is guided by High Anglican beliefs and traditions, the magazine's depiction of duty, sacrifice, and charity as the mainstays of the religious girl is unsurprising. However, Yonge is aware girlhood is mutable. In her introduction, she laments that "if the pretty old terms, maidens and damsels, had not gone out of fashion, I should address this letter by that name to the readers for whom this little book is, in the first place, intended" (i). She recognizes that girls are adopting new labels, and she remains concerned throughout the *Packet*'s run about this instability and its implications for guiding girls toward appropriate behaviour. This volatility suggests that girlhood is, and has already been, the subject of reflection and redefinition.

A clear articulation of the connection between femininity and religion in the *Monthly Packet* can be found in Yonge's series of articles entitled "Womankind," the first of which appeared in July 1874. Yonge discusses a range of subjects pertaining to girls, including the status of women, nursery training, religion, education, and charity. Notably and provocatively, on the first page of this series Yonge writes, "I have no hesitation in declaring my full belief in the inferiority of woman, nor that she has brought it upon herself" (24). This reference to the temptation and subsequent fall of Eve in the Garden of Eden supports the view that Yonge was an antifeminist. However, her depiction of the feminine ideal in the *Packet* is much more complicated than this judgment allows. Her comments on strong-minded women, for example, published in 1876 as part of "Womankind," reflect this complexity:

> Be strong-minded, then. With all my might I say it. Be strong-minded enough to
> stand up for the right, to bear pain and danger in a good cause, to aid others in
> time of suffering, to venture on what is called mean or degrading, to withstand a
> foolish fashion, to use your own judgment, to weigh the value of compliments.
> In all these things be strong. Be the valiant woman, but do not be strong-minded
> in a bad sense in discarding all the graces of humility, meekness, and submission,
> which are the true strength and beauty of womanhood. (NS Vol. 21 476)[11]

A woman can be strong and independent even as she retains the graces of "humility,
meekness, and submission." This paradoxical position of agency and submission
for girls and women is a consequence of Yonge's religious beliefs and her status
as both a professional author and a single woman. The tension between Yonge's
religious life and her professional life makes a compelling case for the paradox of
her feminine ideal. As the editors of Yonge's letters observe,

> The fascination of her story lies in the tension between her conformism and her
> extraordinary achievement: as a bestselling novelist, as an innovative children's
> writer, as a writer of religious works (including fiction), as a successful woman
> journalist, as scholar, biographer and critic, even as a proponent of women's
> rights. (Yonge *Letters* 4)

Like the tension in Yonge's life, the tensions embodied in the religious girl
presented in the *Packet* are equally difficult to resolve. Yonge consistently advises
girls to sacrifice their own needs to ensure domestic harmony, and to understand
that charitable work is the most a girl can expect to do outside the home. In
"Womankind," she describes "what I believe to be the safe and true aspect in
which woman ought to regard herself—namely, as the help-meet of man" (NS
Vol. 17 27). Nevertheless, she believes that a woman is not necessarily defined
by her relationship to a husband. Unmarried women can and should consider
themselves as "pure creatures, free to devote themselves to the service of their
Lord" (NS Vol. 17 27).

Although the serialization of "Womankind" was completed in December
1876, Yonge reintroduced many of its ideas in an 1886 editorial that signals her
discomfort with the way ideals of femininity were changing in the final decades
of the nineteenth century. In the January 1886 article "New Year's Words," Yonge
admits that some might criticize her for repeating herself, which suggests both that
her attitudes about girlhood had not changed and that she believes her readers in
1886 were also reading the *Packet* in 1874. In this regard, it is interesting to note
that in 1866, the word "Younger" was removed from the title of the magazine.
Although the magazine may have been attracting older readers, it is more likely

---

[11]   *The Monthly Packet* run is divided into four series. The first runs from 1861 to 1865
(volumes 1–30). A new series began in 1866 with the change in title to remove "Younger"
and lasted until 1880 (New series, volumes 1–30). A third series was published from 1881
to 1890 (Third series, volumes 1–20). The final series began in 1891 and continued until
1899. (For the sake of clarity, I refer to this as Fourth series, volumes 1–18.)

that the young girls who comprised the original audience continued to read the magazine as they grew up.[12]

While Yonge acknowledges that the world in 1886 is "more for liberty and freedom from restraint" than it was in 1874 and that "to go back is hardly possible" ("New Year's Words" 41), she still yearns for the purity and morality of girls from an earlier age. Thus, even as she recognizes the changes going on in the world around her, she encourages her readers to return to the values of those bygone days. In *Theorizing Childhood* (1998), Allison James, Chris Jenks, and Alan Prout point out that the controls placed on children are designed to contain them within designated spaces and to "restrict the ways in which children can spend their time" (41). Yonge's concerns about sport, fashion, and slang are aimed at controlling girls' conduct since modern girls are most evidently failing to reach her feminine ideal in these areas. She argues that the average young lady of the past "did not want to be a semi-man in sports, talk, and dress, and would have shrunk from seeing men on their own ground, joining them in their smoking-room, or going about with them unchaperoned" (41).

As I discuss more fully in the next chapter, these comments, like Eliza Lynn Linton's in "The Girl of the Period," are intended to be provocative. Both women assert that the girls of the present are less feminine, modest, and pure than the girls from earlier times. Comparing girls continued to be a common method employed in the press, and particularly in girls' periodicals, to encourage debate and thereby increase readership. In the 1902 volume of the *Girl's Empire*, a modern twentieth-century magazine celebrating the possibilities of girlhood, Heloise Edwina Hersey discusses "The Manners of the Modern Girl." As the principal of Miss Hersey's School for Girls in Boston, Hersey was well situated to comment on girls and twentieth-century girlhood. In this excerpt from her 1901 book, *To Girls: A Budget of Letters,* she remarks that "[t]he pulpit and the newspaper vie with each other in regret or admonition over the decay of social graces" (468) of the twentieth-century girl. She reminds her readers to guard against generalizations and affirms that she knows "hundreds of girls whose manners are as elegant as those of the seventeenth century, and withal as genuine as the twentieth century could wish them to be" (468). Like Yonge and Linton, Hersey draws on a comparison with girls of the past, although she suggests that they are all equally well mannered. Yet Hersey also acknowledges that "there remains a great mass of rudeness to be accounted for and dealt with," which arises from "a misconception of the nature of manners and their use in society" (468). While Hersey argues that "gentle manners … are nothing more or less than a set of rules adopted by cultivated people to aid in the playing of their parts in life easily, swiftly, naturally" (469), others have felt that conventional manners were employed to hide one's true nature and used this

---

[12]   The 1860 entry in Mitchell's *Newspaper Press Directory* (the first year that magazines and periodicals were listed) describes the *Packet* as containing "Christian Literature for the Younger Members of the English Church" (14: 114). The 1868 entry has changed to "Tales and General Literature for Members of the English Church" (22: 124).

as an excuse to neglect teaching one's daughters to behave appropriately. Hersey's final advice to her girl readers is to remind them that "[y]ou and I must try to hasten the day when it shall be a matter of course that a woman that makes claim to be thought an educated woman shall be mistress of a decorous and gracious manner, and shall regard it as a precious heritage to pass on to her daughters" (469). Hersey positions girls' manners as timeless and a necessary feminine quality to be passed on to her children. She also hints at the shift in attitudes brought about by changes to girls' education, where increasing access to education is thought to make girls less feminine.

Similarly, Yonge's anxiety in "New Year's Words" arises from how changes in permissible behaviours may cause girls to appear more masculine. Her concerns are explicitly connected with the formation of femininity, a position highlighted in her discussion of Wordsworth's poem "She was a phantom of delight." He calls her "a perfect woman, nobly plann'd/To warn, to comfort, or command" (l. 27–8). Yonge remarks to her readers: "A perfect woman, observe; not an imperfect female man, any more than a weak, sentimental creature, fit for nothing but to be petted" (l. 42). She directly appeals to her readers and uses sensational language to persuade them to follow her advice. She begs them to retain the qualities of modesty, gentleness, charity, and devoutness: "Do not—oh do not, I implore you, throw them away, merely for the sake of being like other people; but be brave in your resistance to that fatal current which is carrying English womanhood away with it, on the impulses of levity, fashion, and daring, into a whirlpool of shame and destruction" (47). The whole of England is at risk if girls, by adopting the new fashions and behaviours of the 1880s, lose their womanliness. Yonge believes that these new behaviours are defeminizing and raises concerns about girls' future roles as wives and mothers, implicitly suggesting Darwin-inspired fears for the future of the English race.

Women's Work

Although Yonge privileged duty, sacrifice, and womanliness, she still believed that middle-class girls needed work to do within the home. Somewhat paradoxically, even as she was constructing this ideal for girls, Yonge herself was doing work which, although it was performed primarily at home, was nonetheless intended for a public audience. The "Correspondence" section in the *Monthly Packet* highlights this contradiction while also presenting the possibility that women were not restricted to domestic and charitable work to the extent advocated by Yonge's ideal. The very first "Notice to Correspondent" section appears in March 1851, after the magazine had been in print for two months. In it, Yonge writes, "E.M.'s first chapter is promising, but the Editor can form no judgment without seeing the remainder of the tale" (208). The next month, "E.M. is thanked for her tale. The editor would be glad to make some comments, if she will be kind enough to give her address" (288). This marks the beginning of a dialogue between Yonge and the potential contributors to the magazine, and subsequent notices indicate the acceptance or rejection of various contributions, thereby highlighting Yonge's role as editor of the magazine, her active participation in the public sphere, and the grooming of a new generation of women writers. As the editors of Yonge's letters note:

> The many letters to other women, including contributors to the three journals she edited, show her encouraging and supporting a large number of other aspirant female writers, mainly encountered via the Tractarian connection, well outside the networks of literary London, who have been barely glimpsed in other accounts of Victorian professional authorship. (Yonge *Letters* 5)

This first notice marks the beginning of a different kind of dialogue between Yonge, a successful writer and editor, and E.M., a woman who hoped to see her own writing in print. No further references to E.M. appear in the "Notice to Correspondents" section, so the correspondence presumably became private. Nonetheless, in responding to this woman, Yonge highlights her active working role as an editor and also alludes to a feminine ideal different from the one she advocates in her own writing. By providing some constructive advice on how to improve E.M.'s writing, Yonge encourages a woman who is attempting to develop her talents beyond the domestic sphere and who thus implicitly contradicts the ideal Yonge circulates in the magazine.[13]

Consequently, in the pages of the *Packet*, a tension exists between the ideal religious girl and the reality of girls' lives. Yonge was not oblivious to the issues of women's work that were being raised by women's rights activists in the 1850s. As June Sturrock argues, the *Monthly Packet* dealt with issues of women and work as extensively as feminist journals like the *English Woman's Journal* and the later *Victoria Magazine*, albeit with a different focus. Rather than highlighting the need for income and the power such income vested in its earner, as Barbara Bodichon does in *Women and Work* (1857), the *Monthly Packet* focused on "the individual's experience of the need for work, relating this need to social and domestic structures—social class and, above all, family hierarchies" (Sturrock "Women" 65). Yonge fully understood and believed in the necessity of work. In "Womankind," she encourages the woman who is single or married to "look for the services that she can fulfil by head or by hands, by superintendence or by labour, by pen or pencil, by needle or by activity, by voice or by music, by teaching or by nursing" (NS Vol. 17 29). Yonge directs her readers toward a variety of different kinds of work and encourages girls to choose tasks that meet their skills and interests. She also encourages them to pursue a detailed course of reading once they are out of the schoolroom.

---

[13]   June Sturrock draws on a more robust sample of correspondence between Yonge and contributor Elizabeth Roberts to demonstrate how Yonge fashioned herself in a "supportive and almost familial" ("Establishing" 267) role.

Girls' Reading

In a magazine aimed at religious girls and edited by a popular writer of children's literature, the importance placed upon reading is hardly surprising. One of Yonge's primary objectives, as both an editor and a writer, is to guide girls towards reading that she feels is appropriate, while also raising their awareness of the dangers and pitfalls of inappropriate reading, in terms of its implications for faith and domestic responsibilities. Although reading is an important occupation for girls, in Yonge's view it could be fraught with danger, especially as religious faith came under increasing scrutiny as a result of the controversy surrounding the Oxford Movement, the subsequent conversions to Catholicism, and the threat posed by interpretations of Darwinian ideas of evolution.

Yonge's belief in the importance of reading to reinforce, rather than question, one's religious faith is echoed in the writing of another writer for children, Sarah Trimmer. As a literary critic, children's writer, and educator in the late eighteenth century, Trimmer believed in the importance of introducing children of the poor to the Scriptures so that they could be closer to God. Her *Guardian of Education* (1802–1806) is widely credited as being the first magazine to methodically review children's books. Yet, as her son Henry describes in *Some Account of the Life and Writings of Mrs. Trimmer*, Trimmer "was always much averse to reading books of controversy; and never liked to disturb her mind by them" (40). In a letter to an unnamed friend, Trimmer writes that, based on her father's recommendation, she has been "avoiding those publications" (41) which might disturb and perplex her mind. She continues, "I have, it is true, read many books of divinity; but very few, that I can recollect, of a controversial nature" (41), preferring instead to build her faith on "the word of God" (41).

In Yonge's first reading-advice column, published in September 1851, she claims to "have been requested to write a few lines of advice" ("A Few Words" 240) on books to read for amusement. Despite Yonge's own liberal reading habits, some books are "so utterly distasteful" that she would never read them; yet she "constantly sees these very books in the hands of young girls, who ought to be ashamed to own they have ever read them" (241). Although Yonge never identifies these books, her message, like Trimmer's, is clear: ignore any book that might cause the reader to question her faith. In fact, Yonge has three very explicit rules: "Never read anything that can at all unsettle your religious faith"; "Read nothing that can affect your loyalty"; and "Never read a badly written book" (241–3). She reminds readers who want to reject her advice that as "the younger members of the Church of England" (241), they are obliged to put aside texts that may cause them to question their faith. To ensure that her readers adhere to the ideal of moral purity, Yonge suggests that they should read only those books of which they have some previous knowledge, "either from reviews, or from some person on whose judgment you can rely" (243), including the reviews found in the *Packet*.

Yonge was particularly concerned that girls did not fritter away their time by reading light-hearted novels. In her account of Victorian women readers, Kate Flint writes that "reading was a form of consumption associated with the possession of leisure time, and thus contributed to the ideology, if not always the practices, which supported the ideal of the middle-class home. Yet it could also be regarded as dangerously useless, a thief of time which might be spent on housewifely duties" (11). Yonge addresses the tension between duty and pleasurable reading repeatedly in the *Monthly Packet* because she feels that girls must understand where their responsibilities lie. She explicitly cautions girls against letting their reading overwhelm their responsibilities in the home. She recommends *In School and Out of School* (1878) because of its value for teachers and schoolgirls "whose learning is in danger of devouring homely duties" ("Hints on Reading" Vol. 6 160).[14] This kind of reading reinforces the domestic responsibilities of girlhood. By suggesting that girls read texts endorsing home duties and that identify the risks of excessive study, Yonge presents a feminine ideal that endorses a girl's responsibilities within the home, while emphasizing the importance of education for a girl's future.

Moreover, the self-discipline necessary for study must be cultivated, especially if a girl has a great deal of leisure time. In 1851 Yonge writes,

> The girl who, after her school-room days are over, is contented to spend every home-morning in light desultory reading, fancy-work, and letter-writing, is frittering away opportunities she will never bring back again, and weakening her own power of mind to such a degree that a few years will make her one of the dull, prosy, mere housekeeping, frivolous women whose company she at present dislikes. ("Hints on Reading" 478)

Study is the best way a girl can avoid becoming a woman who has no "power of mind." The girl at home who merely reads, writes letters, and does fancywork will not be able to achieve the ideal of religious femininity. Furthermore, as Kelly J. Mays explains, "Through the oft-criticized practice of 'desultory reading' in particular, the individual reader, having no principle of organization, no self-coherence, came to mirror the indiscriminate unorganised chaos of [the] texts" (176) she read. Disciplined study is Yonge's answer to the collegiate training that men undergo in order to be fit for active life. While boys have access to colleges and teachers, Yonge's girls should be educated within the domestic sphere.

Although Yonge campaigned steadily for improved reading habits for girls, hers was just one of many voices engaged in guiding young readers towards appropriate reading. In Jane Menzies' *A.1.: A Magazine for Family Reading* (1888–90), the same concerns appear. Like the *Packet*, *A.1.* is also a religious periodical, although generally less overt in its religious message. *A.1.* is one of only three girls' magazines identified by Edward Salmon in his survey of *Juvenile Literature* (1888) that "could be placed advantageously before anybody, to say

---

[14] This book was part of a series called *Magnet Stories for Summer Days and Winter Nights*. Available for 3d., the series was published by Groombridge and Sons.

nothing of girls in their teens" (195).[15] In "Our Monthly Talk: "Railway Book-stalls," Menzies discusses a letter she has received about how respectable people, including women and clergymen, purchase scandalous papers and novels of dubious taste while traveling. The railway bookstall librarian has "tried to sell good books, instead of novels, and *good* Papers instead of *Family Heralds*, etc. ... In the towns, where they live and are known, people buy respectable things; but when they are travelling, they buy *the worst*" (11). There is presumably a class bias here, since cheap weekly magazines like the 1d. *Family Herald* were read by the lower middle classes as well as the working classes. At the same time, the article discriminates against fiction, which was a staple of the *Family Herald*. In a similar vein, *The Mystery of a Hansom Cab* (1888) by Fergus Hume is understood by both the correspondent and the bookseller to contain some of the worst language to ever have been printed. The bookseller asks "how can we librarians respect [clergymen], or profit by their sermons" (11), when we see them buying such books. The quality of one's reading affects how one is perceived, and periodicals like the *Packet* and *A.1.* are intended to "shape the practices of the reading public and to articulate ... the difference between that public and those with the capacity and duty to oversee and guide it" (Mays 169).

Yonge provides regular reading recommendations within the *Packet* throughout her lengthy career, even suggesting other periodicals that girls might enjoy. In April 1868, she recommends the *Churchman's Companion* as well as *Aunt Judy's Magazine* ("Hints on Reading" 415). Yet her recommendations are always directed towards a proper view of the church. She writes in March 1869 that *Good Words for the Young* "is capitally illustrated ... but we are sorry that the usually charming author of 'Lilliput Levee' should have spoilt her fairy wedding with a fairy bishop and fairy curates. Irreverence is always foolish and ugly; and this emphatically so, and most useless" ("Hints on Reading" 310).[16] In Yonge's view, the sneer at the curates should not, and would not, be understood by children. She did not hesitate to criticize material that she felt was not up to the highest of literary and religious standards. Moreover, the periodicals that she recommends are uniformly religious periodicals and, in making such recommendations, Yonge reinforces a reading experience similar to that found within the *Packet*.

From the "Notices to Correspondents" section, the readers of the *Packet* were evidently regular consumers of fiction and other periodicals. In September 1873, for example, "*E.O.H.* would be obliged if another could tell her where she could procure the following back numbers of the *Magazine for the Young*, which are out of print. All the numbers for 1844, and February, May, and September, 1848. She would either pay for them or exchange other magazines" (310). Readers turned to the correspondence section to find other magazines—some long out of print—and to exchange books and magazines for others that they wish to read. In May

---

[15]   The three magazines were the *Girl's Own Paper*, *Atalanta*, and *A.1.*

[16]   Yonge incorrectly assumes that the author is a woman. The collection of poems is by William Brighty Rands.

1874, one woman wishes to exchange her unbound copies of the *Packet* for 1866 and 1867 for any numbers between July 1857 and July 1860. Another wishes to exchange numbers of the *Packet* for numbers of the *Churchman's Companion* ("Notices" 504). The presence of these requests in the Correspondence section is paradoxically suggestive of both the ephemerality of the periodical press and its permanence. Out of print publications, like the numbers of the *Magazine for the Young* from 1844 and 1848, are difficult if not impossible to obtain through normal publishing channels. Yet the *Packet* opens up another channel of distribution, predominately one of barter and exchange, which highlights the possibilities of permanence.

This sense of permanence is one of the aspects of girlhood in the *Packet* that girl readers began to resist. As girls' education improved and their opportunities beyond the home expanded, readers of the *Packet* began to question aspects of its feminine ideal, including the recommendation that readers avoid all potentially harmful texts. Moderated by Christabel Coleridge writing as "Chelsea China," a forum called "Debatable Ground" encouraged the *Packet* readers to contribute their perspectives on particular issues. Coleridge was, by this time, a frequent contributor to the *Packet*. She published her first book, *Lady Betty*, in 1869, and produced a total of 39 novels over her 50-year career. Coleridge had been a member of the Gosling Society, comprised of girls and young women who admired Charlotte Yonge or, as she was called, "Mother Goose." The Goslings wrote and produced a family magazine, the *Barnacle*, which was distributed among contributors. The *Barnacle* could be seen, as Julia Courtney explains, as an "in-house version of the *Monthly Packet*" (73). Certainly Coleridge's longstanding relationship with Yonge was consolidated during this period between 1859 and 1871 when the Goslings flourished. Coleridge wrote collaboratively with Yonge (and others), and she would eventually write the first biography of Yonge in 1902.[17]

In November 1886, "Chelsea China" raises the question of whether reading unsound books could be justified. Unsound books are largely defined as books that might cause the reader to question her faith, and the responses to this question are mediated by "Chelsea China" in three ways. First, she prints arguments against the proposition first, followed by the sometimes qualified affirmatives. This arrangement tends to privilege the negative case since readers may not read all the responses. Second, with the exception of one essay that is printed in full, all responses are summarized. For example, "Chelsea China" summarizes one correspondent's views in the following way: "*Wild Iris* thinks the risk incurred depends upon the religious faith of the reader. People of formed character and firm faith may safely read doubtful books; to others the same book will be a snare" (488). This allows "Chelsea China" to acknowledge the readers' contributions, while also framing the responses as she wishes, although she sometimes quotes

---

[17] The collaborative titles include *The Miz Maze; or, The Winkworth Puzzle, A Story in Letters* (1883), *Astray: A Tale of a Country Town* (1887), and *Strolling Players: A Harmony of Contrasts* (1893).

directly from the letters. Finally, "Chelsea China" concludes the "Debatable Ground" with a statement of her own views, which she presents in the third person: "What she personally thinks unsafe reading for undeveloped young Churchwomen are books in which infidelity ... is taken for granted as the inevitable and matter of course state of mind of all sensible and fair-minded people" (491–2). By using impersonal pronouns, Coleridge effectively distances herself from the message she sends while also reaffirming Yonge's concerns about reading. Although the magazine presents a variety of responses to girls' reading, some of which are openly contradictory to the ideas and values put forth by Yonge, it continues to advocate censorship.

Unsurprisingly in a magazine that presents reading as an important activity, the quality of the literature is a topic of equal importance. Literary authorship is depicted as an acceptable form of work for a religious girl, but only if the writer understands the importance of religion in her writing. In "Barbara's Book," an 1890 short story by Esmé Stuart, pseudonym of Amélie Claire Leroy, Barbara hides the "clever" book she is writing from her friends and family because she fears their disapproval. For her, writing is merely a way to make money, and she suppresses her misgivings about the quality of her book. When Jasper, an army officer, asks her to marry him, she turns him down because she knows he will not understand her decision to write such a novel, and he does not:

> Was this her work, this ghastly story, with its cynical tone, its clever flippancy? It was all the worse because it was clever and powerful, with its Scripture quotations put in to raise a smile. ... [A] bad book was to him one of the great evils of this world, and to have written one the greatest perversion of God's good gifts. On and on he read, till, with a new, strange feeling, he closed the second volume, feeling utterly crushed by the knowledge that the woman he loved had written words which, to his mind, no good woman would care to send forth on the wings of Time. (130)

This excerpt presents, from a male point of view, a perspective that Yonge had long endorsed. Jasper's negative judgement of this kind of fiction supports Yonge's position, reinforcing the need to write and to read quality fiction. In this case, the writing of such a book causes Jasper to question whether Barbara is actually a good woman.

Jasper subsequently falls deathly ill with scarlet fever, ostensibly because he saved a sick young child from being run over by a carriage. However, his illness is clearly a consequence of reading Barbara's book and her refusal to withdraw it from the marketplace. When she finally does take back the book, Jasper takes "a wonderful turn for the better" and "sends his love" (138). By suppressing publication, Barbara acknowledges the ills of writing and reading bad, frivolous books. Moreover, by giving up her right to publish, she gains Jasper's love and a second chance for happiness. Writing morally irreproachable books is imperative for the religious girl who has literary hopes and can even lead to love and marriage. This story signals an important shift in conceptions of religious girlhood in the last decade of the century. The *fin-de-siècle* girl can now consider earning money as long as the methods are consistent with a religious life.

Leroy's theme of religious girlhood is, unsurprisingly, similar to Yonge's. Leroy (as Stuart) contributed a number of short stories to the *Monthly Packet* beginning in 1875 and continuing until 1892. The author of numerous books, she also co-authored *Astray: A Tale of a Country Town* (serialized in the *Packet* in 1885–86) with Charlotte Yonge, Mary Bramston, and Christabel Coleridge. In a January 1894 informational article on "Women Talkers at Leeds," Miss Leroy is identified as giving a paper on the "Discipline of Reading" (Leake 62).[18] At the Conference of Women Workers at Leeds, Leroy cautions her listeners about the importance of a discipline of reading because

> you are influenced, even if you do not recognise it, by every book you read. Some book has made you a truer, grander, a more noble girl or woman, and some other book has lowered your whole moral nature one degree, and has made the next fall of the temperature of nobility easier and more rapid; and in your hands lies the power of falling or rising through the discipline of reading. (Leroy 643)

Much like Yonge's rhetoric about the importance of a disciplined course of reading and the dangers of reading that might cause a girl to question her faith, Leroy similarly believes some texts are "purely controversial and atheistic" and have no benefit because a girl's "pure young faith is more powerful for good than all such literature" (644). The importance and necessity of religion in a girl's life continues to be emphasized in a variety of places in the periodical press, even in magazines not specifically targeted at girls. Even the less religiously oriented *Atalanta* includes an article on Leroy's paper at the Leeds conference, confirming the importance of study in contrast to the principle of *laissez-faire* reading practices. Such freedom is "no blessing, but a curse" (Smith 351) because it prevents girls from reading thoroughly and with careful attention to the text.

Redefining the Religious Girl

Despite the strongly consistent message of God, family, and community in the pages of the *Monthly Packet*, from as early as the 1860s the girl readers of the magazine became increasingly involved in contesting the *Packet*'s definition of girlhood. They did this by writing letters to the magazine that implied or sketched a new religious girl who was more representative of their interests and concerns. Laurel Brake and Julie Codell describe these interactions between the journal and its readers as "encounters in the press," which they define as "any set of articles or letters to the editor in which the writer, whether journalist or reader, responds to a published article in a periodical, often as a reply to special topics or issues of the day, or to other articles with which the respondent agrees or disagrees" (1). Often

---

[18]   Leroy's talk was reprinted in the *Woman's Herald* on 30 November 1893.

in the form of dialogues or debates, they function "as mediations of the topic under discussion" (Brake and Codell 1). The idea—and ideal—of girlhood is the subject of many such encounters in girls' periodicals. In addition to the correspondence in the *Monthly Packet*, in subsequent chapters I also discuss examples found in *Atalanta*, the *Girl's Own Paper*, and the *Girl's Realm*. The frequency of these discussions demonstrates both the topicality of girlhood and the extent to which girls were engaged with its definition.

Through the correspondence section in the *Packet*, girl readers regularly attempt to refine and contest definitions of girlhood, demonstrating the degree to which readers were unwilling to be confined by Yonge's conservative expectations of girlhood. One of the earliest of these "encounters" begins in September 1862, when "Henrietta" seeks advice about the difficulties she experiences as a "young lady district visitor" (332). The following month, a response from "Grandmother" cautions young girls to examine their motives for wishing to do charitable work, to be content to wait if their parents do not wish them to be so "actively useful," and "to do what they can if doing as they wish is impossible for the present" (442). By figuring the girl as ultimately submissive to the will of her parents (and particularly her male relations), this response reinforces a common theme within the *Packet*.[19] In November 1862, "Jane" reiterates the knowledge of fathers and brothers as "better judges of what is suitable than [women] can be" (546) because of their better knowledge of the world. When "Henrietta" responds the following January, she agrees that it is "so much more proper for parents and guardians to arrange work for young people, than for the young to do so for themselves; but the practical difficulty still exists that few parents are to be found who will act in this spirited way" (109). Her subtle resistance to the idea that parents should be the arbiters of every daughter's actions marks the beginning of a tension in the *Packet* over the role that young girls are to occupy within the family and beyond it.

Another correspondent, "Mary," wonders at the busyness of girls' lives and quotes a clergyman who asks, "Where are the young girls of olden times, who cared to sit and sew?" (559). As some girls are exploring new freedoms, other readers of the *Monthly Packet* nostalgically remember the "olden times" when girls were content to remain within the home, free to attend to requests for assistance. Being active is criticized because it implies girls will not have time to be useful to others. The authors of these letters are of course also engaging in the debate, attempting to guide girls' behaviour through their letters. Another contributor, "Mona," explains that the active lifestyle of these girls is "a disease of young ladies newly escaped from the school-room" (217). Her depiction of female activity as a "disease" medicalizes the changing condition of girlhood, in much the same way that Michel Foucault describes the hysterization of the female

---

[19]   Moreover, the use of the pseudonym "Grandmother" evokes earlier series in the magazine such as "Grandmamma's Reflections" (1851) and "Grandmamma" (1859–62). It is possible that Yonge may have written "Grandmother's" contribution.

body, and posits it as something of which a girl may, and should, be cured.[20] In her closing comment, Mona endorses the sentiment of those people "who love to see maidens as they ought to be—'Of a meek and quiet spirit, which in the sight of God is of great price'" (217). By referring to this Biblical passage (Peter 1:3–4), the overactive girl becomes both sick and ungodly and must learn to control her thoughts and her actions in order to demonstrate her health and purity of spirit.

Finally in October 1863, over a year after the conversation about girlhood began, "Velocipede" engages in a spirited defense of the "fast young lady" (445), adopting a common phrase and giving it new meaning. Her pseudonym reflects her modernity, as the velocipede—the precursor to the bicycle—was a human-powered machine invented in 1863. In a letter that is strikingly different in tone from the moral and religious letters of the previous months, this young lady begins by protesting that the *Monthly Packet* is being used "to oppress a large and influential portion of the young ladyhood of England" (444). Although her letter is humorous in parts, the young writer—as a lover of fashion, croquet, and dances—seems almost the antithesis of the young women Yonge is attempting to attract through the *Monthly Packet*. She is, indeed, very similar to the "Girl of the Period" who appears in the *Girl of the Period Miscellany*, as I discuss in the next chapter. Joseph Altholz notes that "[r]eligious periodicals were, for the most part, preaching to the converted" (142) and were intended to reinforce the reader's religious belief. Thus Yonge's decision to publish the letter could well have been because she thought the superficiality and shallowness of its writer would reinforce her message about how girls should behave and subtly warn of the dangers of rejecting the message. Of course, the provocative nature of the letter is also intended to attract readers. Nonetheless, "Velocipede," like "Henrietta," resists attempts by the *Monthly Packet* to control girls' lives. While "Henrietta" asserts the right of girls to do what they can to help others, "Velocipede" refuses the charitable ethic intended to direct girls' activities outside the home. By insisting that her interests lie elsewhere, she suggests that girls should be free to choose their activities rather than being forced down a particular path.

A similarly spirited response from readers appeared after the publication of Yonge's 1886 "New Year's Words," although her declaration of women's inferiority in the 1874 "Womankind" failed to elicit comment in the correspondence section. A number of reasons help to explain this different result. First, owing to the substantial progress in middle-class girls' education, and particularly higher education for women, which I discuss in more detail in Chapter 5, the readers of the *Packet* were better educated than ever before and were increasingly seeking new opportunities. Second, there was a growing awareness that not all women would eventually marry, that they therefore needed some means of supporting

---

[20]   Michel Foucault (in *The Will to Knowledge: The History of Sexuality, Volume 1*) describes "a three-fold process" where the feminine body was "analysed ... as being thoroughly saturated with sexuality" (104) before it became increasingly subject to medical discourses, and was finally placed within the social, familial, maternal sphere.

themselves, and that they were actively seeking more and improved information about employment possibilities. Finally, the rise of the women's movement, which I address in Chapter 6, suggests that the environment into which Yonge was introducing her ideas had changed substantially.

Unsurprisingly, Yonge's "New Year's Words" generated responses over the next six months. The first came from "Middleage," who defends the modern young girl who reads the *Monthly Packet* as "thoroughly sweet, modest, and refined" (191) and more than capable of taking care of herself. "Moonraker" is heartbroken to think that anyone might consider her less than modest and does not want to be "independent" (479). "Modern Girl" agrees with Yonge that "we *are* shorter in manner, more brusque, uncompromising, opinionated—pig-headed if you will—less absolutely feminine even than our mothers are" (480). She argues that education is the cause of these changing signs of femininity because girls are being taught to think for themselves. She makes no apologies for the changing nature of girlhood but assures Yonge that girls' conduct remains "maidenly to the fullest degree" (482).

Through some correspondents' responses to overly restrictive depictions of girlhood, we see the emergence of a new religious girl within the pages of the *Packet*. Some readers are beginning to articulate a modernity at odds with Yonge's ideal of control and containment within the church and the family, reflecting the "provisional free space" of the last decades of the century where girls became aware of "new ways of being, new modes of behaviour, and new attitudes that were not yet acceptable for adult women" (S. Mitchell 3) even if they remained governed by traditional expectations. Although the religious girl of the 1880s has more freedom and choice within traditional hierarchies and is better trained and healthier, she remains constrained within the *Packet* by a mid-Victorian feminine religious ideal. Moreover, as June Sturrock explains, at a time when there were increasing challenges to "established family structures and some relaxation of social controls" as a result of the ongoing debate about the feminine ideal, the *Monthly Packet* promoted "a view of Christian femininity in which these controls could become internalised" ("Women" 71). The *Monthly Packet* addressed the issue of girlhood in such a way as to sympathize with the potential conflict between duty and desire while also reinforcing the need for traditional hierarchies like family and church.

The Final Decade

In the 1890s, owing to the advent of mandatory schooling, improved curricula, and higher quality teachers, girls were better educated, healthier, and increasingly encouraged to participate in the public domain as workers. The girls' periodical press explored different possibilities about how and where girls could participate in the public world. Although the religious press was still expanding at the end of the century, from the 1880s it was increasingly out of touch with the realities of life. Joseph Altholz describes the disjunction between the views of the church and those of a growing population that preferred secular activities to church attendance (142–3). Although the readers of the *Monthly Packet* presumably remained High Church adherents, they felt that the magazine's constraints on girlhood could not be justified. The shifting role of religion in daily life meant that the magazine faced difficulties in guiding its readers toward the religious principles of its earliest days. Recent scholarship, of course, complicates this position. The notion that "a linear and inescapable erosion of faith was at an advanced stage by the second half of the nineteenth century" (Knight and Mason 152) is now viewed with skepticism. Instead, Mark Knight and Emma Mason propose, "it is more constructive, and more accurate, to think about the ways in which Christianity adapted its form and message to engage with widespread cultural change" (153).[21] In light of this assessment, I would like to propose that the *Packet*'s readership declined in its last years not because *fin-de-siècle* girls were less religious, but because the religious girl it endorsed and promoted was out of touch with the period.

The attempts by the *Packet* to remain relevant indicate its editors were aware of the gap between their ideal religious girl and the reality of their readers' lives. The contrasting perspectives regarding the womanly ideal are highlighted in a May 1894 article, "The Fin-de-Siècle Girl." After noting the popularity of the topic, which has resulted in much "cheap writing" (586), Louise Jordan Miln argues that the *fin-de-siècle* girl differs very little from the girl of the past because "womanly women are greatly alike, every where and every time" (588).[22] The *fin-de-siècle* girl is the "logical evolution" of the girl of the past because she is "healthier, more normal, less affected, more broadly useful, more intelligent, more self-reliant, and infinitely more reliable" (588). Although "she is perhaps more assertive, less smooth, less apparently modest," her tremendous advantage over the girl of the past is that she is allowed to develop her own "best talent" (589); thus, "the girl of the day makes a big promise to the girl of the future—a promise of health, a promise of position in the world of doers and thinkers, a promise of limitless intellectual enjoyment—the enjoyment which lasts the longest, is more unassailable, and of which we can never be robbed" (589). This powerful

---

[21]   Jeffrey Cox draws a similar conclusion in *The English Churches in a Secular Society: Lambeth, 1870–1930* (1982). He writes, "Instead of thinking of religion as an inevitable casualty of the 'transition to modernity,' whatever its form, we should think of religion as competing in a free market in ideas whose rules are set by the state. Those rules have changed dramatically since the Reformation. There has always been tension between the Christian churches and the 'secular' world" (266–7).

[22]   Miln's contribution on the *fin-de-siècle* girl is evidence of the changing editorial stance of the *Packet*. This was Miln's only attributed contribution to the *Packet* and she became much better known as a travel writer. Her story of a theatrical tour through Asia, *When We Were Strolling Players in the East*, was also published in 1894 but well after the *Packet* article appeared. Drawing on her own experiences travelling in China, Japan, and Korea with her husband, Shakespearean actor George Crichton Miln, *When We Were* was the first of a number of novels that she published on the Far East.

message presumably would have found support among its target audience of girl readers, yet it includes few references to religious faith. To assert its modernity, the magazine had to retreat from overt religious content.

Despite these challenges, however, the *Packet* continued to construct a feminine subject that was firmly situated within the domestic space. In 1895, a year after she was removed as the editor, Yonge, using her pseudonym of "Arachne," contributes a letter arguing against female suffrage. Yonge argues that women should not be allowed to vote because too many women are "easily roused to popular emotion" ("The China Cupboard" 126) and easily swayed by the opinions of others. Coleridge, as "Chelsea China," admits that she hopes the letter will encourage debate among the readers of the *Packet*, and she must have been pleased with the results. The enthusiasm with which girl readers engaged in this debate not only suggests their comfort with public debate but also the extent to which their ideas diverged from Yonge's on topics, like suffrage, which challenged conventional ideas of femininity.

Over the next few months, readers wrote in to protest against "Arachne's" unjust characterization of women. In February 1895, "Dragon" writes that she considers "Arachne's" arguments invalid, and "Paperknife" comments that "[o]ne cannot argue seriously, after all, for we shall have our votes very soon, and we know how to use them rather better than any of the other classes who got them when they were enfranchised—though that is not saying much" (253). This oblique reference to the enfranchisement of working-class men through the third Reform Act of 1884, which added rural male heads of household and lodgers to the voting rolls, displays an uncharacteristic (for the *Packet*) sense of superiority over men who were less educated. Nonetheless, these respondents set the tone for much of the subsequent correspondence. In March 1895, C.M. Weisskopf writes that "Arachne's" arguments "do not touch the real point at issue, which is, surely, whether women's claim to representation is a just one, and, further, whether it is one we believe God to approve" (376). Similarly, "Amaryllis" argues that "Arachne" "does not meet the arguments for women's suffrage, which are based on justice and right" (377). These letters suggest that few readers endorsed "Arachne's" arguments. Although in the May number "Chelsea China" remarks that she continues to receive "furious denunciations and equally hearty praises" (Coleridge "The 'New Woman'" 619) for "Arachne's" principles, the latter are not published. All of the correspondence that Coleridge publishes unreservedly supports women's suffrage, suggesting perhaps that "Chelsea China" agrees with "Paperknife" that the subject is not worth serious debate. It also highlights Coleridge's attempts to become more topical, since women's franchise is not an issue that otherwise received much attention in the *Packet*. In the final decade of the magazine's run, a tension emerges between the ideas of the magazine's founding editor and the realities of girl readers' lives as the magazine's presentation of girlhood is seen to be increasingly outmoded.

Through a new monthly series entitled "Work and Workers" in January 1891, Coleridge tries to make the *Packet* appear more relevant to its readers. She writes that "[i]t is no new thing for the 'Monthly Packet' to concern itself with the aims and interests of educated girlhood" ("Work and Workers" 66). She evokes the 40-year history of the magazine when she claims that the *Packet* has a history of engagement with the issues and interests of girlhood, thereby attempting to show how the magazine has been, and still is, in touch with the issues affecting contemporary girls. The "Work and Workers" series is a serious attempt to address the question of women's employment in the 1890s and was published in book form as *Ladies at Work* (1893) by A.D. Innes, with a preface by activist Lady Jeune. Each article in the series discusses a different profession—such as music, art, medicine, and journalism—and is written by a woman working in the profession. Despite these efforts to provide information about professional employment, the magazine was anxious to reassure its readers it was not abandoning its core values with an article in July 1891 on working among the poor, a predominant theme throughout the magazine's run. This article urges "the necessity of training" upon potential charity workers and says that "in order to be of any real use to the poor, or indeed to go amongst them without doing positive harm, experience and training are of the greatest importance" (Lonsdale 32). In contrast to the message of "The Daisy Chain," for example, where willing hands and a good heart are all that are necessary to help the poor, now education, work experience, and good health are the best tools with which to assist others.

Through this series on "Work and Workers," a new ideal of religious girlhood is being constructed in the *Packet*. In an article on women's medical work in India, for instance, Fanny Emily Penny demonstrates her knowledge of India. Having lived there since shortly after her marriage in 1877, Penny is familiar with the conditions of and requirements for female doctors in India.[23] She makes clear the need for formal education, and lists the institutions that will allow women to study for a medical degree. She also stresses the need for a "strong constitution to endure such a life with its hard work and comparative loneliness" (Penny 264). The focus on health, which I discuss in Chapter 4, and formal training is new, but Penny reinforces the *Packet*'s Christian imperative in her closing sentence: "For whether she preaches Christianity openly or not, the lady-doctor must of necessity be the pioneer of a higher civilisation, and of a far holier creed than those which now hold India and her millions in their embrace" (265). While women imperialists are uncommon in the *Packet*, their role as female doctors in India is legitimized through a "permissible scope and imperial prestige" enabled by "the opportunity offered by the *zenana* and the imagined passivity of Indian women" (Bell 36). Women could be doctors in India without fear that they are "encroaching on the rights of the sterner sex" (Penny 260). The right of women to become doctors is asserted but also dramatically curtailed: they should practice only in India.

Attitudes towards women's work in the *Packet* remained ambiguous. In an article on nursing, Helen Mary Wilson and R. Wilson fear for "the homes where

---

[23]   Penny also wrote a number of books set in India, including *Caste and Creed* (1890), *The Romance of a Nautch Girl* (1898), and the history of *Fort St. George, Madras* (1900).

parents grow old and brothers are reared ... altogether destitute of a daughter's tender carefulness or a sister's immeasurable influence" (47). This is particularly ironic given that Helen Mary Wilson obtained a medical degree in 1894 and returned to her hometown of Sheffield as "possibly its first woman doctor" (Hall "Wilson"). She practiced privately until 1905, when she retired to become active in the Association of Moral and Social Hygiene. Nevertheless, in this co-authored article on nursing, while necessary qualifications and skills are identified, readers are encouraged to remember their family responsibilities:

> the pendulum of time, which seems to have swung from inactivity and seclusion to the opposite extreme of noisy work, will eventually return to a happy medium, in which those who hear the call to live the highest of all lives—the family life—will strive to make it perfect; while those others—the desolate, the heart-sick, the obliged-to-work, or those who may, or must, stand alone—will find open to them fertile fields of work and interest, which will save them from the 'tragedy of aimlessness'. (47)

Family life is invoked as the "highest" call that a woman can and should hope to obtain, but for those women who are "desolate" and "heart-sick," or "obliged," then work will save them from idleness and aimlessness.

The complex positioning of work is highlighted in the final article in the series, written by Coleridge, about the charitable work of "the Lady of All Work." I find it curious that the co-editor of the magazine is the author of an article about "the Lady of All Work" since, as the co-editor and a published author, Coleridge is clearly not primarily a charity worker. Coleridge published regularly during a career that lasted almost 50 years. Yet, for Coleridge, this "Lady of All Work" is a woman who "picks up the odds and ends, and clears a way for the definite workers who have to confine their energies to one object" ("Work and Workers: The Lady of All Work" 653). This sentiment, and its timing, reflect the conservative view Coleridge would present in her volume of essays, *The Daughters Who Have Not Revolted* (1894), which alludes to both the New Woman debate and Sarah Grand's article, "The Revolt of the Daughters."[24] The "Lady" is "expected to do whatever is wanted" (653) and her primary difficulty is knowing whether doing something imperfectly is better than leaving it undone (655). She is always helping others in the community. According to Coleridge, this vocation is ideal for any girl who does not need to earn money, has no special skills, and feels no special calling towards a particular vocation. The domestic agenda that was an integral part of the early days of the *Packet* has been transformed into a charitable agenda through "the Lady of All Work." A girl should not work for pay if she does not need to and must still help others as far as she is able. The need for training and good health required by many of the professions is not mentioned. Throughout the article, the Christian moral code is assumed. Coleridge writes, for example, that "[t]he

---

[24]	Grand's article appeared in *Nineteenth Century* in 1894.

higher the aim, the less wearisome the work, in spite of all disappointments" (657) because drudgery can be divine.

The tension between the feminine ideal and the reality of women's work is apparent throughout the series of articles. The editors—at this point, Coleridge and Yonge are co-editing the magazine—explicitly highlight this tension between family and work in the same issue as the ambivalent discussion of nursing. A note at the bottom of the page reports that "the Editors do not necessarily *recommend* everything described in this series of papers" (Yonge and Coleridge "Editorial Note" 47). In distancing themselves from the contents of the articles, the editors now occupy a substantially different position with respect to the readers. Whereas Yonge had claimed the role of arbiter of what girls read and authority on how they should conduct themselves, the *fin de siècle* offers so many different possibilities for girls that the editors feel they can no longer adequately advise their readers. However, in granting their readers more autonomy, while nevertheless maintaining key aspects of Yonge's ideal of femininity, they ran the risk that their readers might turn elsewhere for advice and guidance.

Yonge was removed as co-editor in 1894 in an attempt to introduce a perspective more in touch with the girl culture of the 1890s. In a letter to a friend, Yonge describes her removal:

> the Monthly Packet has turned me out except as a contributor. It has been going down. Newbery and Atalanta supplant it, and the old friends are nearly all gone, and the young ones call it goody-goody. So the old coachman who had driven it for forty years is called on to retire! They are very civil about it, and want me to be called Consulting Editor, but that is nonsense, for they don't consult me. It is not Christabel's fault, but A.D.I. wants to be modern, though still good and churchy, and I don't like to be scolded for what I have not sanctioned, so it is a relief in that way. (Coleridge *Charlotte Mary Yonge* 334–5)

In trying to be "modern," Yonge was scolded by older readers who objected to the changes she made to the *Monthly Packet*. At the same time, these changes did not make her magazine sufficiently modern. As Altholz comments, "In an age of mass journalism, the religious press could succeed in keeping a large audience only by diluting its religion" (143). Similarly, Jacqueline Bratton explains that the values passed on by the main religious publishers (the Religious Tract Society and the Society for Promoting Christian Knowledge) changed and the "didactic traditions of writing for children, which had had an independent life for the best part of a century, eventually merged with the literary and other traditions to form one mainstream of juvenile fiction" (*The Impact of Victorian Children's Fiction* 191–2). Yonge's strict adherence to High Church principles meant that this compromise was something she was unable to do.

Coleridge herself astutely recognized that the experiment was unlikely to succeed: "I knew too well how entirely the *Monthly Packet* was the expression of Charlotte Yonge's personality, and the extension of her influence, to suppose that another could supplement it for her own public, and the conditions were not such as to attract a new one" (*Charlotte Mary Yonge* 278). Coleridge distinguishes between Yonge's aging public and new, younger, and presumably larger publics unlikely to be attracted to the magazine. The identity of the magazine was so closely tied to Charlotte Yonge and her construction of the religious girl that it would have been immensely difficult to satisfy the *fin-de-siècle* girl. Moreover, as Coleridge explains,

> the old public was growing older; taste was changing; still more, the conditions of the book trade were rapidly altering. The Monthly Packet was confronted by many rivals; cheap magazines sprang up in every direction; the old negative principle of excluding from a magazine, intended for young women, everything that could be thought less than perfectly suitable for them became more and more difficult to carry out, and perhaps some things were excluded which it would have been well to admit. (*Charlotte Mary Yonge* 277–8)

The marketplace was increasingly competitive, with the appearance of cheaply produced, attractive, illustrated magazines. Girls were surrounded by a plethora of readily available papers peddling many of the views the *Packet* had hoped to exclude. In 1894, Coleridge describes how her desk is covered by "specimen copies of thirty monthlies and weeklies, addressed to women, young women, WOMAN, ladies, young ladies, girls, gentlewomen, and young gentlewomen" ("We. By Us." 454). In contrast to these other magazines, the *Packet* looked increasingly staid, with no photos or illustrations, and it remained burdened by its conservative depictions of girls.

A brief examination of the covers of the monthly magazine demonstrates the attempt to shift the focus from Yonge as editor. Through the Third Series of the magazine from 1881 to 1890, the cover remained the same [Figure 2.1]. Charlotte Yonge is identified in large type on the top right with the title underneath, with the list of Contents appearing below. When the new series with Coleridge as co-editor begins in 1891, there are some significant changes to the cover in both style and format [Figure 2.2]. The large flower that on the original cover occupied the left of the page is replaced by a picture of three girls, leaning over a book: one has a racket in her hand; another wears a scholar's cap and gown; and the third is finely dressed and sits on a chair. Clearly the magazine is trying to engage its younger girl readers with an illustration that speaks to their diverse interests and activities. The contents of the magazine are foregrounded by listing them at the top of the page and the role of the editors is downplayed by moving their names to the bottom of the page where they are partially obscured by the illustration.

The change in the cover in February 1892 [Figure 2.3] suggests that the attempt to engage with younger readers was not successful or perhaps that older readers did not approve of the new cover. Unfortunately, no circulation figures to support these assertions are available, but the style of this cover is quite similar to the Third Series cover when Yonge was the sole editor. The dense foliage emphasizes the remaining white spaces on the page, particularly the names of the two editors, and the image is less implicated in a direct address to its readers, perhaps suggesting

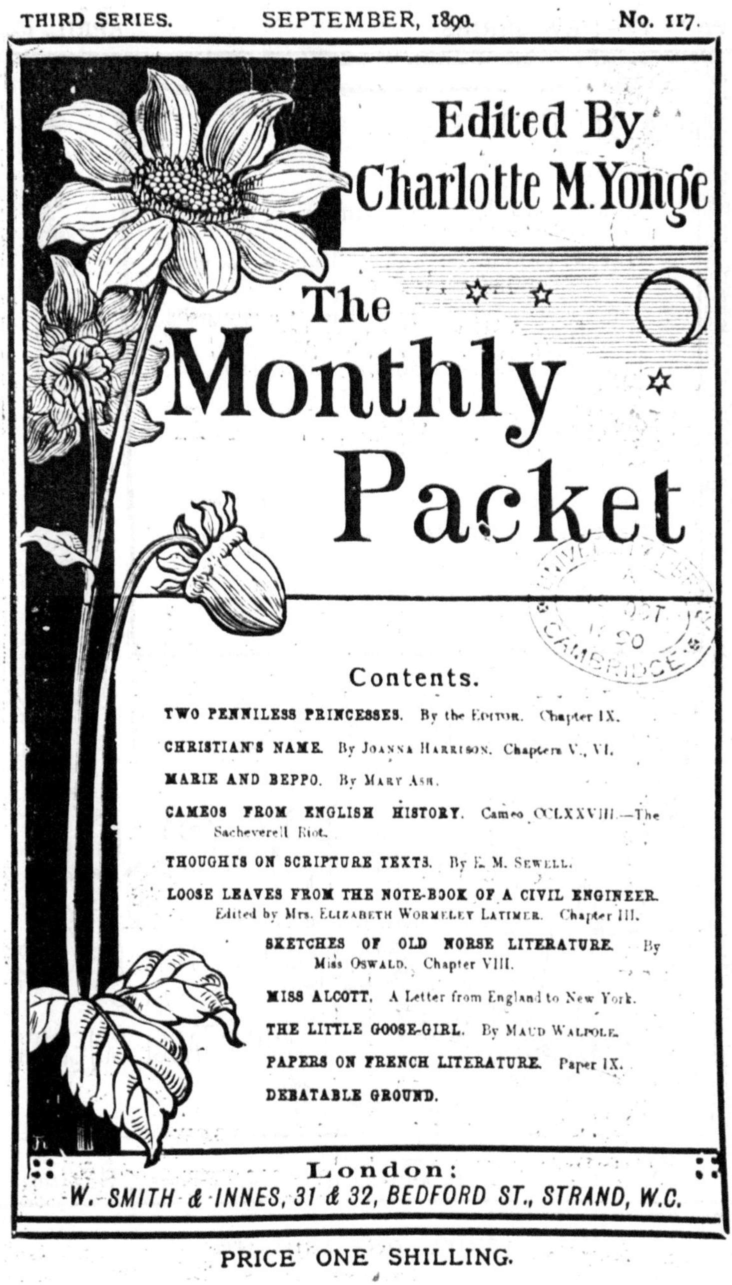

THIRD SERIES. SEPTEMBER, 1890. No. 117.

Edited By Charlotte M. Yonge

The Monthly Packet

Contents.

TWO PENNILESS PRINCESSES. By the Editor. Chapter IX.

CHRISTIAN'S NAME. By Joanna Harrison. Chapters V., VI.

MARIE AND BEPPO. By Mary Ash.

CAMEOS FROM ENGLISH HISTORY. Cameo CCLXXVIII.—The Sacheverell Riot.

THOUGHTS ON SCRIPTURE TEXTS. By E. M. Sewell.

LOOSE LEAVES FROM THE NOTE-BOOK OF A CIVIL ENGINEER. Edited by Mrs. Elizabeth Wormeley Latimer. Chapter III.

SKETCHES OF OLD NORSE LITERATURE. By Miss Oswald. Chapter VIII.

MISS ALCOTT. A Letter from England to New York.

THE LITTLE GOOSE-GIRL. By Maud Walpole.

PAPERS ON FRENCH LITERATURE. Paper IX.

DEBATABLE GROUND.

London:
W. SMITH & INNES, 31 & 32, BEDFORD ST., STRAND, W.C.

PRICE ONE SHILLING.

Fig. 2.1 Cover of *The Monthly Packet*, September 1890

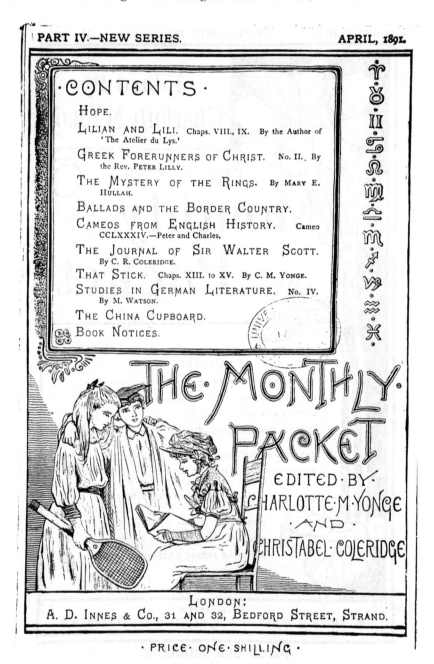

THE MONTHLY PACKET

EDITED BY CHARLOTTE M. YONGE AND CHRISTABEL COLERIDGE

LONDON:
A. D. INNES & CO., 31 AND 32, BEDFORD STREET, STRAND.

· PRICE · ONE · SHILLING ·

Fig. 2.2   Cover of *The Monthly Packet*, April 1891

PART XIV.- NEW SERIES. FEBRUARY, 1892.

The Monthly :Packet:

·Edited·by·
Charlotte·M·Yonge
·&·
Christabel·Coleridge

CONTENTS.

LONDON: A. D. INNES & CO., (LATE WALTER SMITH & INNES), 31 AND 32, BEDFORD STREET, STRAND.

PRICE ONE SHILLING.

Fig. 2.3   Cover of *The Monthly Packet*, February 1892

a reluctance to construct (and define) a picture of that readership. The rapidly changing covers suggest that not only was the magazine equivocating about distancing itself from its close association with its long-time editor, but it was also attempting to refashion itself to meet the needs of its *fin-de-siècle* readership.

In 1893, most likely at the point when plans were beginning to be put into place to remove Yonge as editor, the names of the editors are removed from the cover [Figure 2.4], replaced by the issue's date. In this issue, the only article contributed by Yonge is a single "Cameo from English History." The publisher of the magazine did not act precipitately; it was only in 1894 that publisher Arthur D. Innes replaced Yonge as co-editor. In the first issue edited by Coleridge and Innes, Coleridge writes that "[t]he Editors of the 'Monthly Packet' are fully conscious that no one can ever take the place held for so long by her to whom this magazine has owed its existence, its special characters, and its peculiar influence for forty years" ("The China Cupboard" 115). Despite understanding the difficulty of removing an editor whose influence was so powerful, the co-editors continued to attempt to make changes to retain and build the magazine's readership. The last page of the January 1894 issue lists the new arrangements for the magazine, including the discontinuation of the present series of debates and the introduction of short letters of practical advice from one girl to another. These letters of advice demonstrate how the *Packet* was attempting to engage its readers by encouraging them to speak directly to other girls through the pages of the magazine on topics like society puzzles and college life.[25]

In June 1899, in the final issue of the *Monthly Packet*, a correspondent, "Ema," praises the magazine for its fine writing, but worries that it might be a trifle too up-to-date. Coleridge responds by noting that being "too fin de siècle" ("The China Cupboard" 706) is not an accusation normally levelled at the *Monthly Packet*. Further down on the same page, she begs the "dear friends of the Packet" (706) to get as many new subscribers for July as they possibly can—suggesting declining circulation numbers—but no new issue appeared in July. Instead, the troubled magazine quietly went out of business.

In retrospect, the ousting of Yonge as editor merely signalled the ongoing decline of the *Monthly Packet*. The connections between Yonge and the magazine were too strong to be easily dissolved, and the final years of the magazine continue to have many references to her, either as an occasional contributor or through requests for information about her and her books. Moreover, the religious feminine ideal she spent over 40 years constructing was not easily remodelled to meet the needs of the *fin-de-siècle* readers. The attempts to become more culturally relevant were characterized by slippages between a more contemporary ideal and the values that had characterized the magazine from its early years. The "dear old Packet"

---

25   In Mitchell's *Newspaper Press Directory*, the same anxiety about readership appears. The description of the *Packet* in 1891 is "Tales and General Literature" (46: 217). Between 1892 and 1895, this same description includes "Chiefly for Girls" (47: 218) at the end. In 1896, it becomes "Tales of General Literature for Family Reading" (51: 226).

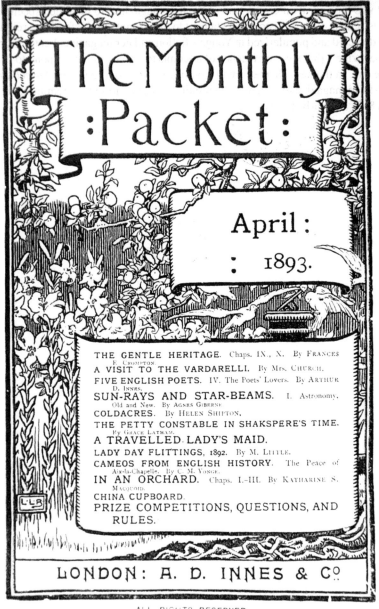

Fig. 2.4   Cover of *The Monthly Packet*, April 1893

was faced with the difficulty of mediating between these two rather different constructions and was unable to do so with any degree of success. Its demise in 1899 was the end of an era for one of the first magazines to be aimed specifically at girls, and its 49-year history is testament to the strength of the feminine religious ideal depicted and popularized in Yonge's fiction and her magazine. Yet throughout the magazine's run, we see evidence of attempts to provocatively respond to issues of the day. In the next chapter, I will examine the *Girl of the Period Miscellany*, a short-lived magazine that signals the rapidly changing notions of femininity in the late 1860s and early 1870s.

Chapter 3
The Latest Sensation:
Girlhood and the
Girl of the Period Miscellany (1869)

In the 5 July 1869 issue of the *Athenaeum,* the *Girl of the Period Miscellany* is advertized as "the Latest Sensation, profusely Illustrated" (775). In a similar advertisement on 10 July, the reader is informed that the *Miscellany* is available from "all Booksellers and Railway Bookstalls" (35). The ubiquity of the "Girl of the Period" in print and in popular culture was, of course, owing to her provocative nature in mid-Victorian England, and this figure sparked a wide variety of responses from both sides of the political spectrum. The monthly production of the *Miscellany* emphasized the topicality of the issue of women's freedoms and rights through extensive illustrations as it responded to this "problem" in a provocative, entertaining way. Not a girls' periodical at all in the traditional sense, the *Miscellany* was aimed at a largely male audience that would enjoy its satirical and parodic representations of the "Girl of the Period." As a consequence, the *Miscellany* highlights the ambiguous definitions of girlhood in the late 1860s and early 1870s, where the "girl of the period" became a label for any girl (or woman) who sought active participation in the public sphere and who demanded opportunities for better education, rights, and legal protection. Moreover, through its extensive illustrations, the "girl" in the *Miscellany* becomes a visual figure who is no longer contained within the drawing room. Instead, she works and plays in public spaces, and she travels in the hands of the men (and perhaps some women) who purchase the periodical. The *Miscellany*'s depictions of the "girl" engaged in a variety of public activities set the stage for illustrated girls' magazines in the last decades of the century, such as the *Girl's Own Paper* and the *Girl's Realm*, where girls' culture is described, visualized, and marketed to girls themselves.

In contrast to the *Monthly Packet*, with its generally conservative depictions of girlhood spanning more than 40 years, the *Girl of the Period Miscellany* represents a transitional moment in the shift from the traditional mid-Victorian feminine ideal of duty, charity, and domesticity into the more progressive *fin-de-siècle* model of femininity. A short-lived magazine appearing in 1869, the *Miscellany* represents the tension between these two ideals, yet the girls in its pages are also alive to the new possibilities for girls and women during this period. Inspired by Eliza Lynn Linton's unsigned article, "The Girl of the Period," the *Miscellany* reworks the Girl of the Period from Linton's object of disdain into a figure who might be humorous, but who was also engaging and sympathetic. The *Miscellany* shifts the register of the Girl of the Period by transforming her into a figure of fun as well as an object of concern, a redefinition that paves the way for magazines specifically targeted at girls, and which are both serious and entertaining.

Who Were the Readers of the *Miscellany*?

The *Miscellany*'s short run signals its uncertain readership—or perhaps its unsuccessful marketing to a specific readership—and may well suggest the extent to which its central theme was in vogue for only a brief moment at the end of the 1860s. While the *Miscellany* was eager to appeal to the provocative nature of the "Girl of the Period," it was also careful to distinguish this modern girl from a girl with loose morals. The 1870 number of Mitchell's *Newspaper Press Directory* vaguely describes the *Miscellany* as containing "Attractive Articles on the Girl of the Period, with Illustrations" (126), failing to clearly identify or define the magazine's target readership. Its illustrations were certainly intended to appeal to those readers seeking a light-hearted, entertaining periodical, but the *Miscellany* advertisements in the high-class literary and cultural weekly *Athenaeum* suggest that the *Miscellany*'s publishers were also trying to attract a sophisticated and well-educated readership.

That the audience for this magazine was unclear is evident in contemporary reviews. The reviewer for the *Era*, a leading theatrical journal, notes, for example, that

> [t]his Miscellany is enjoying a very large share of popularity, and the present number (the fifth) is quite as readable and interesting as any of its predecessors. The Miscellany is designed for the edification of the "girl of period" in various stations of life, and there is nothing in the number before us which the most severe prude could object to. The work is profusely and tastefully illustrated, an engraving to every article being the role apparently laid down by the proprietors of the Miscellany. ("Literature" 11 July 1869: 6)

This review signals the ambiguity of the readership since it suggests that girls in varying classes might read it for their "edification." While the magazine certainly contains some serious pieces, its aim is obviously to entertain rather than to instruct. Significantly, however, the reviewer argues that the magazine's contents are entirely appropriate for these "girls of the period," suggesting that the *Miscellany* contains nothing untoward to which the guardians of feminine purity would object. As I discussed in the previous chapter, the idea that someone might need to approve its contents suggests that the *Era* reviewer understood women as part of the magazine's target readership.[1] The "girl" who responds to the controversies inspired by Linton's "Girl of the Period" article could be, then, anyone who was interested in the Woman Question.

In contrast to the *Era*'s positive reviews, the *Derby Mercury* is less enthused with the *Miscellany*. The reviewer of the first number notes that the "girl of the period" is "positively irrepressible, and we doubt whether the publication of this class of serials is the best means to reform them—if that is the object of their

---

[1]   Kate Flint has demonstrated the extent to which women's reading was subject to scrutiny in *The Woman Reader, 1834–1914* (1993).

promoters" ("Literature" 24 March 1869: 6). The reviewer is uncertain about the expected readership and wonders whether it will be effective in "reforming" these girls, even though the fictional editor, Miss Echo, suggests that these girls are not her intended readers. Nonetheless, the *Miscellany* is a publication in which "the idlers of society may find amusement" (6). By the time the seventh number appears, the *Mercury* reviewer is severely critical of the material, claiming that there are "several articles in this number that can serve no other purpose than to minister to a vitiated and prurient taste" ("Literature" 18 Aug 1869: 6).[2] The final review in the *Mercury* condemns the content of the magazine as nothing more than "'fast' writing to suit 'fast' girls and silly men" ("Literature" 20 Oct 1869: 6). The use of "girl" here suggests an audience of women (young or otherwise) whose reading is no longer subject to the censorship of her parents.

Regardless of its readership, the *Miscellany* has an important role in this overarching discussion of girlhood between 1850 and 1915. It signals a significant shift in the constructions of girlhood in the late 1860s, which otherwise has few magazines specifically targeting girls or discussing their behaviour. By this point, the *Monthly Packet* had renamed itself to remove its reference to "Younger" members of the Church of England, suggesting both its aging readership and its attempt to attract a wider group of readers. Other children's magazines in press at this time, like *Aunt Judy's Magazine*, were aimed at a mixed audience of both boys and girls.

When Linton's article appeared in the *Saturday Review* in March 1868, it reinvigorated the debate about the role of women in British society. The 1860s saw improvements to girls' education, the establishment of the first college for women, and increasing agitation for women's suffrage and property rights. A series of Contagious Diseases Acts (in 1864, 1866, and 1869) were designed to prevent the spread of sexually transmitted diseases by forcing women believed to be prostitutes to undergo mandatory medical examination and treatment. Issues of sexual freedom, educational advancements, and employment opportunities lie at the heart of discussions about women and girls during this decade. Linton's article polarized these discussions when she described the "girl of the period," who had little in common with the chaste, virtuous "ideal" (356) girl of the past. Instead, the modern "girl of the period" was like a member of the *demi-monde*, concerned only with fashion and pleasure.

The widespread conversation, debate, and satire inspired by Linton's article were phenomenal, indicating the centrality of Linton's concerns to Victorian readers (Helsinger et al. 113). Items as varied as cows, horses, and ships were named "The Girl of the Period," and she spawned parasols, comedies, waltzes, and cartoons, as well as publications like the *Girl of the Period Miscellany*. In her comments about the commercialization of the Girl of the Period, Nina Rinehart notes that "the satirical thrust of the original article was ignored by the commercial

---

2   Linton herself uses this term in her description of the "Girl of the Period": "Nothing is too extraordinary and nothing too exaggerated for her vitiated taste" (357).

exploiters since the products using Linton's title as a label were presumably aimed at the same fashionable young women Linton had attacked" (4). Nonetheless, the Girl of the Period occupies a central role in discussions about femininity in the early 1870s and provides an example of how girls' concerns could be addressed in a sympathetic light.

The issue of self-definition is at the heart of this debate about the "Girl of the Period." The immense "textual and commercial proliferation" of the Girl of the Period "suggests a need to codify and contain 'representative' woman" and also "points to a general concern about England's self-definition" (Boufis 98). The surge of popularity in the Girl of the Period arose in part because of the middle-class girl's desire to have "fun" (N. Anderson 118). This desire marks a different kind of emancipation than movements toward higher education or women's suffrage because it upsets the prevalent model of femininity.[3] These girls "gloried in self-display" (N. Anderson 118) and conspicuous consumption became a predominant occupation. The Girl of the Period became a lightning rod for anxieties about traditional feminine roles as she made decisions for herself about her conduct and her appearance in public spaces. Unable to control her appearance or her behaviour, the British periodical press increasingly demonstrated its concern that the changing nature of girlhood was a sign of moral decline and degeneration.

The advertising in the pages of the *Miscellany* itself is generally geared towards a female audience. It contains ads for chocolate, "Ladies' Hats in English Taste," women's fashions, "Wyatt's Golden Hair Wash," babies' clothing, and bridal squares. Yet it also includes ads for the gun and rifle manufacturer E.M. Reilly & Co. and the Railway Passengers Assurance Co., which were presumably targeted at a male readership. The advertising thus suggests a degree of uncertainty about the nature of the magazine's readership, while also reflecting the nature of the controversy. Men and women were both invested in the discussions of the Girl of the Period, and the *Miscellany*'s publishers were most interested in gaining readers, regardless of their gender.

The *Girl of the Period Miscellany*

In an *Era* review, the *Miscellany* is commended for its

> very extensive circulation from the first, and the success is likely to continue while the contents are so attractive as they are at present. Articles written in a light and amusing tone are, of course, to be looked for in a magazine of this

---

[3]   In *Notes and Queries* in 1908, Edward Heron-Allen notes that the *Miscellany* was issued in close imitation of *Punch* and comments, "As a skit upon the fashions of the day it is a valuable contribution to history … and as a link in the history of the suffragette movement it is at once illuminating and pathetic" (467). His link to the suffragette movement is more suggestive of the early twentieth-century period in which he was writing. Although the magazine is clearly implicated in the ongoing discussion of women's roles in the 1860s, to suggest that it is engaged with the issue of women's suffrage seems to me to be a great leap.

special class, but others of a more solid kind are wisely introduced from time to time. To commence with, in the August number is the third of a series of papers entitled The Plain Gold Ring, and in it are to be found some exceedingly sensible remarks on the superficial and altogether faulty education given to the young ladies of the present day. The changes are continually run on the "Girl of the Period," but monotony is cleverly avoided, and to conduct a magazine which has one principal theme to be kept constantly in view is no easy task. ("Literature" 29 August 1869: 6)

The "special class" of the magazine refers to its role as a comic journal, but also its lavish illustrations. As Barbara Onslow has noted, "At mid-century, illustrations were becoming a major selling-point across the middle-class market" for periodicals, and they also "became an important feature of children's magazines" (*Women* 157–8) in the 1860s. Each of the *Miscellany*'s ten 32-page numbers include a variety of illustrations. In the March issue, for example, there are ten illustrations ranging from a quarter page to a full page, including one fold-out. These illustrations are important to constructions of girlhood in the periodical press. For the first time, and despite their ambiguous definition, "girls" were being portrayed visually in the print culture of the period as they worked, played, and socialized. The "visual pleasure" (*Magazine* 90) that Margaret Beetham ascribes to the inclusion of these kinds of illustrations in women's periodicals is true in the periodical press more generally. As the technology improved, illustrations became increasingly vital to the success of periodicals from the 1870s onwards, a shift that I discuss in further detail in the next chapter on the *Girl's Own Paper*.

The *Era* review also notes how the *Miscellany* focuses on one topic, the Girl of the Period, but cleverly avoids becoming monotonous. The provocative nature of this Girl is central to her popularity. In her discussion of Eliza Lynn Linton's contribution to the rise of popular journalism, Andrea Broomfield demonstrates Linton's ability to profit from the "fluid, dynamic nature" ("Much" 268) of the mid-century periodical press and how Linton capitalized on the sensational by making "worn-out themes and clichéd phrases fresh and provocative" ("Much" 271). The contributors to the *Miscellany* similarly capitalized on the freshness of the "Girl of the Period," creating first the *Girl of the Period Almanack* in 1868, and following up with the *Miscellany* in the wake of the *Almanack*'s success in March 1869. Its run lasted just nine months before culminating in another *Almanack*.[4]

The *Miscellany*'s ability to transform what was effectively a single issue into a varied periodical that attracted readers from month to month was a sign of its journalistic adeptness. Yet its brief run also suggests that the magazine was only able to capitalize on the "Girl of the Period" while readers found something new and provocative in its pages. There is, of course, a stark contrast between the vilified Girl of the Period found in *Saturday Review*, *Punch*, *Tomahawk*, and elsewhere,

---

[4] The *Almanack* is strictly focused on representations of different "girls of the period." In contrast, the *Miscellany* contains a wider variety of assorted articles. Both contain numerous illustrations.

and the multifaceted Girl of the Period depicted in the *Miscellany* who is modern but also capable, attractive, and entertaining. Yet, like Linton in her intentionally provocative article, the *Miscellany* used the controversial nature of the "Girl of the Period" to attract and retain a readership. The "Girl of the Period" is a journalistic construct, like the figure of the New Woman that I discuss in Chapter 6.

Each issue is composed of a variety of different materials, including poetry (much of which was illustrated), articles about "Girls of the Period" from different countries (including those from Scotland, France, America and Ireland), and numerous illustrations. Regular features include Miss Polly Glott's "Contributions to a Dictionary of the Future" and "The Grumbler," a humorous one-page correspondence section.[5] A single serialized story, "The Wooing and the Winning; Or, the Best and the Worst of Him" by an Ex-Girl of the Period, typically took at least six pages of each number and remained unfinished as of the last number.[6] The periodical was undoubtedly "ephemeral" (Layard 143), but its importance lies in how it portrays girls in its pages and in how it capitalizes upon the controversy about girls, modernity, modesty, and the *demi-monde*.

The cover of the magazine [Figure 3.1] is dominated by an illustration of three girls of the period. Each girl holds a different item: croquet mallet, fishing rod, and riding whip. Depicted within the oval border that identifies the title of the magazine, the girls are contained within the admiring gaze of the reader. They are fashionably, yet modestly, attired, as are the girls in the small illustrations in each corner. These smaller illustrations show girls dancing, riding, playing croquet, and getting married, reinforcing the idea that although the Girl of the Period is interested in sports, she is also interested in feminine concerns like dancing and marriage. This illustration is accompanied by the poem, "The Graces of the Period," inside the first number. The three traditional graces are Aglaia, Thalia, and Eurphrosyne, and they bring brightness, flowers, and joy and mirth, respectively. In this poem, they are mirrored by the three personified "Sister-Graces" of Britannia, Caledonia, and Hibernia (or England, Scotland, and Ireland). Britannia is the "favourite in the race" (l. 6), which could mean the croquet game, but actually refers to the "coming Matrimony Stakes" (l. 12). Caledonia is the angler who "baits the hook" (l. 13) and by whom "[m]ost fish are proud of being caught" (l. 18). The mounted Hibernia begins her errand "gaily;/To gallop over fifty hearts" (l. 20–21). Each Sister-Grace is associated with love, courtship, and matrimony, and the final stanza encourages these girls of the period to "make all the havoc that you can" (l. 29), although "[t]he present bard's a married man!" (l. 30). The humour and fun associated with the Girl of the Period is emphasized through the comic tone of the poem and the narrator's joking reference to himself as already married, and thus removed from these courtship games.

---

[5]   Entries included "ALTAR, *n.* a woman's starting-point in life; the matrimonial knotty point" and "AGE, *n.* a vice, which no woman ought ever to acknowledge; a horrible thing, a calamity; a shame" (67).

[6]   This serialized story does not appear to have been printed in book form.

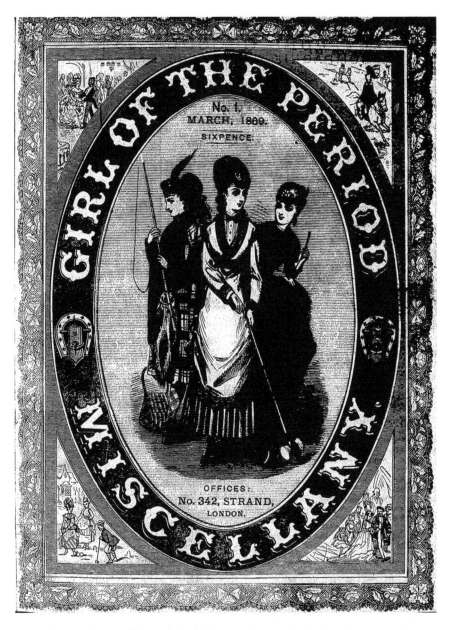

Fig. 3.1   Cover of the *Girl of the Period Miscellany*, March 1869

Nonetheless, the *Miscellany*'s role as a comedic journal complicates the reading of the Girl of the Period. The *Miscellany* certainly emerges from the tradition of comic journalism that arose from the early nineteenth-century literary magazine and the journal of political satire was instantiated with the arrival of *Punch* in 1841. However, as Alvin Sullivan notes in his discussion of Victorian comic journals, "rival comic weeklies" tended to resemble *Punch* "more closely than comic monthlies, which are generally less political and less satirical" (501). Donald Gray similarly observes the characteristic weekly nature of the British comic periodical, also noting that it generally sold "for a penny or two, rarely more than three" (2). A 6d. monthly magazine that was designed to attract readers interested in the latest controversy about modern girls, the *Girl of the Period Miscellany* is involved in an alternative project. Rather than engaging with Whig and Tory politics, the *Miscellany* addresses the contentious issues of gender and femininity. As Gray notes, "Increasingly, in the course of the century, what can be called social topics began to be given more space" (2) in comic journals.

The humour in the *Miscellany* sometimes functions as a distancing device. As readers, we can enjoy the Girl of the Period and sympathize with her, but we do not have to treat her too seriously. Furthermore, the irony in its pages allows readers the space for self-reflection on the provocative question of girlhood and modernity in Victorian England. The fictional editor, Miss Echo—whose name raises questions about whose voice and which ideas are being echoed—declares that girls are "everywhere. You cannot go into society, you cannot go to church, you cannot visit the theatre, you cannot walk the streets, without meeting girls. These girls are all girls of the period, because they exist at the present hour" (33). Importantly, however, they are "by no means all of them Girls of the Period in the high typical sense which the phrase has acquired since it first found publicity" (33). They may dress preposterously, but they are "*not* Girls of the Period in the bad sense. They are good, kind, gentle, modest creatures to-day, just as they were a year or more ago, before they would have been wearing such dresses" (33). Readers can "cherish a sneaking kindness for her" because it is "barely possible to unwomanize a woman" (34). This declaration invites the reader to join in on the joke, appreciate the foibles and idiosyncrasies of the Girl of the Period, and celebrate her "elastic" (34) womanliness. Thus, unlike the comic journal *Punch*, which actively satirized politicians and politics, the *Girl of the Period Miscellany* is capitalizing on the furor raised by the provocative Girl of the Period.

Linton's "Girl of the Period" is rather different to the multitude of different girls found in the *Miscellany*. As Yonge does in the *Monthly Packet*, Linton compares the modern girl unfavourably to the pure, virtuous girl of the past. She describes a "fair young English girl ... who could be trusted alone if need be, because of the innate purity and dignity of her nature" and "who was neither bold in bearing nor masculine in mind" (356). She is "generous, capable, and modest;" "a tender mother, an industrious housekeeper, a judicious mistress" (356). Linton's definition of "girl" is as broad as the *Miscellany*'s. Girlhood can extend from the teenage years to a time when she is married with children and keeping her own home. However, in contrast to this model of feminine perfection from the past, the Girl of the Period desires "plenty of fun and luxury" (356).

The article provocatively laments the disappearance of the innately pure and virtuous English girl. She is a mere memory, and England must wait for her return until "the national madness has passed" (360). Nationhood is intricately tied to its girls because of their future roles as wives and as mothers of the next generation of children. In her role as the spiritual and moral centre of the home, a girl will influence everyone around her. Linton waits hopefully for England's girls to "come back again to the old English ideal, once the most beautiful, the most modest, the most essentially womanly in the world" (360). The Girl of the Period's deviation from the ideal of the past makes her less feminine and less womanly. Her lack of modesty is connected to a heightened sense of feminine sexuality that makes her less womanly.

Linton's *Saturday Review* article reflects her astute navigation of the increasingly fluid commercial periodical press. By adopting inflammatory antifeminist rhetoric, she was able to mobilize fears about the Woman Question. As Broomfield explains, "Marketing controversy for profit, a staple modern media practice, was thriving in the 1860s when John Douglas Cook [the editor of *Saturday Review*] and other like-minded editors took advantage of stamp reforms to create a commercial press that championed scandal and controversy to generate interest and sales" ("Eliza" 254). Moreover, the vehement popular response to the "Girl of the Period" meant that other periodicals, like *Macmillan's Magazine*, *Punch*, the *Eclectic Review*, *St. Paul's Magazine*, and *Tinsley's Magazine*, which had formerly been "apathetic to the subject of women's rights (or to any subject pertaining to women, for that matter)" (Broomfield "Much" 280), scrambled to address the topic. Thus Broomfield concludes that "Linton did in one short essay what several women's right activists had immense trouble doing: she popularised most of the debate's tenets" ("Much" 279).

The frequency of articles on the "Woman Question" in contemporary periodicals demonstrates the extent to which nineteenth-century readers were interested in this issue. In the *Monthly Packet*, for example, editor Charlotte Yonge argues that girls must sacrifice their own needs for the benefit of family and church, yet they must also have useful and meaningful activities to occupy themselves.[7] Emily Faithfull's feminist *Victoria Magazine* (1863–80) endorses the need for education and training for girls and women so that they can support themselves, and provides details about employment available to women. This discussion became sharply focused after the appearance of Linton's article. Underlying many of these responses is a tacit acceptance that the feminine ideal endorsed by Linton is superior to the modern girl. In the February 1869 issue of *Macmillan's Magazine*, for example, an upper-class "Girl of the Period" agrees that the modern girl is inferior to the girl of the past, but she argues that this is the result of limited choice. In George Worth's history of *Macmillan's Magazine* (2003), he explains that the magazine

---

[7]   See Charlotte Yonge's "Grandmamma: 'My Life, And What Shall I Do With It?'", appearing in April 1861 in the *Monthly Packet*.

lacked a consistent approach to women's issues during the 1860s. Yet, "at the end of the decade, *Macmillan's* played its part in a controversy regarding the position of women that dwarfed the liveliness" (84) of anything else it published about educational, professional, or political reforms. The magazine was somewhat late to the party, with nearly a year passing before *Macmillan's* took part "in the commotion" (Worth 85). Penelope Holland, young wife of a clergyman, anonymously published "Our Offence, Our Defence, and Our Petition," in which she argued that a girl in fashionable society must choose between a life of "reckless dissipation" (Holland 324) and a convent life. Assuming that most girls will not choose to enter a convent, she explains how limited opportunities for girls lead to a life of "useless self-indulgence" (325). This Girl of the Period "feels herself falling farther and farther from her own girlish ideal," (326), but she never questions the validity of the ideal or the assumption that the modern girl represents a lack—a lack of modesty, purity, and femininity. According to Patricia Meyer Spacks, Holland's argument "raises familiar feminist issues: male control of all avenues of possibility, the absence of choice in female experience—both urgent problems for adolescent girls full of vague aspiration" (193). Holland's solution is for more "liberty of choice" (327) so that girls can spend a "portion of their young lives in the service of their God and of their fellow creatures" (331). Although her letter identifies a variety of possible solutions, including paid employment and higher education, she views charitable work as the primary occupation by which a girl can become the "fair young English girl" of the past.[8]

Linton is concerned that the modern girl is ungovernable and presents only two possible positions—the virtuous woman of the past or the prostitute of the present—for the modern girl, thereby "reducing the complicated issues involved in the woman question to an accessible level" (Broomfield "Much" 270). Linton ignores "the increasing numbers of respectable women who reject both angel and whore roles and want to extend woman's sphere without forsaking true womanhood" (Helsinger 112). Lyn Pykett notes that "[p]erhaps the most interesting aspect of Linton's rhetoric is the way that the norm from which the [Girl of the Period] supposedly deviates can only be recalled nostalgically" (*The "Improper"*

---

[8]   Linton's link between the girl of the period and the prostitute was provocative, and it led to a variety of responses in the periodical press. Two of the most famous responses came from Mary Elizabeth Braddon and Henry James. Braddon, a popular sensation novelist, blames modern young men for changes in modern girls. In a *Belgravia* article entitled "Whose Fault Is It?," she argues that the "moral deterioration of the modern young man" (214) has caused the fast girl of the period. In an 1868 review of a collection of Linton's essays appearing in the *Nation*, James condemns "The Girl of the Period" as "a wanton exaggeration in the interest of sensationalism" (334), which blames women unjustly for the state of civilization. James situates the Girl of the Period as a construction of the increasingly sensational journalism of the era and notes that these changes to girlhood are part of a broader shift in gender relations—owing in part to vigorous debate about the Woman Question—and particularly the feminine ideal. James' defense of the Girl of the Period is interesting given his anxiety about more advanced forms of first-wave feminism. See Alfred J. Habegger's *Henry James and the "Woman Business"* (1989) for more detail.

Feminine 70). Linton focuses on the changing representation of girls but does not examine the reasons for these changes. Modern girls are exercising their power to choose what to wear and how to conduct themselves rather than living according to a traditional ideal of femininity and domesticity. The changing styles of beauty, fashion, language, and behaviour reflect the evolving expectations of feminine conduct.

The *Miscellany* capitalized on the free-ranging debate about women's rights by exploiting "its incendiary or entertaining elements" as "enterprising editors and journalists alike recognized that it could be watered down to maximize its entertainment potential and minimize its threat to the social order" (Broomfield "Eliza" 257). The *Miscellany* focuses on the modernity of the Girl of the Period as it celebrates the changes to girlhood and encourages these "girls" to embrace new possibilities for work and play, while continuing to reassert their femininity and virtue, thus reconfiguring them as positive sites for change and growth.

Who is the Girl of the Period?

The pages of the *Miscellany* are devoted to French, Irish, Scottish, and American Girls of the Period. There are London Girls of the Period, Evangelical Girls of the Period, and Tourist Girls of the Period. A cursory review of the *Miscellany* demonstrates the difficulty of identifying common characteristics among these girls. Indeed, the very form of the *Miscellany* "resists the singularity of the concept" (Fraser, Green, and Johnston 22). There is not just one Girl of the Period, but many. Moreover, the uncontrolled behaviour that Linton critiques is at the heart of the *Miscellany*'s Girl of the Period. This Girl of the Period enthusiastically supports the new freedoms of girlhood. Liberated from the domestic sphere, she plays croquet and flirts with both captains and curates. In a poem appearing in the first issue, "Awfully Nice" (31), we learn that the life of a girl of the past was "shamefully slow" (l. 2) because it placed limitations on her behaviour. A girl's life in the present is "better by far" (l. 12) because girls have "freedom to roam;/We have not to sit always moping at home" (l. 15–16). This poem rejects the nostalgic ideal of the past and embraces the reality of girlhood in the present, while emphasizing the relatively innocent nature of freedoms enjoyed by girls of the period.

The narrator in "Awfully Nice" is eager to leave the feminine space of the home. Instead of worrying "about stockings, or buttons, or needles and thread" (l. 18), she invokes John Stuart Mill and his treatise on women's rights. Dismissing concerns that freedom might cause a young girl to become "a bad wife" (l. 30), the narrator jokingly argues that her life is full of "hard, lady-like work" because "we crochet, we tatt, and till eyeballs are sore,/O'er horrible crimes in new novels pore" (l. 36–8). The Girl of the Period loves these useless activities, yet she understands that finding a husband is still a primary concern. Even a fun-loving Girl of the Period must present herself as an attractive and marriageable girl.

Although the Girl of the Period is concerned with marriage, she challenges Linton's feminine ideal and redefines it for the purposes of a modern young woman. The narrator is untroubled by her household management skills, nor is she concerned about her family responsibilities. The emergence of girls into the public sphere suggests that the social expectations governing the behaviour of middle-class girls are changing, with girls no longer willing to confine themselves to traditional spaces. As Linton fears, the Girl of the Period "has done away with such moral muffishness as consideration for others, or regard for counsel and rebuke" (357). Of course, the humour in "Awfully Nice" also lies in the fact that, at her worst, the actions of the Girl of the Period are relatively harmless.

The Girl of the Period, then, is problematic because she transgresses the norms of privacy and control. As she enters the public domain, seeking new fashions and entertainment, she moves beyond the containment of the domestic sphere. Critics like Mary Poovey in *Uneven Developments: The Ideological Work of Gender in Mid-Victorian England* (1988) have addressed the separation of the public and private spheres and the extent to which women were contained within the domestic sphere. Poovey concludes that the binary opposition of the sexes, which was "socially realized in separate but supposedly equal 'spheres,' underwrote an entire system of institutional practices and conventions at mid-century, ranging from a sexual division of labour to a sexual division of economic and political rights" (8–9). In this system, middle-class women are self-sacrificing, moral, impervious to sexual desire, and located within the domestic space. Men, meanwhile, want women to create a home as a respite from the cares and concerns of the commercial sphere.

With the arrival of the Girl of the Period, the activities of the private sphere began to spill into the public sphere. The freedom associated with the Girl of the Period can be found in an illustrated double-page spread of "Un-Posted Valentines." Entitled "Girls Who Play" [Figure 3.2] and "Girls Who Work" [Figure 3.3], these pages appear somewhat unexpectedly between a three-page article on "Miss Mary Roseneath's Wedding" and a two-page article on "Irish Girls of the Period." Each page is divided into quarters, with each quarter occupied by a different girl. The Croquet Girl, The Nautical Girl, The Hunting Girl, and The Archery Girl are the representatives of "Girls Who Play." Each illustrated girl is accompanied by a poem and together they celebrate girls outside the home, engaging in physical activities. These activities are not especially masculine and are unlikely to be attacked for their defeminizing potential. Croquet was seen as a feminine activity and the "Nautical Girl" is merely standing on the ship, gazing out to sea. The significance of the illustrations lies in their outdoor settings; these girls are not contained within the domestic interior. As I will discuss in the next chapter, the second half of the century saw a shift in attitudes towards girls' health and the growing belief that outdoor activity was an important aspect of the healthy girl. Furthermore, these girls—with the exception of "The Hunting Girl," whose exceptionally short skirt and billowing cigarette smoke signify her lack of femininity—are all elegantly dressed for their activities and maintain their femininity through their appearance. Girls who play can be modern in their behaviour while still retaining their feminine virtue.

Fig. 3.2   Un-Posted Valentines: Girls Who Play, *Girl of the Period Miscellany*, March 1869

Fig. 3.3   Un-Posted Valentines: Girls Who Work, *Girl of the Period Miscellany*, March 1869

The "Girls Who Work" features girls who are employed outside the home as a "Ballet Girl," a "Lady's Maid," a "Refreshment-Bar Girl," and a "Sewing-Machine Girl." While these occupations are all typically female, their public nature makes them less traditional, and they are clearly working-class occupations. The barmaid and the ballet girl have long been associated with an uncertain sexual status, and the sewing girl is also a figure of sexual vulnerability. Yet the magazine portrays these girls as successfully and happily employed. "The Sewing-Machine Girl," for example, sings and sews "with a merry sound" (l. 1) and can even find time "to prattle, smile, and flirt" (l. 4). The working conditions for "The Sewing-Machine Girl" have changed substantially since Thomas Hood described the toil as nothing but "Work! work! work!" (l. 9) in his poem "Song of the Shirt" (1843). In the *Miscellany*, the Sewing-Machine Girl is no longer a poverty-stricken working-class girl; the girl's clothing and the illustrated background may suggest she is pursuing a hobby at home, rather than working for a living. The illustrations represent newfound opportunities in public spaces for girls of the period. Although these images seem like deliberate attempts to recuperate working girls, the success of these images is somewhat mixed. The *Miscellany* is uncertain about depicting working girls in its pages because employment was a difficult facet to incorporate within the feminine ideal of virtue and purity. The moral and spiritual center of the home could be contaminated by a girl's exposure to the business world.

With its reference to "Un-Posted Valentines," the *Miscellany* highlights the tradition of comic valentines that began in the 1840s. Unlike sentimental valentines, which were printed on high-quality paper and sometimes hand-painted, satirical comic valentines were printed on cheap paper and often sent anonymously. The *Miscellany* differs from this tradition because of its sincerity; although humorous, the illustrations of "Girls Who Play" and "Girls Who Work" are not comic exaggerations. Instead, these girls are attractively feminine and successful in their pursuits. Why, then, are the valentines un-posted? Possibly there may be no one to receive them, the world may not be ready to make jokes about these girls, or their "un-posting" performs a kind of modesty on behalf of these adventurous girls. Because the Girl of the Period is displayed so positively elsewhere in the magazine, I would argue that these valentines are intended to portray the Girl of the Period as an attractive, albeit humorous, figure. The primarily male readers of the *Miscellany* are the intended, hypothetical, senders. The verse associated with "The Archery Girl," for example, refers to the sender's pleasure of being with "staid Marian" in "Sherwood's deep glades" (l. 3), where he can "press her and call her my own!" (l. 4). While the narrator in "The Nautical Girl" would gladly "sail the whole world over" (l. 2) "with such a skipper for my boat" (l. 1), the narrative associations with the working girls are less intimate. Although "The Ballet Girl" is "my sunny-haired girl" (l. 8), she is clearly identified as a flirt who causes "joy" (l. 1) and "rapture" (l. 2), while "The Refreshment-Bar Girl" is a "charmer" of whom the narrator is "intensely fond" (l. 1) because she is "well trained" (l. 3). These illustrated girls are representations of Girls of the Period, yet the male reader engages with these models of femininity only as "an object of his gaze" (Beetham *Magazine* 91). These are not "real" girls of the period in any legitimate sense, thus the valentines remain un-posted because the readers are not supposed to, or do not, know these kinds of girls. Instead, like the other girls of the period found in the *Miscellany*, they are only imagined models of femininity.

The freedoms associated with girls of the period in the *Miscellany* remain constrained within marital and maternal obligations. Significantly, given the provocative language of promiscuity associated with constructions of the Girl of the Period in the press, she *will* be able to marry, suggesting that her virtue is unquestioned. The modernity of the Girl of the Period does not extend to liberal sexual behaviour and is thereby limited to play and work. Although her childbearing responsibilities are often implicitly tied to her marriage, they are never made explicit. For example, no "Mother of the Period" appears in the *Miscellany*. Thus, the Girl of the Period is sexualized through the focus placed on marriage, yet this sexuality manifests itself independently of the traditional maternal role. In the *Miscellany*, "The Fast Smoking Girl" [Figure 3.4] stands holding a pool cue and smoking a cigarette. Elaborately coiffed and dressed, she describes her favourite activities, which include balls, concerts, and sensation novels as well as singing and dancing. In her art studies, she rejects the "tame subjects" of landscape, fruit, or flowers, and instead studies the "glorious masculine figure ... all day" (l. 31–2). The sensual, sexual pleasure she describes certainly suggests a male readership. However, the concluding stanza reminds the reader that a girl's sexual desire will be contained through marriage. The Fast Smoking Girl tells her mother, "Shut up, and don't preach about marriage" (l. 33) because she will "hook a rich stupid old husband,/And *I*'ll promise—but *he* shall *obey*!" (l. 47–8).

Despite the Fast Smoking Girl's declarations to the contrary, the radical possibilities embodied in the figure of the Girl of the Period in the *Miscellany* can be limited through marriage. One of the final contributions is a poem, "Lines to 'A Girl of the Period'" (303). The love-struck narrator disregards the gossip that his Girl of the Period has smoked, talked slang, gamed, and diced, and concludes, "'Girl of the Period!' be it so, but matrimony/With one you love will make you amply steady" (l. 19–20). Marriage reclaims the traditional feminine ideal and also suggests that it will tame and subdue the unruly woman. The Girl of the Period will become more "steady" through marriage. She has only to change her name, not her nature. The competing discourses about modernity and morality operate on the Girl of the Period, and her radical potential can be contained through marriage because even the Girl of the Period wants a husband and children. The feminine ideal of the past is reconfigured to include the possibilities embodied by the Girl of the Period, yet the traditions of marriage and maternity remain an important part of this new girl.

The *Demi-Monde* and the "Extreme" Girl of the Period

Issues of sexuality, femininity, and modernity are intertwined in both Linton's and the *Miscellany*'s discussions of fast girls of the period. Both worry about girls who go too far and can no longer be seen as pure and virtuous. However, while

THE FAST SMOKING GIRL. 137

The weekly accounts may be filed ;
How can I have time for one glance,
When dear Monsieur Chassez is coming
To teach me that jolly new dance?
He says : "Mees, you must *élever votre jupe*
Vos très-petits pieds to deesplay."
When he twirls me about in the *trois temps*
From earth we seem floating away !

Oh, bother the children ! You know
At South Kensington, Ma, I am due,
That exquisite cast of Apollo
To draw with my master till two.
"Draw landscape, fruit, flowers." No, thank you ;
Such tame subjects are not in my way :
The glorious masculine figure
Is the model *I* study all day.

Shut up, and don't preach about marriage ;
Of spoons you well know I've a host ;
When I come to your old fogey age
I sha'n't have to mourn over time lost.
The neighbours may gossip, and welcome ;
I don't mind two pins what they say ;
I'll hook a rich stupid old husband,
And *I*'ll promise—but *he* shall *obey !*

MODERN IRISH MELODIES.—No. II.

Air—"I saw from the Beach."—TOMMY MOORE.

I SAW from my window, when Morning was smiling,
A "Girl of the Period" come tripping along,
When, sudden, the wild blast like fury came howling—
The girl was still there—but her "chignon" was gone !

Ah ! such is the fate of the wigs we put on us !
So fleeting the false hair of which we're so proud :
Our darling excrescence the rough wind blows from us,
And leaves us exposed to the jeers of the crowd.

MODERN IRISH MELODIES.—No. III.

Air—"The harp that once in Tara's halls."—TOMMY MOORE.

The girl that oft in lighted halls
Enchantment round her shed,
Now sits neglected by the walls
Her bloom and temper fled.

So fades the belle of garrisons
Till she becomes a bore,
And hearts that once beat high for her
Now feel that pulse no more.
AN OLD BACHELOR.

THE FAST SMOKING GIRL OF THE PERIOD.

DESCRIBED BY HERSELF.

I'M a filly just rising eighteen,
Lots of life I'm determined to see ;
Stow "Markham and Mental Improvement"—
No more of such rubbish for me.
Balls, concerts, 'drums, sensation-novels,
Are the cheese for us girls of to-day :
And I'll do a mild weed on the quiet,
For that is the new-fashioned way.

Slow Sophia may sew herself blind ;
With Herr Trompette I'll try the duet
We have practised so many times over,
But never sang perfectly yet ;
"Come, let us be happy together,
For where there's a will there's a way,"
In the Lost One or La Traviata
He'll make me quite perfect some day.

Fig. 3.4   The Fast Smoking Girl of the Period, *Girl of the Period Miscellany*, July 1869

Linton provocatively identifies all girls of the period as too modern and too fast, the *Miscellany* believes that the "extreme" girl of the period is a rare creature. The illustrations in the *Girl of the Period Miscellany* are intended to reassure male readers that middle-class morality and chastity can be inscribed on the female body. Its representations of girls of the period demonstrate the many varieties of girls who remain virtuous. Miss Echo explains in "The Irony of the Situation" that "in the extreme, the noisome sense, the Girl of the Period is a rare being. At all events, it is not for her that this *Miscellany* is provided" (33). Implicitly, she suggests that the *Miscellany* is intended for those readers who believe English girls to be recognizably "the true old English type—the well-knit, supple frame; the breezy apple-bloom on the cheek; the honest, brave, yet tender eye; the warm and kindly, yet not sensual lips; and the nameless, indescribable chaste freedom of carriage so different from boldness" (33). Miss Echo believes these girls to be "beautiful" and "uncorrupted," yet she also discerns "hints, or, as some would say, threats" (33) of change.

In contrast, Linton argues that sexualized "modern" (356) girls are no longer content "to be what God and nature had made them" (356). The girl who uses artificial beauty aids like cosmetics and hair dyes is replacing the "natural" feminine ideal. A source of embarrassment and dismay, she imitates the *demimonde* world of prostitutes. Linton explains that "it cannot be too plainly told to the modern English girl that the net result of her present manner of life is to assimilate her as nearly as possible to a class of women whom we must not call by their proper—or improper—name" (359). The blurring of lines between the *demi-monde* and respectable middle-class society betrays an anxiety about class boundaries and their permeability. Moreover, because the modern English girl wishes to make a good marriage, she willingly forsakes love to engage in the "legal barter of herself for so much money" (358). It is a short leap from the "legal barter" of marriage to the exchange of money for sex common among the *demimonde*. Thus Linton takes a feminist critique of marriage, the legal barter, and transforms it into an anti-feminist stance.

Although the *Miscellany* agrees that Linton's Girl of the Period exists, it also insists that she is rather uncommon. The *Miscellany* distinguishes "good, kind, gentle, modest creatures" from that girl

> who paints her face, who takes too much wine, who smokes, who habitually (and not as a matter of occasional humour, when it is quite innocent) talks slang, who is rude to her parents, who is coarsely allusive in her conversation with men, who is wilfully impudent in her style of dress, whose whole *manière d'étre* is a solicitation dashed with defiance. (Echo 33)

The *Miscellany* simultaneously acknowledges and dismisses the existence of Linton's Girl of the Period. Thankfully, according to Miss Echo, this extreme Girl of the Period is "very uncommon" (33) and consequently she is beyond

> the pale of tolerant criticism and discussion; she is simply a fair mark for the lance of invective when she shows herself, and it may with some plausibility be

said that she is so truly by nature a creature of the social twilight, who carries within herself the seeds of dissolution, that it is better to leave her alone than to talk about her. (Echo 33)

The *Miscellany* sidesteps the difficult issue of Linton's sexually wayward Girl of the Period by insisting that she is beyond redemption, implicitly reprimanding her at the same time. She "carries within herself the seeds of dissolution" and is thus "naturally" a member of the *demi-monde*. The behaviour of the "extreme" girl of the period can never be contained.

The *Miscellany* reinforces the image of the pure, chaste Girl of the Period by refusing to discuss alternatives. Although she acknowledges the extreme Girl of the Period, Miss Echo invites the reader, *"Non ragioniam*, then ... and pass on with us to ask who, for our own purpose, the Girl of the Period really is" (Echo 33). By invoking Canto 3 from Dante's *Inferno*, the author compares extreme Girls of the Period to the souls who will never be received in either Heaven or Hell, and then dismisses them from further consideration. Only the "real" Girls of the Period in the *Miscellany* are worth discussing. The liminal figure of the sexually experienced girl has no place in the magazine. In addition, by explicitly excluding the extreme girl, the *Miscellany* could entertain its readers without fear of offending them.

The *Miscellany* satirizes expectations about female sexual behaviour through articles like "The Flirt of the Period," in which the flirt is another type of Girl of the Period to be celebrated. "We are," the narrator claims, neither "much worse or better than our grandmothers or great-grandmothers ... We love, marry, ogle, enjoy a sly kiss or so, now and then, and a little hand-squeezing, maybe, just the same as they did" (287). Contrary to Linton's nostalgic assertion about the purity and modesty of girls of the past, the author claims that they were equally as likely to flirt. The girls of the past were sometimes even more sensational than the girls of the present because they openly violated "the rules of propriety in a shocking way" (287).

Rather scandalously, the Flirt of the Period uses her intelligence to compete with the "unacknowledged rivals" of the *demi-monde* by "taking hints from them" (288) on fashionable dress. The narrator notes that borrowing fashions from "the excommunicated sisterhood" is one of the points that "her adversaries urge most strongly against her" (288). This author argues that "men bring all this on themselves" (288) because "they obtrude these people on her notice everywhere" (288). Elsewhere in the *Miscellany*, men are held accountable for their behaviour. In an article entitled "A Lady's Remonstrance," for example, "a lady" argues that "women are what men make them" (179). Once again, the feminine ideal and the ability to read that ideal on the body are unquestioningly accepted. The Flirt and the "lady" contravene fashionable decorum by taking dressing tips from women of doubtful reputation.

This resistance to conventional expectations makes the *Miscellany* a fascinating contribution to discussions of mid-Victorian girlhood. These girls of the period are provocative, yet imagined, depictions of femininity. They open themselves to attack when they adapt their dress or their behaviour based on examples from the *demi-monde*. They reject Linton's moralizing just as they reject the idea that the changing nature of girlhood is a sign of moral decline and degeneration. Contravening accepted norms is a key facet of the Girl of the Period. The successful management of the tensions between the ideal of the past and the radical possibilities of the present owes in part to the *Miscellany*'s successful integration of femininity, purity, and virtue into its various representations of girlhood.

Contradictions in Feminine Roles

In catering to its primarily male audience, the *Miscellany* clearly wished to be provocative. Yet a strong focus on marriage and the domestic is presented alongside the humorous yet appealing Girls of the Period. In her discussion of the periodical press, Margaret Beetham reminds us that each issue of a magazine contains articles by different contributors. Thus, a single issue of a periodical, much less its entire run, is unlikely to present a unified or coherent view on a given topic.[9] The feminine role in the *Miscellany* demonstrates this incoherence, as does the structure of the magazine itself. By its very nature, it is comprised of "miscellaneous" articles by a variety of male contributors.

One of these contributors, Joseph Ashby-Sterry, describes the *Miscellany* as "one of those ephemeral publications that are thrown away as soon as read" (Layard 143). Like the contents of magazine itself, the contributors were similarly varied. Ashby-Sterry wrote lyrics for *Punch* and published volumes of verse such as *Boudoir Ballads* (1876) and *The Lazy Minstrel* (1886), which both achieved quick success (Miles 521).[10] James Vizetelly, the *Miscellany*'s editor, owned and ran the Vizetelly Brothers printing, engraving, and publishing business with his brother Henry.[11] His brother, Frank Vizetelly (1830–83), was a travelling correspondent and illustrator for the *Illustrated London News* during the American Civil War. In 1867, Frank and James started the weekly periodical *Echoes of the Clubs: A Record of Political Topics and Social Amenities*, for which Frank drew most of the cartoons. When it ceased in 1868, the two brothers found

---

[9]   See Beetham's "Open and Closed: The Periodical as a Publishing Genre" in *Victorian Periodicals Review* 22.3 (1989) for her discussion of the complexities associated with analyzing the periodical.

[10]   Ashby-Sterry wrote the 'Bystander' column for the *Graphic* for over eighteen years ("Death of Mr. J. Ashby-Sterry" 5), and he contributed verse to *The Broadway*.

[11]   Ashby-Sterry identifies James Vizetelly as the *Miscellany*'s editor in a letter to George Somes Layard, author of the 1901 biography *Mrs. Lynn Linton: Her Life, Letters, and Opinions*. Ashby-Sterry writes that "[t]he publication ... first began with the *G.P. Almanack*, which sold wonderfully. Then came the *Miscellany* every month for a year— then another Almanack. After that came the *Period*, which I think was not very successful and did not last very long. The *G.P. Miscellany* was edited by James Vizetelly—who I fancy was also proprietor" (qtd. in Layard 143).

a new opportunity with the *Girl of the Period Almanack* and then the *Miscellany*, where Frank provided illustrations.

Mortimer Collins, Augustus Mayhew, H. Savile Clarke, and Edward Draper were the other contributors to the *Miscellany*. A novelist, journalist, and poet, Collins contributed to a variety of periodicals including *Punch*, *Belgravia*, *Aunt Judy's Magazine*, and *Temple Bar*. He also published a number of novels and collections of poetry.[12] Augustus Mayhew wrote comic novels such as *The Finest Girl in Bloomsbury: A Serio-Comic Tale of Ambitious Love* (1861). He also wrote plays and farces, and co-wrote with his brother Henry some highly successful serials.[13] H. Savile Clark was a *Fun* contributor and first contributed to *Punch* in 1867, although the bulk of his work appeared after 1880 when he was encouraged by editor Francis Burnand to write regularly.[14] Edward Draper contributed articles to the Savage Club's short-lived penny weekly *Colman's Magazine* as well as to the second volume of *The Savage-Club Papers* (1868), which was used to raise funds to support authors and their families in times of need.[15]

In addition to Frank Vizetelly, the illustrators of the *Miscellany* were "Miss Claxton, E. Barnes, and William Brunton" (Layard 143). "Miss Claxton" undoubtedly refers to Florence Claxton, a professional artist living and working in London and a frequent contributor to the periodical press, who provided illustrations to *Aunt Judy's Magazine* among other periodicals. William Brunton was "an artist of fertile power in humorous design" ("William Brunton" 145) and a frequent contributor to humorous magazines like *Fun* and *Funny Folks*.

---

[12] He was harshly criticized in the *Tomahawk* for his 1868 novel, *Sweet Anne Page*, which, according to the reviewer, was intended to "induce decent persons to look into the book, expecting to find a sweet subject, pleasantly and tastefully treated, instead of a coarse, tedious chronicle of the doings of the vicious of both sexes" ("A Sullied Page" 71).

[13] With his brother Henry, Augustus wrote *The Good Genius that Turned Everything Into Gold; Or, The Queen Bee and the Magic Dress* (1847), *The Greatest Plague of Life; Or, The Adventures of a Lady in Search of a Good Servant* (1847), and *The Image of His Father: A Tale of a Young Monkey* (1848). Their *Whom to Marry and How to Get Married; Or, The Adventures of a Lady in Search of a Good Husband* (1848) is similar in tone to "The Wooing and the Winning; Or, the Best and Worst of Him" by "An *Ex*-Girl of the Period." The farce *Christmas Boxes* (written by Mayhew and Henry Sutherland Edwards) appeared at the Strand Theatre in January 1860 and was reviewed favourably in *John Bull and Britannia*, where it is described as "a pleasant imbroglio of married life, well constructed, [and] written with appropriate freedom" ("Theatres and Music" 43).

[14] In a letter to M.H. Spielmann, Savile Clark explained his lack of enthusiasm for unsigned contributions, since the chance of gaining reputation was very small (Spielmann 435). He wrote the very successful *Alice in Wonderland* operetta (first produced in 1886) with music by Walter Slaughter.

[15] Draper was a member of the Savage Club, which "celebrated the bohemian literary culture which flourished during the mid-Victorian expansion of periodical publishing" (Secord). A September 1862 photo of the "Members of the Savage Club" including Draper is held at the National Portrait Gallery.

This eclectic group of illustrators and journalists repositioned the provocative Girl of the Period into a figure of humour and enjoyment. Yet not all the content in the *Miscellany* was humorous. In an occasional series entitled "The Plain Gold Ring," for example, the author strongly supports traditional values:

> [A] woman *is* positively and distinctly created in order that she may become a wife and mother. If she misses this destiny, there is something wrong somewhere—it may be in herself, it may be out of herself. But a woman is a most complicated piece of mechanism, as clearly intended for wifehood and motherhood as the eye is intended to see. You may make an old maid, or a nun, or nurse all her life of her; but if you do, she is *qua* woman, a failure, whatever great and noble things she may do, or whatever she may accomplish to raise the standard of human effort and kindle the lamp of human hope. (277)

The tone of this article is surprising because humorous references to the Girl of the Period have been replaced by a more severe tone, rejecting feminine imperfections or spinsterhood. The message is also surprisingly direct after the many coy references to marriage. Any lack of clarity about the importance of marriage and domestic skills has been eliminated. A woman's roles as wife and mother are part of her feminine function because a woman is a "mechanism" intended for marriage and motherhood. Echoing Linton, the author describes the female body as a symbol of her natural feminine functions. The subversive and comical possibilities of the female body have been replaced by its sexual and maternal functions.

Elsewhere in the *Miscellany*, other articles support the idea that girls are exclusively meant to be wives and mothers. In the first issue, one contributor wonders, "What shall we do with our surplus women?" ("What is the Girl of the Period For?" 6), an echo of two controversial 1862 articles by W.R. Greg and Frances Power Cobbe.[16] The author argues that only emigration to the Colonies "meets the case so far as the ideal of a woman's career—wifehood and motherhood—is concerned" (6). This vocal support for traditional female roles is curious in the first issue of the *Miscellany*, which was intended to celebrate modern girls. The male readership is likely to identify with this humorous male position where even emigration is an unsatisfactory solution because "it hurts one's feelings as a man to think of exporting women; having them examined like government stores, and carried off in batches like Sheffield or Manchester goods" (6).[17] Moreover, the lack of marriageable British men is problematic for women because the long disuse of the "feminine functions" will cause a woman's hair to be

---

[16]   In "Why are women redundant?", Greg proposes that the problem of surplus women be resolved through emigration. Cobbe's November 1862 *Fraser's Magazine* article, "What Shall We Do with Our Old Maids?" also explores the Woman Question, arguing against the imperative of marriage and encouraging women to develop interests beyond motherhood.

[17]   These sentiments are similar to Thomas Hood's "I'm Going to Bombay," in which a woman moves to India to find a husband after being jilted in England.

"short and straight, her bust flat, her shoulders broad, and the whole of the existing pyriform aspect of her form [will] disappear" (6). A woman's reproductive role is linked to her femininity, a topic I address in more detail in Chapter 4, and the lack of a husband and children will cause her to become increasingly masculine. The feminine ideal on which a woman's social and reproductive roles are based is reinforced through its connection to her physical appearance. In contrast to the humorous articles about the Girl of the Period, this article associates girlhood with maternity and marriage and demonstrates the fear that the activities of the Girl of the Period may be defeminizing.

However, the predominantly humorous view of the female body in the *Miscellany* distances the Girl of the Period from the *demi-monde*. Intended to be seen as a spectacle and sometimes a joke, the female body and its adornments are subject to comment and critique, as well as humour. The ridiculousness of certain styles is highlighted on a page of hairstyle illustrations. In "Prize Chignons from 'The Horticultural'" [Figure 3.5], the exaggerated hairstyles, including the use of false hairpieces, demonstrate the fashionable extremes to which the Girls of the Period will subject themselves. Instead of imitating the "extreme" girl, these girls use comic styles to become spectacles and the objects of the male gaze, which helps them in their quest to find suitable marriage partners. Although the magazine pokes fun at ludicrous styles, it does not explicitly endorse a more prim and proper figure. Readers are invited to love and laugh with the Girl of the Period. Other contemporary periodicals, like the *Monthly Packet* or *Victoria Magazine*, offered depictions of girls as models of appropriate behaviour. In contrast, the *Miscellany* is more interested in humour. Although humour can also be used correctively, here the reader is to be amused and entertained, especially since the *Miscellany* is not explicitly targeted at girls or women. The magazine is more interested in the humorous follies of the Girl of the Period than the supposed disorder she might cause. The poem accompanying the illustrations, "My Chignon" (185), celebrates the chignon for its ability to protect the wearer after a fall down six flights of stairs, and to create a bird's nest with stray twigs. The chignon also provides an opportunity to entrap a man when he becomes entangled. The Girl of the Period is sensational because of her affinity for foolish, yet amusing, fashions rather than her similarities to the "extreme" girl of the period.

The Need for Education

The use of humour in the *Miscellany* allows it to be more progressive, endorsing positions that might otherwise be considered too controversial, such as girls' education. Although many Girls of the Period in the magazine are foolish, one article explicitly supports the need for women's higher education. In "The Education of Women: Science or the Confessional?" the author asserts that "[w]e are going, this very moment, to be profoundly earnest, and we beg that no girl will laugh, or even giggle. The commonplace sobriety of the title of this discourse—we mean this article—is a guarantee of seriousness of intent" (69). This introduction

Fig. 3.5   Prize Chignons from "The Horticultural", *Girl of the Period Miscellany*, August 1869

to the earnestness of the subject is done with tongue firmly in cheek, yet beneath it lies a serious, thoughtful message. As we will see in Chapter 5, the discussion of higher education in the *Miscellany* is neither as extensive nor as serious as Emily Davies' in *The Higher Education for Women* (1866). However, this article similarly argues that "there is nothing necessarily unwomanly in profound culture" (69) and the changes to girl's education "will do no harm, and will assuredly do some good" (70).

The article contains little information about where to access higher education, in part because the first college for women is yet to be founded.[18] Yet the *Miscellany* demonstrates its relevance through its discussion of poor quality girls' education that eventually led to the establishment of high quality secondary schools like North London Collegiate School and Cheltenham Ladies' College, founded in 1851 and 1853, respectively. The *Miscellany* mocks women for their inferior education, reminding readers that "the extent of territory we have to conquer" for women to be considered properly educated is "enormous" ("Education" 70). The author encourages men to educate their wives because,

> Seriously, though we all love to see women innocent, does any man care to see them silly? or fetichistic? or blindly submissive (except, of course, to their husbands)? If not, let us look—to put it at the lowest—let us look leniently upon the movements for their better education. The gulf between a highly cultivated man and a woman of society of only ordinary culture is, in our own day, far too great. ("Education" 70)

The article, despite its jokes about feminine capability and the need for a "submissive" wife, strikes a balance between humour and seriousness and explains the benefit of improved girls' education. Through its humour, the magazine endorses girls' education and positions it within a feminine ideal of purity.

The subtitle of the article, "Science or the Confessional," situates education in opposition to religious faith. The author concludes that "in view of the active and stealthy efforts which are being made to ecclesiasticise" women, "it is in our interest, not less than [women's], that they should have access to forms of culture which are particularly unfavourable to ecclesiastical tendencies" (70). Improved education is seen as antithetical to religious indoctrination, to which women and girls are believed to be particularly susceptible. Although "the natural tendency of the female intellect is not scientific, and never will be" (70), scientific education will reduce the likelihood of women being persuaded by superstition. Although the Pope had criticized the scientific education of girls for its potential to cause religious doubt, this author feels girls' critical thinking skills will improve, allowing them to resist the indoctrination of the High Church.

The mixture of humour and seriousness found in "The Education of Women" is used to the same effect in an article on female doctors. In "Aesculapius in Petticoats," the author feels that women are capable of practicing medicine and

---

18 Hitchin College (later Girton College) was founded on October 16, 1869.

should eventually be trained to become medical doctors. However, this Medical Girl of the Period is "in advance of the age" (110). The author jokingly refers to those women who, like Dr. Elizabeth Blackwell and Dr. Elizabeth Garrett, have been "licensed to kill" (110). This jest seems pointed at women doctors in particular, rather than at the medical profession in general, although student doctors were often the subjects of jokes.[19] The article concludes that the Medical Girl "must confine herself to amateur doctoring, in the course of which she will probably inflict agonies on her family and friends" (111). The seriousness of the intent lies underneath the jokes, but the author states that "under certain conditions" women should be granted access to hospitals and lecture rooms "for if woman asks in earnest to be admitted to any trade or profession, it is surely a hardship to refuse her" (111). With articles like this, a spark of revolution and reform is apparent in an otherwise humorous magazine of the period. Although few women are likely to take up the offer of a medical education, the author presents the possibility. This article differs from the more openly encouraging articles on medical education for women that appear later in the century in magazines like *Atalanta* and the *Monthly Packet*. Because the tone of this magazine is more light-hearted, the contributor balances the support of medical education with humour. A relatively progressive stance is presented and endorsed, yet the use of humour allows readers to reject those ideas that they find objectionable.

Healthy and Active Girls

In the *Miscellany*, the Girl of the Period is increasingly healthy and active, but the magazine uses humour to reinforce the femininity of this healthy girl. A girl's femininity can be enhanced by her active lifestyle, yet there were fears about its potentially defeminizing effects. In a fictionalized letter to the editor entitled "A Muscular Maiden" (79), for example, a man describes an incident where two boys try to rob a young governess walking to work. The narrator admires the young woman's pugilistic ability when she gives one boy a black eye, and punches the other in the stomach. The accompanying illustration depicts the young woman thanking the narrator for offering his (unneeded) his assistance. She "quietly" replies that she has "arranged the matter" (78). Both her quiet response and her neat dress emphasize her femininity, while the boys at her feet suggest her masculine capability. Significantly, the illustration does not depict her as she punches the boys. Instead, it emphasizes her ability to look after herself, while also maintaining her femininity. The narrator inquires of Miss Echo whether there is "no one among your staff like this fair Amazon to whom you can introduce me? I do not know the muscular one's address, and besides, she probably has a lover, and I want to have the field all to myself. But I want a muscular wife" (79). He explicitly sexualizes the woman's capabilities by explaining how, as

---

[19]   Earlier in the century, for example, Charles Dickens mocks student doctors in *The Posthumous Papers of the Pickwick Club* (1837).

husband and wife, they can "playfully practise pugilistic feats upon each other, and amicably settle all conjugal differences by putting on the gloves" (79). She is implicitly sexually attractive, for he believes she already has a lover, and her masculine pugilistic abilities make her an ideal sexual partner. He is, of course, parodying mid-Victorian expectations of female passivity and ill health, which I discuss further in the next chapter.

Similarly, the "The Tourist Girl of the Period: The Climbing Girl" [Figure 3.6] is admired for her ability to climb mountains and remain feminine. The author assures the reader that this girl is "a new adaptation of femininity. For basis you must take an active, courageous English girl. Let her have plenty of health. Let her have a hearty hatred of all kind of humbug. Let her have a wholesome love of change, movement, and adventure" (197). This "new adaptation" suggests a different feminine ideal than the prototype that Linton provocatively identified. Highlighting the changing circumstances of girls' lives, this girl welcomes the challenge of climbing mountains. Although the text supports this new femininity, the accompanying illustrations are inclined towards humour. Although the girl wears a shorter dress and carries a walking stick, she is clearly unsuitably attired for climbing mountains, with a fashionable hat and inappropriate shoes.

This humorous portrayal of femininity is further reinforced when the author concludes that the "Final Cause" (197) of the Climbing Girl of the Period is to marry the Climbing Young Man of the Period. The author reassures his reader that marriage is the proper conclusion, even for this new feminine adaptation. Despite this traditional rhetoric regarding marriage, this Climbing Girl is nonetheless a unique figure. As she climbs high mountains with only a walking stick, she embodies free and independent living. She does not depend on men, yet she retains her feminine figure. Her femininity remains uncompromised by this new activity and, like the Muscular Maiden, her traditional role is enhanced by these new abilities. Moreover, the irony in both the description and the illustration of the Climbing Girl presents a space of subjective freedom for the Girl of the Period. She is free to dress and behave as she wishes, yet the Climbing Girl embodies the tension between the traditional feminine ideal and the modern girl of the period that is present elsewhere in the magazine. While the *Miscellany* endorses the Girl of the Period, it is also careful to depict her as appropriately feminine and virtuous.

Femininity Remains

In its approach to the Girl of the Period, the *Miscellany* never veers from its appreciation of her foibles and her many attributes, although it grapples with a variety of contradictions in its discussions of education, health, marriage, and motherhood. The Girl of the Period is multifaceted. She can ride a bike, climb mountains, flirt, disarm a threat, get married, use slang, and make her own choices. A point of humour and a site for sober discussion, she represents many things to many readers, and she sparks an unprecedented debate at the end of the 1860s.

Fig. 3.6   The Tourist Girl of the Period: The Climbing Girl, *Girl of the Period Miscellany*, September 1869

Inspired by the discussion of the "Woman Question," she leads the way for a broader conception of girls and girlhood in the final decades of the nineteenth century. Her popularity demonstrates the extent to which she captivated the public imagination. Yet even as the *Miscellany* redefines Linton's homogenous Girl of the Period into a series of figures who are appreciated for their wit, daring, and adventure, the magazine keeps the pure and virtuous feminine ideal intact. The Girls of the Period in the magazine could cross many boundaries, but they remained feminine and virtuous.

The *Girl of the Period Miscellany* is part of the mass popularization of the Woman Question in the late 1860s and early 1870s. By moving the question of women's rights into the popular press, new discussions and debates about women's roles in Victorian England became possible. This, in turn, enabled the publication of clearly identified girls' periodicals in the last two decades of the century that addressed the multifaceted nature of girlhood in the form of fiction, and in articles on health, education, modernity, heroism, and sexuality. The appearance of the *Miscellany* signals a shift in girls' periodicals from small, niche publications like the *Monthly Packet* to mass-market magazines like the *Girl's Own Paper* because the idea of the girl became increasingly central to definitions of femininity in the last decades of the century. In the next chapter, I will demonstrate how health was incorporated within definitions of girlhood in the pages of the *Girl's Own Paper*, which was faced with a variety of challenges as it modelled its feminine ideal on purity and virtue while also exploring new behaviours intended to help girls stay healthy.

Chapter 4
The Healthy Girl:
Fitness and Beauty in the
Girl's Own Paper (1880–1907)

The *Girl's Own Paper* was undeniably the most popular girls' magazine of the century. In some ways, with its extensive serialized fiction, informational articles, and correspondence section, this evangelical periodical that focused on morality was little different from other magazines of the period. Yet, for the first time, the importance of the popular and the visual became embedded in a girls' magazine. The lavish illustrations provided girls with images of themselves, in a magazine designed especially for them. Editor Charles Peters hoped "to foster and develop that which was highest and noblest in the girlhood and womanhood of England" (Klickmann 1). Priced at one penny and appearing weekly, the popular and long-running *GOP* offered girls "stories of their own" (Briggs and Butts 158).[1] Moreover, the presentation of a girl's health as an important facet of her femininity reflects a significant shift in girls' periodicals. The healthy girl is active, physically capable, and beautiful; thus health in the *GOP* is both an aesthetic category and a feminine ideal. This chapter will argue that the *GOP* developed girls' health as an aesthetic ideal as well as a feminine ideal while also placing limits on girls' behaviour to ensure their modesty and decorum. Retaining these aspects of femininity was essential to the successful expansion and redefinition of girlhood to include health. Exercise and beauty are intertwined to depict a girl whose good health is visible on her body and whose health is part of her feminine appeal. Girls' participation in the male domains of sport and fitness was met with unease, and the magazine refigured some traditionally male activities to reflect girls' desires for freedom and health, while maintaining the bounds of acceptable femininity.

Mid-Victorian middle-class ideals rarely considered health an important component of femininity, yet the last decades of the century were marked by Social Darwinist concerns regarding the health of the British race. Imperialism became increasingly central to ideas of British nationalism, as did the ability of women to produce healthy offspring and raise healthy children. Female health was also vital for women who sought paid employment to support themselves and their families. The public perceptions of girls' health began to shift, in part owing to the publication of Darwin's *On the Origin of Species* (1854) and *The Descent of Man*

---

[1] The *Girl's Own Paper* continued under Peters' editorship until his death in 1907, when Flora Klickmann became editor and changed it to the monthly *Girl's Own Paper and Woman's Magazine*. It continued under various titles until finally ceasing publication in 1956.

(1871), which prompted fears of racial degeneration. Medical professionals were concerned that excessive physical activity or higher education would defeminize women, and they would be unlikely to marry and unable to bear children. These fears of degeneration are pivotal to understanding how and why the *Girl's Own Paper* endorses and redefines the healthy girl. As Kathleen McCrone notes, exercise and health were increasingly promoted in the late nineteenth century out of "a desire to assure the production of healthy mothers who would protect England against racial degeneration" (10). Towards the end of the century, this focus on the healthy girl would help to counteract the aestheticization of decay that was found in the *fin-de-siècle* Decadent movement.

The *Girl's Own Paper*

Unlike the other magazines under consideration here, the *Girl's Own Paper* had a unique marketing strategy when it began in 1880 as both a weekly and a monthly periodical, which was part of a sophisticated and complex plan by its editor, Charles Peters, to attract both working- and middle-class girls as readers.[2] As a weekly magazine priced at one penny, it was more affordable than the more expensive monthlies. Yet as a monthly number, it was also able to compete for middle-class readers. Because of its frequency, the *GOP* was more current and topical than the longer and less frequent monthly magazines, like the *Monthly Packet* or the *Young Ladies' Journal*. In addition, unlike these magazines, the *Girl's Own Paper* had neither the religious didacticism nor the focus on homemaking. Instead, it "stressed information" by carrying "more articles dealing with practical and personal problems confronting readers in their daily lives" (Drotner 150). Each issue of 16 pages includes the latest chapters of a serialized novel—which would often last the entire year—and a shorter piece of fiction, with fiction occupying approximately half of the issue. Informational articles about history or natural sciences or on topics such as health, employment, etiquette, and education are set alongside one or more poems and at least a page (and often more) of answers to correspondents.

The regular competitions and weekly correspondence sections encouraged girls to write in to the magazine, thereby gaining a dedicated readership that waited each week to see their contributions in print. Similarly, the serialized fiction enticed readers to purchase each week's issue so they could read the latest installment and was written by authors such as Evelyn Everett-Green, Anne Beale, Emma Brewer, Beatrice Harradan, Helen Burnside and Edith Nesbit. The *GOP* annuals often include a list of contributors to attract new readers. These lists contain aristocratic names such as the Countess of Buckinghamshire and H.R.H.

---

[2]   The complexities of this dual readership are particularly evident in the magazine's attitudes towards employment. See Kristine Moruzi and Michelle Smith, "'Learning What Real Work ... Means': Ambivalent Attitudes Towards Employment in the *Girl's Own Paper*."

The Princess Mary Adelaide as the magazine tried to leverage their contributors' cultural capital. Many of these names also appear in other girls' magazines of the period, demonstrating how writers, especially women, clearly had a network of publications to which they contributed. Mary Cadogan and Patricia Craig describe the offerings for girls under Charles Peters' editorship as "domestic fiction, rather drab school stories and gentle anecdotes about the childhood of Queen Victoria" (74), but they underestimate the significant contribution of this magazine to girls' reading. The magazine was "the first broadly successful magazine for girls" (S. Mitchell 27) and its popularity is testament to Peters' adept management of the dynamic terrain of girlhood.

When the Religious Tract Society (RTS) first began publishing the *Girl's Own Paper* in 1880, it was responding to two troubling trends it perceived in the publishing industry. The first was the appearance of inexpensive, weekly penny dreadful magazines, full of lurid stories of murder and intrigue. The second was the frequency with which girls were reading magazines intended for boys, including the RTS' *Boy's Own Paper*. The last decades of the century were marked by an increasingly gendered children's literature market. Ostensibly aimed at working-class and lower-middle-class children, the RTS intended the *Boy's Own Paper* and its companion *Girl's Own Paper* to provide entertaining content for children while also providing uplifting, morally appropriate messages. According to its advertisement in Mitchell's *Newspaper Press Directory*, "The want of a pure and elevating Magazine for Girls has long been felt" (223). The publishers of the *Boy's Own Paper* responded to this need, intending that "[l]iterary and artistic talent of the highest order will be brought to bear upon the work, and it is therefore hoped that it will receive the hearty support of our British maidens, and of those, also, who desire to further their best interests" (C. Mitchell 223). These two magazines were immensely popular, perhaps because the RTS concealed the religious origins of both magazines by publishing them under the auspices of "The *Leisure Hour* Office."[3] Because of its long history of publishing and distributing improving evangelical religious tracts to the working classes, "the name 'RTS' would be more likely to suggest patronising middle-class interference than trustworthy information" (Fyfe 180).

While the adventure stories of the *Boy's Own Paper* appeared only infrequently in the girl's magazine, the *Girl's Own Paper* was nonetheless attractive for its focus on girls and their lives. Sales of the *GOP* soon overtook the *BOP*, and Edward Salmon's 1884 survey of girls' reading shows it to be the favourite magazine for girls by a large margin.[4] Salmon describes the *Girl's Own Paper* as one of only

---

[3]   Advertisers, however, were clearly informed of the Religious Tract Society's involvement. The *Girl's Own Paper* is advertized in Mitchell's *Newspaper Press Directory* as part of a suite of magazines published by the RTS, including the *Leisure Hour*, the *Boy's Own Paper*, the *Child's Companion and Juvenile Instructor*, *Sunday at Home*, and *Cottager and Artisan*.

[4]   The *Girl's Own Paper* received 315 votes; the *Boy's Own Paper* placed second with 88 votes.

two magazines "that could be placed advantageously in the hands of anybody, to say nothing of young ladies in their teens" ("What Girls Read" 520) because of its tone and subject matter.[5] Its moral tone meant that adult reviewers considered it acceptable reading for girls.

Invalidism and the Healthy Girl in Fiction

The feminine ideal endorsed by the magazine is designed to encourage girls to be healthy and explicitly links beauty, fitness, health, and womanliness. Wendy Forrester points out that health and beauty are often connected in the *Girl's Own Paper*.[6] These aspects of femininity encourage the creation of what Foucault calls "docile bodies" (*Discipline and Punish* 135). In his discussion of disciplinary practices, Foucault describes "a policy of coercions that act upon the body, a calculated manipulation of its elements, its gestures, its behaviour" (138). Influenced by the rise of the New Woman and the racial degeneration fears of the Social Darwinists, the discourses of health, beauty, and femininity in the *GOP* guide girl readers toward appropriate behaviours and toward a feminine ideal of strength, capability, and decorum.

Defining the limits of girls' activities was one of the most challenging problems confronting the *Girl's Own Paper* as it tried to expand the definition of femininity in its pages to include considerations of health. J.S Bratton notes the "extraordinary argumentative contortions" ("British Imperialism" 197) required to reconcile the competing spiritual and biological notions of femininity in the late nineteenth century. The middle-class woman was the spiritual center of the home and reigned there in a "state of iconic passivity" (196), often subject to weakness and ill health. Yet girls and women were looking beyond the domestic sphere to the world of higher education, which I discuss further in Chapter 5. They were encouraged to be useful in the home and beyond it, and girls needed their health if they were to contribute to the home and the economy through their labour. For the middle-class woman, strength and fitness were increasingly vital to her success as a mother, wife, and worker. The *GOP* reflected these new directions in femininity by including regular contributions by "Medicus," who argued that girls need healthy bodies to accompany educated minds, and including features about sports for girls. However, the magazine had concerns about girls entering typically male domains. Walking and, late in the century, cycling were acceptable activities for girls, but their participation in team sports was often more problematic. The fitness and fun of cricket and hockey were contrasted with the potentially masculinizing aspects of competition and excessive levels of fitness. The *Girl's Own Paper* reflects the tension between valuing feminine modesty and decorum while also reframing its feminine ideal to reflect the realities of girls' lives.

---

[5]   The other magazine is *Every Girl's Magazine*.

[6]   In *Great-Grandmama's Weekly*, Forrester's thematic chapters include one on "Health and Beauty."

As public perceptions of the feminine ideal began to shift, improving girls' health became an important theme in the *Girl's Own Paper*, especially alongside the debate about women's higher education. The *GOP* was not especially supportive of the move towards higher education for girls, yet its articles on health reflect concerns that excessive study could cause physical deformity and weakness. As I shall discuss in Chapter 5, the medical establishment was mobilized to fight the demands of higher education by confirming "the biological and mental inadequacies" (Heilmann 49) of women. Medical professionals were concerned that higher education would defeminize women and they would be unlikely to marry and unable to bear children. Contemporary fears of racial degeneration are pivotal to understanding how and why the *GOP* endorses and redefines the healthy girl.

The need for health was accompanied by a shift in the aesthetics of the feminine ideal. According to Darwinian theory, all species have the possibility to evolve, and those characteristics that enable a species' survival will be passed on to succeeding generations. Medical professionals consequently defined the characteristics that would enable the human race to progress. Angelique Richardson points out that "[a]s the language of biology was shaping the debates on poverty and the role of women in society, so it underpinned new aesthetic discourses in the second half of the century, equating the ugly with disease and the beautiful with health" (80). Novelist and journalist Grant Allen was a significant proponent of this physiological aestheticism. With the publication of his book, *Physiological Aesthetics* (1877), Allen identified how the human form was allied with function, intending "to exhibit the purely physical origin of the sense of beauty, and its relativity to our nervous organization" (2).[7] The success of his volume suggests that the notion of a feminine aesthetic was not unwelcome. In the pages of the *GOP*, notions of health informed this aesthetic.

Yet the attempts within the *Girl's Own Paper* to describe the healthy feminine ideal are problematic and occasionally contradictory. Although health could be used to authorize a variety of new behaviours for girls, contributors to the magazine try to define a narrow list of acceptably feminine activities. Moreover, the new aesthetic of beauty is entwined with moral qualities, robust health, and physical capability instead of an abstract idea of beauty. Thus the aesthetic appeal of the healthy girl is explicitly connected to her usefulness and her character, particularly in the fiction of the magazine. Although few fictional pieces in the *GOP* discuss the healthy girl, two stories suggest the competing attitudes towards girls' health. The artist Frank Warren is horrified by the specimens of femininity on display at a party in the 1887 serialized story, "Transformed." Recently returned from a European tour, he has become "very fastidious, having spent so much of [his] time amongst the most perfect statuary and amongst people who have the highest

---

[7]   Yet Peter Morton points out that Allen's attempt was problematic because by defining principles of taste, he was "fixing them, implicitly, as objective and immutable" (25). The physical ideal of beauty is, of course, subjective and Allen exposes his "cultural and personal prejudices" (25).

ideals" (698) of art as a true representation of Nature. Presumably referring to statues he has seen in European art collections, he applies a classical ideal of aesthetics to the Victorian female body. His friend, Charley, who is studying to be a doctor, likes to see a girl with "a good figure. I like to see her carry herself well, and be able to move gracefully. I know nothing about art, but I think I know a little about health ... and ... I like to see a girl look nice" (698). A girl is graceful and beautiful because she is healthy. Both men, of course, reveal the subjective nature of aesthetics and find it difficult to define their aesthetic ideal. Charley describes a healthy girl's figure as "nice," suggesting something undefinable yet inherently attractive about a healthy girl.

The protagonist, Cicely, rightly concludes that she does not satisfy their aesthetic ideal. She first appears as an invalid, temporarily laid up with a sprained ankle. She realizes that "my figure was execrably bad; I knew that I was round-shouldered, narrow-chested, that I stooped, and that I walked in a listless, ambling sort of fashion" (699). Her subsequent transformation into a healthy, active, capable girl allows her to leave behind her "invalidism." In the *GOP*, girlhood can be a site of transformation from chronic invalidism to health, beauty, and productivity. Cicely also understands that aesthetics, character, and intellect are entwined when she acknowledges that she is "entirely without character" (699).

Both men perceive only one girl at the party, Matilda [Figure 4.1], as beautiful. While Frank acknowledges Matilda's "singularly plain face," he nonetheless feels that she is his ideal feminine form:

> Look how full of spontaneous grace every motion is! What a magnificent turn of the head! What a carriage! There is pride, and yet there is no pride, in it ... I tell you there is character in every gesture. I tell you this woman—and I use the word in its most dignified sense—must have a beautiful mind, if she has not a beautiful face. Look at her now, as she is lifting that golden-haired child in her arms, and holds him up to look at that picture on the wall. With what grace she raised the dumpling from the ground! What firmness in the pose! What lightness and elegance in the balance of the body! (699)

Matilda is both physically and mentally beautiful because physical strength and grace are associated with mental ability. Her strength is balanced by "lightness" to demonstrate her femininity. Moreover, by lifting up a child, her aesthetic appeal is aligned with maternity, thus reinforcing the healthy body as enabling motherhood. Health and femininity are united as the healthy girl is depicted as beautiful, intelligent, maternal, and useful. Cicely is inspired to travel with her family to Sweden, where she trains in the Swedish system of gymnastics and transforms herself from a weak, foolish, and unattractive girl.[8] She takes control of her body and improves her aesthetic appeal and her health.

---

[8]   Per Henrik Ling's system was intended to "promote the harmonious development of the whole body through a system which progressed in its demands upon strength and skill, and included simple, free-standing exercises as well as work with apparatus" (Fletcher 17).

"'WITH WHAT GRACE SHE RAISES THE DUMPLING FROM THE GROUND.'"

Fig. 4.1　　Matilda from "Transformed", *Girl's Own Paper*, 1887

The embodiment of health and beauty in the female body is an important precursor to mental development. Cicely is delighted with the changes in her body and wishes to "put [her] newly-found energies to use—to do something good and glorious" (715), a theme that recurs in the *GOP*. Girls are encouraged to be useful and guided towards certain kinds of occupations, such as nursing, and Cicely trains to become a nurse in her parish. Both the type and the location of Cicely's labour are significant. As a nurse, she conforms to "Victorian notions of woman's innate nurturing and domestic skills" (Swenson 17), thus reinforcing her femininity. By nursing locally, rather than in a sisterhood or nursing home, she embodies Christian charity for the poor while also reinforcing her position in the domestic sphere because she remains at home to pursue her new vocation. The feminine ideal she portrays is one of strength and capability, yet she remains within carefully constructed boundaries. Unlike Ethel in Yonge's "The Daisy Chain," whose scholarly ambitions are deemed inappropriate, Cicely's ambitions are suitably feminine. Her improved health does not threaten the traditional limits of the home. Moreover, as the embodiment of his aesthetic feminine ideal, Cicely inspires Frank's art when she reencounters him while nursing. They marry and Cicely is able to bear healthy children, deflecting fears about the health of the English race by reinforcing the connection between health and maternity.

The possibilities and potential of health are conveyed directly in the story's afterword. The anonymous author writes that "I would have every girl and every woman as healthy and as strong as she can possibly be" (805) through a daily exercise regime and rational dress that allows for freedom of movement. Without physical health, a girl can live only "a half-developed existence, or an unproportionately developed one, with some powers exaggerated and others left quite in abeyance" (805). Although the author does not identify the exaggerated powers, she is likely referring to girls who study to the detriment of their physical health. Without a good balance, many girls and women tend to "a chronic state of *apathy*, which is so universal as to be almost considered a desirable 'ladylike' thing" (805). This direct address to the readers is unusual in the *GOP*, yet the afterword provides an intriguing example of a real girl who suffered from the invalidism and apathy that the author critiques in the story. It reinforces the optimistic conclusion that transformation is possible with good health.

However, improved feminine health is also a concern in the *GOP* because it enables transgressive possibilities for girls as they gain the strength and capability to make their own decisions about the limitations imposed by the traditional feminine ideal. Mary E. Hullah's 1892 cautionary tale, "Stand and Wait: An Invalid's Story," uses invalidism to punish a girl who dares to seek useful

---

It was introduced into English schools by Madame Bergman Osterberg, who trained in Ling's Royal Central Gymnastics Institute in Sweden before being appointed to the London School Board in 1881 to superintend the physical education of girls in metropolitan schools.

occupation outside the domestic sphere.[9] At eighteen, Madeline leaves her aunt's home against her advice and moves to London's East End to work among the poor, where she soon becomes ill. A male doctor rescues her and suggests that she may have mistaken her vocation. In this case, health enables a girl to make her own decisions, yet they are flawed because she ignores her domestic responsibilities and refuses to be guided by her elders.

The male medical professional can help girls understand their abilities and the limitations of their bodies. Patricia Vertinsky notes that "[t]he medical system and medical science have occupied and continue to occupy a central place in women's experiences of themselves as women" (6). In "Stand and Wait," a male doctor whom Madeline has never met turns his expert gaze on her and judges both her fitness and her capacity for charity work based on extremely limited knowledge.[10] Yet Madeline accepts his medical determination that she is unsuited to this kind of labour, especially after he tells her, "They also serve who only stand and wait" (622). This reference to John Milton's poem, "When I consider how my light is spent," reminds Madeline that she can serve God from anywhere. She concludes that "it had not pleased God to give me the strength to carry out my plans" (622). Her health has been compromised; she is now a chronic invalid. Yet this results in a new relationship with the local villagers, and she finds new purpose in her home life: "Gradually the old longing to try first one scheme and then another left me, and I learnt to be content" (622). Properly chastised, she acknowledges her responsibilities to the local community and accepts her ill health as a consequence of her poor decision.

Good health is often associated with working-class girls, not only because they need their health in order to perform their jobs, but also because they are typically more active than their middle-class counterparts. In Lewis Novra's 1882 poem, "Contentment," for example, Kitty "trips lightly o'er the mead,/Flush'd with the sweet fresh morning gale,/A type of health indeed!" (l. 10–12). In contrast to those with untold wealth who lie "dreaming of their hoarded gold" (l. 19), Kitty is content because she has "happiness and health" (l. 24). Accompanied by an illustration of her crossing a creek while carrying a milking pail, Kitty is a strong, healthy young woman whose health enables her happiness. She is able to do her work each day, and she desires nothing more. Health is similarly written upon the

---

[9]   Mary Hullah was an occasional contributor of serialized fiction to the *Girl's Own Paper,* including "No" (1886), "Forbidden Letters" (1889), "Ella's Experiences" (1890), and "A Daughter of the House of Tregaron" (1891).

[10]   Charlotte Perkins Gilman's "The Yellow Wallpaper" (1892) famously explores the potentially devastating influence of medicine on women's lives. A young woman suffering from post-partum depression wonders if "*perhaps*" (31) the reason she does not get better is because her husband John is a physician. She suffers under the dictates of the male medical establishment since both John and her brother agree upon the "proper" treatment, yet she knows that only through her writing and with intellectual stimulation will her good health be restored. Unlike Madeline, this young woman never learns to be content but is instead driven insane by the circumscribed conditions of her life.

country girl with "the glow of health upon her cheek" (l. 3) in the Rev. William Cowan's 1890 poem "All For Love." Young Pauline picks flowers along country lanes to give to cheer the "lonely couch" (l. 17) of a dying woman living in town. Moreover, the city can be an unhealthy place, particularly for the working classes. In the 1888 poem "Hampstead Heath" by G.C.H., the heath is a "blest spot, so near to London's din and smoke" (l. 1) because it lies within easy reach of London's "poorest folk" (l. 2). On the heath, the "toiling thousands" (l. 27) can "breathe health-giving air" (l. 28). The pastoral location frees London's workers from the cares of employment and provides an uncontrolled space that they can inhabit as they wish.

These stories and poems highlight the tensions in the *GOP* about the healthy girl. The working-class girl is almost always healthy, because her health is vital to her employment. For the middle-class girl, however, although health makes her capable and confident, it can also be dangerous. Without proper guidance, she may abandon her duties in the home, with the attendant consequences for her health and her future as a wife and mother. A more appropriately healthy girl understands the need for health but will not exceed the proper bounds of feminine behaviour by abandoning her family or her home. In fact, her health is a critical component of her femininity because it makes her more beautiful and more capable. Her aesthetic appeal operates in tandem with her moral and physical strengths to make her a suitable, and desirable, wife. The male doctor in "Stand and Wait" also signals the important role that the male medical professional plays in the magazine.

Medicalizing Girls' Health

The *GOP* promotes the idea of the healthy girl through the frequent contributions of "Medicus," the pseudonym of retired Royal Navy assistant surgeon Gordon Stables, in which he instructs girls about appropriate behaviours designed to improve their health. In addition to his boys' adventure stories and health articles for the *Boy's Own Paper*, he also wrote regularly for the *Girl's Own Paper*.[11] As Terry Doughty remarks, a former naval doctor is a "curious qualification for a writer on girls' health" (161), but the longevity of his contributions suggest that his advice was popular. Between 1880 and 1908, he contributed over 200 articles, averaging more than 6 articles on girls' health every year.[12] His voice is a predominant and pervasive one in the pages of the magazine as he established himself as a knowledgeable, jovial, and somewhat paternal figure. His pseudonym certainly reinforces his medical expertise.

In the *Boy's Own Paper*, he uses his own name, rather than "Medicus." In addition, his contributions are more varied, including a number of serialized

---

[11]   Curiously, despite frequent and regular contributions to the *Girl's Own Paper* between 1880 and 1908, only Stables's health articles in the *Boy's Own Paper* are noted in his entry in the *Oxford Dictionary of National Biography*.

[12]   Stables published *The Girls' Own Book of Health and Beauty* in 1891.

articles about pets, such as "Boys' Dogs and All About Them" and "The Boy's Own Museum; Or, Birds and Beasts, and How to Stuff Them." His fiction—he was a prodigious novelist—also appeared in its pages, beginning with "The Cruise of the Snowbird" in 1881. His articles on health in the *BOP* have a rather different tone as well. In "Common Sense About Health and Athletics," Stables provides "a few common-sense words of advice" (591) about hygiene, boyhood complaints, and how to become strong.

The advice "Medicus" provides to his girl readers highlights his somewhat ambiguous attitude towards girls. Although he believes girls should be active, healthy, and capable, he also believes they must be treated gently and that they have both less interest in, and less ability to understand, scientific and physiological facts about the human body. Consequently, he adopts a different approach with his girl readers. He writes,

> If I were writing for a class of young men students I should at once set about proving in a scientific and physiological manner the value of exercise of the human frame. I would explain the actions of the heart, and the functions of the brain and nervous system generally, and even describe minutely and anatomically the mechanism of the great but sadly over-worked gland the liver. But my audience is a gentle one, and I must deal gently with it, in the matter of hard words and scientific language. ("Exercise" 218)

Although he has the necessary medical knowledge with which to justify his advice, he chooses to exclude that knowledge because girls will find it boring and difficult. His readers are expected to accept his recommendations because of his qualifications rather than his demonstrable knowledge of medicine.

Although "Medicus" never explicitly discusses higher education for women, he fears that excessive study will adversely affect a girl's health because she will not take time from her academic pursuits for sufficient exercise. In "Beauty Hints" in 1901, he writes that some girls devote too much attention to their studies:

> [T]hey succeed in injuring themselves mentally and bodily. Over-much study in any one line or branch does not tend to fit the mind for the battle of life. A world of blue stockings and specialists would not be a pleasant one to live in. I like a Robinson Crusoe kind of girl far more than a specialist. And that is the sort of lass that gets best on in life, and that makes the best wife and the best mother, ay, and the best mistress of a household. (85)

Despite endorsing a feminine ideal of marriage and motherhood, "Medicus's" reference to a "Robinson Crusoe kind of girl" is intriguing because he supports a capable feminine ideal while attempting to contain this behaviour within the home.[13] This limitation is implicitly paradoxical since a Crusoe girl is presumably

---

[13]   As I discuss briefly in Chapter 7, Stables's story, "The Girl Crusoes: A Tale of the Indian Ocean," appeared in the *Girl's Realm* in 1902.

cast upon her own resources outside the traditional domestic sphere.[14] When "Medicus" rejects excessive study, he suggests that the feminine ideal of the healthy girl will be compromised if physical and mental capabilities are not developed in tandem. He reasserts the connection between femininity and health by insisting the active and capable Crusoe girl will make "the best wife and the best mother." Curiously, the resourcefulness of the Crusoe girl is contained within the feminine and the domestic but her Crusoe-like capabilities will assist her to become "the best" because, as a healthy girl, she will attract a good husband and have healthy children.

In his earliest contributions "Medicus" establishes and maintains his project of redefining femininity to include health. Along with strict injunctions against tightly laced corsets, perfumed or coloured soaps, and artificial beauty aids, "Medicus" rejects invalidism and insists that femininity equals capability. Exercise is a key component of a girl's health. In "Exercise, and How to Benefit By It" in 1883, "Medicus" is unsurprised when three young women have poor appetites and a "general air of languor and *ennui*" (218). Because these middle-class girls belong to a family "in which work or labour of any kind was not by any means compulsory," they devote their time, "when not reading, or playing, or writing, to sewing, knitting, [and] embroidery" (218). "Medicus" critiques these inactive hobbies but acknowledges that his readers may be unaware that "exercise is a necessity of life, and one of the best means we possess of keeping sickness at bay and ensuring long life" (218). With no hobbies to keep them active and no encouragement to pursue outdoor exercise, the health of these girls is understandably poor.

"Medicus's" advice gives girl readers control over their bodies and encourages them to exercise. Instead of relying on draughts and medicines, for instance, "the real tonic needed [is] plenty of wholesome exercise in the open air" ("Exercise" 218). They should go for regular, vigorous walks. Combined with light clothing that "should not be tight in any way" (219), girls are encouraged to move beyond the confining (and unhealthy) limits of the home and into public spaces to maintain their health. This ingenious strategy allows girls to use this male medical opinion to justify new behaviours to adults who might otherwise disapprove of their conduct. At a time when information about female biological and reproductive functions was limited, "Medicus" provides practical advice upon which girls could begin to manage their own health. Kirsten Drotner explains the significance of these articles for girl readers: "Assessed within the heated debate" about girls' capabilities and responsibilities, "Gordon Stables' articles to many must have acted as a welcome antidote, strengthening their beliefs in their own physical powers. Lacking sexual advice, it may have been a consolation just to consider one's own health in a legitimate way" (154). The empowering focus on health in the *Girl's Own Paper* thus gives girls an alternative to incapacity and incapability.

This empowerment manifests itself most obviously in the "Answers to Correspondents," where "Medicus" responds to written enquiries about health.

---

[14]   Michelle J. Smith discusses these female figures in more detail in "Nineteenth-Century Female Crusoes: Rewriting the Robinsonade for Girls."

Girl readers regularly wrote to the magazine for health advice, which would have been both easier to obtain and more affordable than arranging to visit a doctor. In one such response to "Ross," he writes, "We are at a loss to understand why so many girls are demented on the subject of the natural plumpness which nature bestows on youth. It is a sign of health" (272). For "Medicus," the health of the female body is much more important than its shape or appearance. "Medicus" also encouraged girls to refer to articles that had already appeared in the magazine. He tells "Cora Orman" to "Read 'Health and Beauty for the Hair,' which appeared in vol. i" and "An Only Child" concerned about her hair falling out is told to "See page 624, vol. i" (351). The articles on health appearing in previous numbers of the magazine are seen as a resource to which girls could return to learn more about particular health matters.

The health advice provided in the "Answers to Correspondents" also encouraged girls to seek proper medical attention when warranted. In one such case, "Meg," a victim of abuse from her parents, is advised on how to negotiate access to a doctor by suggesting how her poor health interferes with her ability to complete her work:

> Tell your father how much you suffer from headaches, and that, apart from the suffering and state of health producing them, you find them to interfere with your daily work, and ask him to let you consult a doctor. If you can see the latter privately, you had better confide to him the blows you receive, and get him to tell your parents that any blows on the head are dangerous, and carefully to be avoided (without betraying that he knows how they were given). (367)

In this case, "Meg" is encouraged to seek medical advice in the hopes of reducing violence in the home. The implication is that the doctor may be able to influence other adults' behaviour through his authority as a medical professional, and he can act as "Meg's" advocate, hopefully in ways that do not expose her to additional violence. In the face of physical abuse, "Meg" has written in to the magazine for assistance and support, which "Medicus" provides. While we have no way of knowing whether this advice is successful, "Meg's" example demonstrates the extent to which the *GOP* operates as a venue through which girls could take control of their bodies and obtain information. Moreover, "Medicus's" suggestion that "Meg" appeal to her father on the grounds of her productivity highlights the changing nature of girls' work.

These changing attitudes towards women's work are one reason why health is successfully incorporated into the feminine ideal in the last decades of the century. In the 1880s and '90s, women were increasingly entering the workforce to support themselves and their families, and because they desired useful occupation.[15] As

---

[15]   In the 1880s and '90s, the *GOP* also firmly supported the idea that both working- and middle-class girls should consider emigrating to the colonies as domestic servants. Health was a critical factor for their success in gaining emigration assistance. See Kristine Moruzi, "'The freedom suits me': Encouraging Girls to Settle in the Colonies."

the amount of domestic work in the middle-class home decreased, middle-class girls had less to occupy themselves. The *Girl's Own Paper* regularly contains articles about women's employment, including details about the required skills and training. One such article appears in the *GOP* in 1902 in which a laundry owner observes that, after years of hard work in the schoolroom, girls are "utterly unfit … to commence at eighteen or nineteen years old an aimless existence" ("My Laundry" 42). The author speaks with such authority on the lives of middle-class girls that she appears to have come from a similar background. When the focus and purpose of the schoolroom is replaced with an aimless life, a healthy girl turns into "a complete nervous invalid" (42). In this article, and elsewhere in the *GOP*, health is guaranteed through work. The laundress concludes that "those who lose themselves in work and in the lives of others … find their own true life" (42). A girl's "true life" will be discovered through work and service to others. As I discussed in Chapter 2, this ideal of service and duty is consistent with a traditional feminine ideal, but the focus on work is a significant difference. The feminine ideal is expanding to include both health and work because a healthy girl can and should have a useful occupation that contributes to the family's well being.

The feminine ideal of beauty and health is not employed in discussions targeted at working-class girls. For these girls, work is aligned with health to enable girls to support themselves. In "Healthy Lives for Working Girls" by "Medicus" in 1886, health is a critical aspect of the life of a working girl for it may be "the only capital" she possesses. For these girls, "loss of health means loss of work, loss of wage, anxiety, … and perhaps serious privations to those in any way dependent upon their exertions" (77).[16] In "Remove the Cause," "Medicus" declares that the two main causes of working girls' ill health are "too much faith in physic" and "injudicious food," by which he means the lack of "strengthening food in sufficient quantity" (7). He explains the types and quantities of desirable food, oblivious to questions of affordability, and prescribes his traditional advice of regular sleep habits, daily exercise and cold baths. He also eschews "silly novels, especially those pretty little stories of love and murder" and instead advises "useful and amusing" (8) light reading. Aside from this glancing reference to working-class girls' reading, "Medicus" provides a series of suggestions designed to improve a girl's health. A steady course of fresh air and exercise will improve the appetite, and girls will be able to eat "more and better food" (8), which should nevertheless be easily digestible. He promises that "[i]f you do all I tell you in this paper regularly for six weeks, you will in all probability have completely removed the cause of your trouble" (8). For working-class girls, health is imperative for their work, but not an important aspect of their femininity.

---

[16] Although "Medicus" connects health and usefulness in his articles, he is not generally concerned with the working-class girl. In fact, his reminder in 1888 that "this is a working girl's paper, and so I have to deal with working girls' troubles" ("Remove the Cause" 7) is somewhat surprising, since many of his earlier articles refer to idle, pale, unhealthy girls who have little to occupy themselves and are presumably middle class.

In contrast, the "Medicus" articles aimed at middle-class girls contain the healthy feminine ideal within the traditional boundaries of work inside the home, expectations of usefulness, and the duty to be beautiful. In "Work Versus Idleness," he harshly informs his readers that "[i]dle people do not live long, and when they die they are never missed, for the simple reason that they are not the salt of the earth and nobody ever really loves them" (622). An idle girl is unnatural because she ignores the "example set by Nature" (623), where all creatures work. Moreover, "idleness, indeed, is a kind of a moral cancer that eats away all nervous power and ends by totally destroying both health and happiness" (623). Although "Medicus" does not explicitly support the idea of middle-class girls' paid employment, he nonetheless encourages girls to "work with a will at whatever are the duties her station in life makes incumbent on her" (623). A girl is unlikely to be healthy without work, and will be "deceiving herself" (623) if she thinks otherwise because neither her complexion nor her eyes will be as healthy as they could be if she were usefully occupied. Thus, in the *GOP*, depictions of girlhood employ the idea of health in different ways and to different effect. Health is a crucial factor for working-class girls because it enables them to support themselves. For middle-class girls, however, health is presented as an important component of their femininity.

The Aesthetic of Health

The middle-class girl's beauty is also a function of her health, with the image of the healthy girl aestheticized in the *Girl's Own Paper*. Ken Montague identifies a "fundamental redesign of the ideal female figure" (91) in the medical, aesthetic, social, and anthropological discourses of the late nineteenth century. For example, not only does "Medicus" wish to improve girls' health so that they will be stronger and more useful, but he also depicts the healthy girl as more beautiful. He encourages girls "never to sit or stand in a bent or uncomfortable pose" ("Work Versus Idleness" 623) and compares girls' postures to two "stops" used by writers and printers, the question mark (?) and the exclamation point (!). He critiques girls' fashion when he inquires, "Which of these stops would you like to grow like—the crooked one that asks questions, or the tall, stately one that marks an exclamation?" (623). This critique follows a similar campaign in *Punch*. An 1870 comic illustration, "The Venus of Milo; Or, Girls of Two Different Periods" [Figure 4.2], highlights the folly of women's fashions and also illustrates "Medicus's" point about posture. The title refers not only to women of different historical periods, setting Victorian women alongside a classical Roman statue, but also to Eliza Lynn Linton's provocative article on the Girl of the Period (which I discussed in Chapter 3) where she criticizes the modern girl. A group of fashionably dressed women surround a status of the Venus de Milo, criticizing her large feet, regular-sized waist, and her tiny head with no chignon. The Victorian women, of course, look ridiculous—unable to stand up straight, with tiny waists, elaborate hairdos, and feet encased in high-heeled shoes. They embody the "?" posture that "Medicus" critiques, while the Venus de Milo represents the more rational "!" posture developed through healthy, active living.

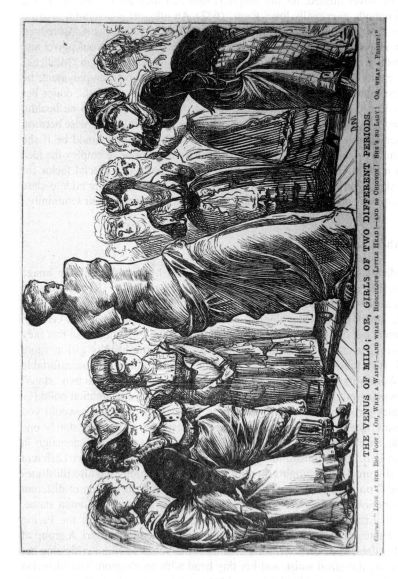

Fig. 4.2   The Venus of Milo; Or, Girls of Two Different Periods, *Punch's Almanack for 1870*

In Sharon Marcus's discussion of Victorian fashion plates, she emphasizes how "those who sell fashion ... create simulacra of femininity not for men but for *women and girls* to scrutinize, handle, and consume. To market femininity to women is to use hyperfeminine objects to solicit a female gaze and to incite female fantasy" (4). She interprets this *Punch* cartoon as an opportunity for women to "scrutinize female figures, make aesthetic judgments, and wield the social powers of denigration and exclusion" (16). In contrast, when "Medicus" describes the "?" and "!" postures, he hopes that girls will see the folly of the "?" and will instead endorse the "!". In developing his female aesthetic, he wishes his readers to reject any ideal that contorts the body into an unhealthy position and prevents free movement of the limbs.

The female body is a site for display, critique, and improvement in the *Girl's Own Paper* and elsewhere in the periodical press. The corset plays a central role in these discussions because of how it physically shapes the body and for its adverse health implications. The overlap of aesthetics and health is apparent in two separate, yet interrelated, discussions of the corset. *The Art of Beauty* (1878), one of three books by Eliza Haweis on domestic décor and the dangers fashion poses to health, describes the tightly-laced corset as "a tyrant ... crushing in the ribs, injuring the lungs and heart, the stomach, and many other internal organs" (49).[17] She includes two illustrations, one of the natural form and the other of the "fashionable form" of the ribs and spine, to demonstrate how the tightly-laced corset results in "the grotesque outline of the body—and many a dire disease" (48). In "Medicus's" "health-sermon" (which suggests a curious mixture of medicine and religion) on "Health, Strength, and Beauty," he describes "a hornet, or something that looked very like one" (758) while walking in the country. This hornet figure echoes the 1869 *Punch* cartoon, "Mr. Punch's Designs After Nature" [Figure 4.3], which declares that "wasp-waisted" young ladies might advantageously adopt the costume of a wasp. "Medicus" criticizes the lady he sees "coming mincingly along up the hill ..., slowly, mind. Oh, she could not have walked quickly to save her sweet and precious life. She was what is called 'fashionably dressed' ... and she carried a cane—I daresay she needed its support" (758). He condemns tight lacing from a "health point of view" (758) and hopes that "every little word from a medical man" will help to encourage the end of this fashion and the rise of "a due appreciation of what is really beautiful" (758). He employs his medical credentials and his medical knowledge to encourage girls to abandon tightly-laced corsets and articulates his own aesthetic for beauty by insisting that a girl whose blood is insufficiently aerated "can possess neither health, strength, nor beauty" (758).

These critiques of tight lacing demonstrate the extent to which the female body was figured as a site for foolish fashion and for beauty. Importantly, however,

[17] Haweis was a writer and illustrator. She published a wide range of books, including *Chaucer for Children: A Golden Key* (1887), that combined her interest in art and literature. *The Art of Beauty* (1878) was followed by *The Art of Dress* (1879) and *The Art of Decoration* (1881).

MR. PUNCH'S DESIGNS AFTER NATURE.

MIGHT NOT *WASP-WAISTED* YOUNG LADIES ADOPT THIS COSTUME WITH ADVANTAGE?

Fig. 4.3   Mr. Punch's Designs After Nature, *Punch*, 1869

neither "Medicus" nor Haweis call for the elimination of the corset entirely. As a signifier of "fashionableness in middle- and upper-middle-class women" (Finch 343), the corset was also used to represent the virtue of its wearer. Thus, while tight lacing was considered by some to be foolishly dangerous to a girl's health, the sensibly worn corset reinforced the feminine ideal of health and beauty.[18] Moreover, it might have been problematic if "Medicus" had called for the abandonment of the corset, since corset makers were advertising in the magazine. Izod's Corsets [Figure 4.4] claims its product is "[m]odelled on the most artistic and hygienic lines," suggesting beauty and health can be improved through the use of a corset. Like the *GOP*, the corset advertisers aligned beauty and health on the female body and transformed these aesthetic categories into a form of consumption.

Although "Medicus" frequently decries tight lacing, most of his observations about feminine beauty pertain to healthy living rather than fashion. Regular exercise, a proper diet, and good hygiene will make girls healthy, and healthy girls are beautiful. Beautiful skin, for example, is "one of the signs of health" and is possible if girls would live "more naturally" ("A Beautiful Skin" 643). "Medicus" chastises girls who wish to be more beautiful: "Silly thought—you have health. Health can make the plainest girl pleasant to behold" because it "causes the rich blood to mantle in the cheeks, brings the gladsome glitter to the eye, brightens the complexion, gives music to the voice, a charm to the smile, litheness and vigour to the limbs, and sprightliness and grace to every motion" ("Our Bodies" 218). A healthy body is beautiful, then, because of its physical attributes (in the form of pink cheeks, sparkling eyes, and clear skin) and because it enables physical capability (in the form of a graceful, vigorous body). Thus, "Medicus's" feminine ideal includes health and transforms the healthy girl into an aesthetic category.

This female aesthetic also includes moral beauty, which is designed to ensure that the healthy girl remains suitably feminine through her obligations and responsibilities within the home. In her study of nineteenth-century fashion, Valerie Steele describes the connection between moral or spiritual beauty and physical beauty, noting that, for some religious writers, spiritual beauty is so overwhelmingly important that physical appearance becomes "irrelevant to true beauty" (105). Similarly, "Medicus" encourages behaviours that are unrelated to physical health and beauty, but which guide a girl towards moral beauty. For example, he opposes idleness because it "often leads to moral ruin, while the habit of exaggeration when conversing may teach you habits of untruth, and bring upon you misery and wretchedness untold" ("Our Bodies" 218). He reinforces traditional mid-Victorian (and religious) ideals of femininity when he asserts that one of a woman's missions in life "is to soften, refine, and ennoble" ("Things" 70). He encourages "girls to do good, if good there may be done, because it is everyone's duty to do so, because the sense of having done your duty causes happiness, and because happiness begets health, and health beauty" ("Things" 71).

---

[18] As Valerie Steele points out, however, the frequency and degree of tight lacing are subject to interpretation and debate.

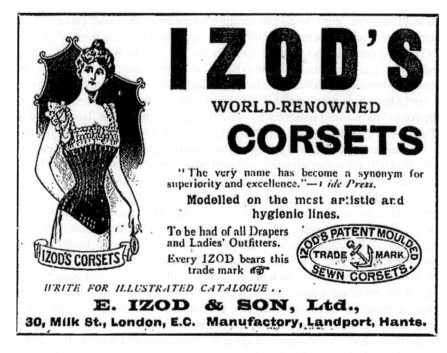

Fig. 4.4   Izod's Corsets, *Girl's Own Paper*

He explicitly connects service and duty with happiness, health, and beauty, where the healthy girl in the *GOP* is incorporated within traditional notions of duty and charity. Encouraging girls towards moral and physical beauty reflects the tension between the feminine ideal of the past and the healthy ideal of the present because the healthy girl presents a disturbing possibility of agency and determination. Consequently, the magazine guides girls towards morality and duty, while also attempting to contain the healthy girl within carefully prescribed boundaries.

Physical Culture for Girls

As the idea of the healthy girl became increasingly popular, the *Girl's Own Paper* also explored a range of possibilities by which girls could develop their physical capabilities. As early as 1882, and continuing well into the twentieth century, the magazine contains numerous informational articles about girls' sporting activities. In articles on gymnastics and callisthenics, hockey, golf, cricket, and cycling, girls are increasingly active outside the home. Yet, even as the feminine ideal expands to include health, the sporting articles display an anxiety about the defeminizing potential of these activities. In her study of women and sport in the nineteenth century, Kathleen McCrone notes that "[s]port is a complex phenomenon which acts as an important agent of both social change and social control and modifies and defines female roles in society at large" (1). The sporting activities presented in the *GOP* demonstrate the tension between understanding that girls need to develop their physical capability and fearing that girls might cross the boundaries of acceptable femininity as they became stronger.

Other print culture of the period explores the same challenges of liberating girls from mid-Victorian constraints while also ensuring that they remain suitably feminine and virtuous. Herbert Spencer, a strong proponent of physical exercise for girls, attacked the idea that girls given access to sports would become wild and uncontrollable. In a series of *Essays on Education* (1859), he wonders "why should … sportive activity prevent girls from growing up into ladies?" (137). He encourages girls to take up enjoyable sports. Whoever forbids these activities, he writes, "forbids the divinely-appointed means to physical development" (138). Spencer disapproved of gymnastics for girls, suggesting that they were repetitive, boring, and artificial. Although the movement towards gymnastics and callisthenics—which marks one of the earliest stages of girls' physical education—became extremely popular in the 1880s when it was first introduced, Spencer highlights the problematic nature of its disciplinarity. While gymnastics are initially promoted in the *GOP* in stories like "Transformed," this exercise soon gives way to activities that people like Spencer considered much more enjoyable for girls. McCrone notes that the teaching approach of the Swedish gymnastics system emphasized "the identification of individuals with a group and the repetition of identical movements. Excessively regimented, it gave little thought to individual or imaginative ways of moving, or to the idea that exercise should be enjoyable" (102). The references in the *GOP* reinforce the idea that gymnastics are not intended to be enjoyable but are necessary for a girl's physical wellbeing. Health is positioned as yet another responsibility of girlhood along with a girl's responsibilities to her home and family. In an illustration entitled "The Gymnasium of the North London Collegiate School for Girls" [Figure 4.5], for example, the exercise is neither liberating nor, seemingly, entertaining. Instead, this disciplined work ensures a girl's health.

Despite the magazine's support for girls' health, sporting activities are viewed with some anxiety. Although new, health-promoting activities are generally encouraged, some contributors express concerns that are intended to restrict the healthy girl to activities that are considered suitably feminine. In June 1894, for example, respected physician and scientist Sir Benjamin Ward Richardson reminds his readers that recreation should not "interfere with duties and functions especially belonging to the woman" (546), particularly those relating to the home and motherhood.[19] He adopts a Social Darwinist perspective when he insists

---

[19] Richardson was known for his involvement with public health and the sanitary movement as well as a number of innovations in anaesthetic practices. He published scientific works throughout his career, including *Diseases of Modern Life* (1876), and the Utopian novel *Hydeia: A City of Health* (1876). A committed teetotaller, he also published widely about the dangers of drink.

THE GYMNASIUM OF THE NORTH LONDON COLLEGIATE SCHOOL FOR GIRLS.

[See page 104.

Fig. 4.5   The Gymnasium of the North London Collegiate School for Girls, *Girl's Own Paper*, 1882

> that if the race is to progress [girls] must someday become mothers, that they
> must undertake special maternal duties, and that for home to be home they must,
> within the sphere of home, display domestic talents, and do domestic work
> which comes exclusively under their control. They must remember, moreover,
> without thinking of giving up recreative pleasures and exercises as matters of
> necessity, that every attempt to pass in recreation beyond a certain bound of
> natural womanly duties, is to pass into a sphere with which such duties are
> utterly incompatible. (546)

Recreation is acceptable and necessary as long as it strengthens and prepares a girl to become a wife and mother. Excessive sport and extreme physical strength are incompatible with a woman's proper role. Consequently, certain types of recreations are suitable for girls because they are not vulgar and they promote the equal development of the body, a key characteristic of Richardson's feminine ideal. When he writes that "[t]here are recreations which lead to general beauty, and there are recreations which divert from general beauty" (546), he aligns his rationale with racial progress and an aesthetic ideal of beauty.

In contrast to the control and discipline of gymnastics, other forms of physical culture liberated girls from the constraints of the gym and offered more opportunities for freedom and fun. At the same time, girls participating in these activities retained their feminine appeal. "Medicus" offers his advice on the appropriate exercise for girls, especially in "Useful Pastimes for Health and Pleasure" in 1895, and he selects activities because of their feminine qualities. "[P]astimes" (and significantly not "sports") should be outdoors, "non-exciting," and have "value as mental tonics and calmatives" (557), yet his emphasis on the calming aspects of recreation is inconsistent with his frequent advice to get the blood stirring. His advice reinforces McCrone's observation that while commentators on women's activities

> manifested an obvious concern for the health of women and a genuine desire that
> women take more exercise, they lacked any semblance to a feminist perspective.
> Almost all considered females naturally inferior to and weaker than males. They
> cautioned constantly against overstrain and were obsessed with worry about the
> effects of exercise on maternity and propriety. Their recommendations were thus
> exceedingly cautious. Few indicated any sympathy for the idea that women had
> a right to develop their bodies as fully as possible, and none saw sport as a means
> of their doing so, since sport was inevitably equated with masculinity and threats
> to true womanliness. (11)

In the *GOP*, excessive sport is feared to encourage increasingly masculine behaviours, such as competition, and could defeminize girls. Concerns about a girl's appearance are consequently paramount. "Medicus" recommends tricycling rather than cycling because a girl can dress like a lady, not like a "mounteback" (558); a girl's healthful exercise must reinforce, rather than undermine, her femininity. Thus "Medicus" generally supports individual activities (rather than team sports) where feminine decorum and dress can be maintained easily, such as golf, walking, and boating. Fishing and gardening are to be commended for their "calmative" properties. The only team sport he endorses is cricket, though he limits this to those girls with large families or at large schools for "I do not believe in girls and boys playing the game indiscriminately" (558). As McCrone observes, "men's and women's sports, with a few exceptions, remained strictly segregated" (13).

This segregation is a significant aspect of the redefinition of the feminine ideal to include health. Girls' exercise, if it involves others, is usually conducted within female, homosocial groups, and rarely includes the highly competitive aspects of team sports. In an illustration appearing in 1892/3 [Figure 4.6], four nicely dressed young women skate together. They exclude the three men in the background as they hold hands. They enjoy themselves as they maintain their dignity and modesty. The caption, "Healthful Exercise," reinforces their participation in a healthful activity while also maintaining their feminine decorum. Similarly, an 1894/5 illustration reinforces health and modesty. In "Healthy Recreation" [Figure 4.7], a young woman is about to hit a golf ball, while a female friend watches and a young male caddy carries the clubs. For the girls, golf is a leisure activity, while it offers employment for the male caddy. Both young women are demurely dressed, yet the figure of the golfer is strangely static, especially in contrast to the ease of movement in the skating illustration.

This illustration and an 1890 article on ladies' golf demonstrate the ambivalence with which the public viewed these shifts in exercise for girls and women. In "Ladies' Golf," the anonymous author describes how only recently

> ladies have—with much more becoming and feminine taste than inspires them to compete in the more masculine sports of cricket and football—taken up a game which has, especially in the modified form in which they usually play it, nothing but favourable points to recommend it, embracing as it does all the advantages of open air, healthy exercise, education of the eye, and, like most games, developing control of temper and general judgment in deciding the best method of overcoming the various obstacles and 'hazards' of the links, which might well be applied to the ups and downs of life generally, with beneficial effect. (273)

The author critiques girls' participation in the traditionally male domains of cricket and football and suggests that golf is more appropriate, particularly when the "fair ones" do not follow the "more energetic play of the men, with their longer links and herculean 'driving'" (273–4). Instead, these female players are "content" with putting, the "more delicate part of the game" (274). The accompanying illustrations show women making small, careful putts while men watch [Figure 4.8]. Female golfers are transformed from active participants into the subjects of the male gaze, even as they reject the vigorous play of the game to remain appropriately feminine. Of course, the health benefits of golf are considerably muted when the game is limited to putting, but this modified game highlights the tensions between health and femininity operating in the magazine. Sheila Scraton argues that

HEALTHFUL EXERCISE.

Fig. 4.6   Healthful Exercise, *Girl's Own Paper*, 1892

HEALTHY RECREATION.

Fig. 4.7   Healthy Recreation, *Girl's Own Paper*, 1894

VOL. XI.—No. 527.]   FEBRUARY 1, 1890.   [PRICE ONE PENNY.

BEFORE THE STROKE.

LADIES' GOLF.

THE ancient game of golf is fast becoming a very popular pastime in England, though it may possibly be some little time before it reaches that popularity which it obtains on more northern shores, where, so great is the enthusiasm of players of all ages, and "all sorts and conditions of men," women, and children, that in such places as St. Andrews, which has long been considered its head-quarters, golfing seems to be the one absorbing subject of interest and conversation from morning to night; and even the natural beauties and historic charms of the ancient city alike appear to be of secondary interest to this engrossing pastime of our Scotch brethren.

The name of golf (pronounced "goff") apparently had its origin in the German word kolbe, or Low Dutch kolf (a club), and the game itself is considered by the best authorities to be of very ancient origin among the natives of North Britain. In the reign of James II. it had already become a popular game in Scotland, for in an Act of Parliament

dated 1437, in favour of archery, it is "decreeted and ordained that the weapon-scha-winges be halden be the Lordes and Barronnes, Spirituel and Temporal, foure times in the zeir, and that fute-ball and golfe be utterly cryit downe and not be used."

It is, however, only of late years that ladies have—with much more becoming and feminine taste than inspires them to compete in the more masculine sports of cricket and football —taken up a game which has, especially in the modified form in which they usually play it, nothing but favourable points to recommend it, embracing as it does all the advantages of open air, healthy exercise, education of the eye, and, like most games, developing control of temper and general judgment in deciding the best method of overcoming the various obstacles and "hazards" of the links, which might well be applied to the ups and downs of life generally, with beneficial effect.

Wisely, the fair ones who of late appear apt to follow too closely the "lords of creation," are willing, except in few cases, to ignore the

AFTER THE STROKE.

Fig. 4.8   Ladies' Golf, *Girl's Own Paper*, 1890

> [m]orality and modesty—sexually appropriate behaviour—remained the firm
> responsibility of girls and young women through their appearance and behaviour.
> Physical education, although liberating women from many bodily restrictions
> and conventions of dress, was careful to protect the sexuality of young women
> with a reaffirmation of 'feminine' modesty and 'desirable' dignity. (35)

Although girlhood in the *GOP* includes new expectations about health and
beauty, the magazine remains concerned about how this new feminine ideal can
be incorporated within a girl's modesty and decorum. The liberating impulses of
exercise and sport are constrained by the need to ensure the morality and purity of
the girl readers.

Sport thus occupies an intriguingly contested space in the pages of the *Girl's
Own Paper*. McCrone writes that "[i]ts masculinity makes it an obvious sphere
for women to attempt to penetrate—or at the very least to challenge by creating
parallel worlds of their own—in their efforts to counter external definitions of
female physical and emotional frailty" (2). In the article on "Ladies' Golf," of
course, the putting portion of the masculine game of golf is redefined as essentially
feminine, becoming a space women can enter without appearing to compete in a
male domain. To a certain extent, golf is more easily defined as an acceptable sport
for girls because it lacks the vigor and excitement of more obviously competitive
team sports like cricket. The *GOP* encourages sport as an important aspect of girls'
health, yet the types and locations of these activities are defined to ensure that
girls' femininity is not compromised.

This ambiguity is, in part, owing to the *GOP*'s status as a middle-class
magazine. Although, as Hilary Skelding points out, Charles Peters and the *GOP*
contributors were "keen to stress the universal appeal of the magazine, which
deliberately targeted a wide audience" (39), the feminine ideal depicted in the
magazine embodies predominantly middle-class expectations. Feminine ideals
of purity and morality were more firmly invested in middle-class girls and
women and consequently became the subject of more intense scrutiny. McCrone
specifically excludes working-class women from her examination of women and
sport, explaining that, "[w]ith only a few exceptions, between 1870 and 1914 sport
among working-class women was virtually non-existent since the requisite leisure,
schooling and money were lacking" (ii). Certainly the types of sport that girls in
the *GOP* were encouraged to pursue, from lawn tennis to skating and golfing,
would have been available only to girls with sufficient income to purchase the
necessary equipment and to access the required sporting arenas. Most working-
class girls lacked the time and the resources to engage in these activities.

Like the comic journalism in the *Girl of the Period Miscellany*, humour is
occasionally employed to mute the potentially destabilizing effects of girls' team
sports. An 1888 article on "A Girl's Cricket Club," for instance, positions girls
playing cricket as a joke. The author attempts to minimize objections to cricket
"as a most unladylike and improper game for girls to play at" by insisting that
"if the girls behave quietly, and only have friends for spectators," there "can be
no serious objection" (33). The secretary of the club amusingly relates how the

little town of Shepstock has "no idea of healthy rational amusement" for there is no tennis or skating and "the more sensible ones among them seemed to think that girls were meant to do housework, parish work, or needlework the whole day through" (33–4). The girls are uncompetitive, running from the ball so that no one gets "killed" (34). When they compete against men wielding broomsticks, the men let the girls win. In fact, the male referee bowls the final over for the girls to ensure their win. The story suggests the imminent demise of the cricket club since the men in the town "have decided to make a tennis ground somewhere, in which case we shall probably change our game" (36). These girls are merely enjoying the liberty offered by new opportunities for physical exercise and pose no threat to the masculine world of sports. Instead, they retain their femininity and quickly abandon their attempts to enter the masculine domain of cricket. Although the author flippantly suggests a lack of dedication to cricket when tennis is presented as an alternative, the men who control their access to sport are directing the girls toward more socially acceptable physical activities. While the *GOP* emphasizes the morality and modesty of the girls, it offers the realm of physical culture as a space to explore the freedoms and the limits of girlhood.

While the efforts of girls to enjoy sports that were perceived to be too masculine were marginalized in the magazine, their dedication to cycling is much more predominant. Scraton argues that "the vigorous physical activity needed for team games was the antithesis of femininity" (28), and even the emerging healthy feminine ideal was not able to contain team sports. This ideal was, however, sufficiently malleable to include the notion (and motion) of girls' cycling. McCrone notes that "bicycling—not a sport at all in the competitive sense— ... provided women with their most significant experience of physical exercise and did more than any other activity to break down conservative restrictions" (177). The appearance of the cycling girl in the *Girl's Own Paper* aligns her with health, mobility, and the New Woman. Sarah Wintle explains how the bicycle literally and symbolically offers "freedom, physical independence and [a] sense of personal control" (66). The first articles on cycling appear late in the century, but they uniformly support cycling as an appropriate and healthy sport for women. In Dr. A.T. Schofield's "The Cycling Craze," for example, he notes the "very unique character" of bicycle exercise and identifies "many points in its favour" (185), including fresh air and the freedom to travel.[20] "Medicus" describes cycling as "a glorious institution when ruled by reason" ("Cycling" 722) and only warns against "cyclomania" (723), an obsession with cycling, as a potential problem. Cycling, then, is enthusiastically supported within the magazine because its weaker associations with masculine activity. In fact, the acceptability of cycling as a female sport is highlighted through an advertisement in 1902/3 for Dunlop Tyres [Figure 4.9]. The ad begins with the encouraging phrase, "When ordering

---

[20] Dr. Alfred Taylor Schofield, a neurologist, wrote a number of books, including the *Manual of Personal and Domestic Hygiene* (1889) and *How to Keep Healthy: Familiar Chats on Hygiene of Daily Life* (1891). In later years, he turned to psychology and religion, writing *The Knowledge of God: Its Meaning and Power* (1903) and *Christian Sanity* (1908).

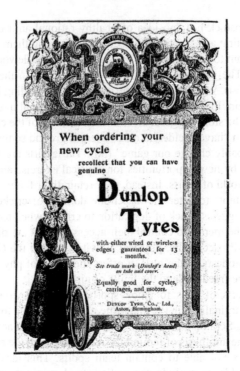

Fig. 4.9   Dunlop Tyres. *Girl's Own Paper*, 1902/3

your new cycle," and depicts a fashionably dressed woman holding onto a bicycle. The presence of this kind of advertising in the *GOP* emphasizes the suitability and pervasiveness of women's cycling.

Although there were concerns about the appropriate dress for the female cyclist and her mobility was sometimes perceived to threaten the social order, those concerns were elided when the cycling girl appeared in the *Girl's Own Paper*.[21] The magazine's positive portrayal of cycling is highlighted in a 1908 illustration of "The Modern Traveller at Eastertide" [Figure 4.10]. Girls and women are shown cycling and riding in automobiles. Unaccompanied by any text, the "Modern Traveller" has expanded the boundaries of the feminine ideal to include greater freedom and health. Moreover, the girls in this illustration retain their femininity and decorum as they go about the business of their daily lives. These new boundaries have not compromised the ideal of beauty and morality. Instead, girls are healthy and capable as they travel into the twentieth century.

The last decades of the nineteenth century are consequently marked by substantial changes to the image of the girl in the *GOP*. In an 1894 article on

----

[21]   See "Individual Sports: Lawn Tennis, Golf and Cycling," in McCrone's *Sport and the Physical Emancipation of English Women, 1870–1914* (1988), especially pages 177–85, for details on the rise of women's cycling.

Fig. 4.10   The Modern Traveller at Eastertide—With Cycle and Motor, *Girl's Own Paper*, 1908

"Women's Work: Its Value and Possibilities," F.H. highlights the changing nature of the physical and mental feminine ideal. The weak, insipid girl of the past has been replaced and

> should she return to the 'Book of Beauty,' she would find her place usurped by a type, distinct, with characteristics utterly unlike her own. In place of her rounded, irresolute chin, she would find a chin, firm and resolved; her mouth with its drooping lips would be displaced by one as beautiful, but indicative of self-control and energy; her expression, inane and colourless, would be overshadowed by one of intelligence and character. And the new type is as perfect in beauty as the old. But where was only weakness there is now strength and purpose. (51)

This new girl looks and acts differently from girls of the past. Equally beautiful, she shows strength, intelligence and character. Her physical beauty is enabled through the inclusion of health in the feminine ideal and is complemented by learning. In the next chapter, I will show how the move to include health within the feminine ideal of the *Girl's Own Paper* was matched in *Atalanta* by an equally pervasive desire to improve girls' education. As Cicely demonstrates in "Transformed," physical capability is often accompanied by the need for useful, productive work. A healthy girl in the 1880s and '90s was physically and mentally capable of attending to more than domestic concerns, and she sought to expand her knowledge through equal access to higher education. Yet, just as the move towards health in the *GOP* includes some resistance and unease, *Atalanta*'s support for girls' higher education is sometimes undermined by concerns about how these new mental capabilities could be incorporated within a feminine ideal that promoted marriage. Like the *GOP*, *Atalanta* managed these tensions by reinforcing notions of femininity and virtue.

Chapter 5

The Educated Girl:
Atalanta (1887–98) and
the Debate on Education

The debate about women's higher education continued throughout most of the second half of the century and much of it occurred in the periodical press. In the 1927 *Times* obituary for women's higher education activist Emily Davies, the reporter concludes that "[t]here is no subject of vital human concern about which public opinion has changed so much in the last seventy years as it has about the education of women" ("Emily Davies and Girton" 10). In the 1840s and '50s, "the current ideas about the duties and position of women were those which are so admirably set forth in the novels of Charlotte Yonge, and which were much more crudely expressed in some of the periodical literature of the day" (10). Yet towards the end of the century, discussions about education also appear in the girls' periodical press. The middle-class girls' magazine *Atalanta* is one such magazine. It emphatically supported improved education for girls, but often betrayed its uneasiness about the impact of this learning. Unlike the *Monthly Packet*, which until its last years reflected Charlotte Yonge's objections to girls' education outside the home, L.T. Meade's *Atalanta* adopted a more progressive stance, a notably different focus from other girls' magazines of the period. The *Girl's Own Paper*, for example, rarely addressed the need for girls to be adequately educated, although numerous inquiries from correspondents suggest its readers actively sought out practical information about educational opportunities. In contrast, when *Atalanta* first appeared in 1887, it targeted middle-class girls who were interested in study. From its earliest days, it included a regular monthly section entitled the "Atalanta Scholarship and Reading Union," highlighting the scholarly nature of its intended readership. The magazine also contained a number of articles on higher education, including specific descriptions of Girton and Newnham Colleges, two of the first colleges established for women.

Despite its support for girls' education, however, *Atalanta* was troubled by conflicted and sometimes contradictory responses to these changes in girls' learning. Although it favoured education for girls, it remained cautious about the impact of this education and simultaneously tried to reinforce the traditionally feminine role of wife and mother. Through its opinion articles and some of its fiction, *Atalanta* often reinforced traditional roles that were at odds with its depictions of girls elsewhere in the magazine. Moreover, its final years, before ceasing publication in 1898, are marked by a change in focus from education to fashion, suggesting an attempt to shift its readership away from scholarship and towards consumption instead. The girl in the pages of *Atalanta*, then, understood the need for education, but was less clear about how this intellectual life could be integrated with a life of marriage and motherhood.

The Education Debate

The debate on girls' education traces its roots to late eighteenth-century texts such as Mary Wollstonecraft's *Thoughts on the Education of Daughters* (1787) and *Vindication of the Rights of Woman* (1792). The subject was revitalized in the 1850s and '60s by Emily Davies, one of the most famous nineteenth-century advocates for women's higher education. She wrote about the importance of equal opportunities for women in *The Higher Education of Woman* (1866), a text that reflected many contemporary anxieties about how and why girls ought to be educated. Davies argues that girls should be educated to the best of their ability because "the object of female education is to produce women of the best and highest type, not limited by exclusive regard to any specific functions hereafter to be discharged by them" (7–8). Prevailing attitudes encouraged girls to be trained for their future roles as wives and mothers. According to Davies, this did girls a great disservice because although they may eventually need to support themselves, they "seldom receive any adequate training for their future work" (36). Moreover, girls who do eventually become wives and mothers wish to be better educated. Consequently, Davies argues, girls should be educated to the same standards as boys, regardless of their future occupations. This argument struck at the "separate spheres" ideology, which tended to enshrine women within the domestic space as mothers, wives, and caregivers who were the moral superiors, but also the intellectual inferiors, of the men inhabiting the public world. The idea that women could and should be trained to occupy more than this domestic space threatened the fabric of gender relations for many middle-class men and women.

The debate about higher quality girls' education raised questions about whether educated women could be adequate wives and mothers and whether these women would choose marriage and motherhood if other opportunities were available to them. Both Patricia Marks and Martha Vicinus note the significant threat posed by educated women. In *Bicycles, Bangs and Bloomers: The New Woman in the Popular Press* (1990), Marks writes that the girl who sought the equivalent education to her brothers was

> attempting to become, so to speak, the author of her own story. In so doing, she was literally planning for the contingency of not marrying, a state that no young lady might admit to pursuing but one that every young lady expected. She was, in fact, entertaining the notion of an independent life, one in which she might earn her own sustenance by using her head as well as her heart. (91)

As women argued for more political, social, and economic rights, the girl who was "the author of her own story" was a significantly destabilizing force. An independent woman did not need a man—husband, father, or brother—to care for her. Instead, she could care for herself and wished to control her own life. Her personal skills and desires would direct her decisions about her role in British society. She is a threatening figure, then, because she may not choose a role consistent with marriage and motherhood. Similarly, the educated girl in *Atalanta* is troubling because she does not fit easily within the constraints of marriage and maternity. The magazine thus had to balance its support of education with more traditional expectations of femininity as it redefined girlhood to include mental capability.

The collegiality and community associated with college life were important facets of this redefinition of the feminine ideal. In a discussion of women's colleges, Martha Vicinus writes that these institutions offered "a unique opportunity for intellectual women to join others who shared their delight in study; they were expected to take responsibility for their own time and studies" (124). Moreover, "within the precincts of the colleges [women] were freer and more independent" (124) than virtually anywhere else in English society. The freedom afforded by college life was embraced in *Atalanta*. In an 1890 article about the "Schools of Today," Dorothea Beale, the principal of the Cheltenham Ladies' College from 1858 until her death in 1906, speaks highly of the intellectual life at schools and colleges: "To learn with others, to feel the intellectual sympathy of numbers, to measure one's strength with companions: this is stimulating and invigorating" (311). The lived experience of life at a women's college varies from the solitary one that appeared elsewhere in the press. Margaret Birney Vickery explains in her study of the architecture of women's colleges that "these colleges are a unique blend of domestic and collegial traditions" (xii), in which they employed the idea of domesticity in their design and structure "as a reassurance and guard against abnormal or undisciplined behaviour" (6). The physical layout of the college was intended to reinforce the domesticity of family life while also enabling the girls to focus on their studies.[1] *Atalanta* promoted these positive aspects of higher education through informational articles and fiction that encouraged girls to develop their mental skills through a disciplined course of study at college. At the same time, however, the magazine reinforced the idea that these educated girls remained pure, virtuous, and feminine.

The establishment of colleges for girls nonetheless marked a significant change to the educational landscape. Girls were entering the public sphere to study, which had ramifications for their conceptions of themselves and their responsibilities. College life "was a glorious interlude; a special women's space in which duty to

---

[1]   As Emily Davies was planning Girton College, for example, she knew her best chance of success lay in distancing herself from the more radical women's movement. She stressed the domestic arrangements at the college and assured critics that the students would be under the care of a lady. There was a common room for rest and relaxation (but which also served as a lecture hall) and a dining room. The initial five students rebelled at Davies's arrangement of a "High Table" in the dining room, insisting that such an arrangement was absurd with so few students and in such a small space. The girls were unwilling to abide by highly formal arrangements in a space that was exceedingly domestic in its layout and structure.

self and community took precedence over all outside obligations" (Vicinus 124). The lack of emphasis on family would prove problematic for Davies as she sought support for the college. Charlotte Yonge cited this changing notion of a girl's duty as one of the reasons for rejecting Davies's request. Yonge writes:

> I am obliged to you for your letter respecting the proposed college for ladies, but as I have decided objections to bringing large numbers of girls together and think home education under the inspection or encouragement of sensible fathers or voluntarily undertaken by the girls themselves is far more valuable intellectually and morally than any external education I am afraid I cannot assist you.

> I feel with regret that female education is deficient in tone and manner, if in nothing else. Superior women will always teach themselves and inferior women will never learn enough for more than home life.[2]

Yonge's position is antithetical to Davies's because she fears that girls might forget their duty to their families. In contrast, Davies wanted her proposed college to be located outside the center of Cambridge so that the students would not be faced with the challenges of managing their studies and their morning callers. She wanted them to dedicate themselves to their studies and be free from the usual responsibilities and cares of family life. Yonge, of course, was also quite concerned that the "tone and manner" of public school would be inappropriate for impressionable girls.

Joyce Senders Pedersen argues compellingly that public education resulted in significantly less familial control over the girl as the school's influence increased. She notes that "when girls entered public schools or colleges they experienced a new type of authority, less subject to their family's influence, less mindful of family interests, more impersonal, more bureaucratic" (76). The changing nature of authority was problematic for critics of women's higher education. The students were situated in a domestic setting, presided over by a headmistress who occupied the maternal role to a limited extent, but without a corresponding paternal figure. The college students thus operated in an alternate space outside male control.[3]

---

[2]   Ironically, subscribers raised funds for a college scholarship in Yonge's name in the *Monthly Packet* in the 1890s.

[3]   Some fiction of the period reflects similar concerns about public education for girls. In *Six to Sixteen* (1875), for example, Juliana Ewing uses the intelligent Eleanor and her orphaned friend Margery to demonstrate how domestic space is the best place for girls to further their education, provided this education is accompanied by opportunities to explore the natural world. In this story, which originally appeared serially in *Aunt Judy's Magazine* in 1872, Margery's cousin Matilda becomes seriously ill while at boarding school with Margery and Eleanor. Inattention causes Matilda's illness to go undiscovered for some time, and she never fully recovers. Meanwhile, an outbreak of scarlet fever necessitates the closure of the school, and Eleanor and Margery return to Eleanor's home in the north, where they revel in the freedom of the family home and the undisturbed hours in which to pursue their own studies. The school, then, is an unhealthy place of disease and containment. The

Despite opposition from a number of sources, in 1869 Davies founded Hitchin College, which was associated with the University of Cambridge.[4] It was moved and renamed Girton College in 1873. Around the same time, the discussions in the periodical press on the impact of higher education became more medicalized. As I discussed in the previous chapter, just as some sport was considered too masculine to be incorporated into the ideal of the healthy girl, some critics raised concerns that excess study would be defeminizing. Dr. Henry Maudsley, a medical psychologist, was a vocal opponent of equal education for women and maintained that although women could succeed in their intellectual pursuits, their success came at the expense of their femininity and their reproductive capabilities. In 1874, he discusses the physiological effects of higher education on women in the *Fortnightly Review*, asserting that women are "marked out by nature for very different offices in life from those of men, and that the healthy performance of her special functions renders it improbable she will succeed, and unwise for her to persevere, in running over the same course at the same pace with him" (468). Employing Darwinian undertones, Maudsley suggests that higher education will make women unable to perform their "special" reproductive functions. Education should thus be adapted to women's "foreordained work as mothers and nurses of children" (471). Elizabeth Garrett Anderson, a successfully accredited doctor in England, rejects his arguments in her *Fortnightly Review* response.[5] She insists that those who wish to learn about women's higher education should examine the evidence themselves, rather than basing their decisions on information provided by medical men who "seem to be afraid of this higher education" (594).[6] She

same studies can be pursued more fruitfully at home under an educated maternal influence. Moreover, Eleanor's future prospects as wife and mother are improved by her education. Her active, able lifestyle contributes to her health, vigour, and beauty. The novel itself ostensibly arises out of a project that Eleanor and Margery set for themselves to document the stories of their lives. In a very real sense, they are writing their own stories.

[4]   Women were allowed to take the same examinations as their male colleagues, but it was not until 1947 that Cambridge University granted them degrees. Barbara Stephens' *Emily Davies and Girton College* (1927) and M.C. Bradbrook's *'That Infidel Place': A Short History of Girton College, 1869–1969* (1969) both provide useful, and complementary, histories of Davies's campaign to obtain equal access to higher education for women.

[5]   Garrett was the first woman qualified in Britain to be listed on the medical register, the first woman to obtain an MD from the University of Paris, and the only woman admitted to membership in the British Medical Association until 1892. The latter was "one of several instances where Garrett, uniquely, was able to enter a hitherto all male medical institution which subsequently moved formally to exclude any women who might seek to follow her" (Elston). In the 1850s and early 1860s, she was an active member in the Langham Place circle.

[6]   For further details about the medicalization of the education debate, see Joan Burstyn's "Education and Sex: The Medical Case against Higher Education for Women in England, 1870–1900" (1973) and also *Victorian Education and the Ideal of Womanhood* (1980). In *Victorian Education*, Burstyn addresses how the changes to education for girls undermined the feminine ideal of womanhood that was prevalent throughout most of the century.

suggests that Maudsley fears the implications of higher education and his medical perspective is not to be trusted. Implicitly, Garrett Anderson uses her own personal example—as a woman, a wife, and a mother—to refute his claims about women's unsuitability for higher education.

Atalanta

Atalanta's predecessor was *Every Girl's Magazine* (1877–87), a girls' magazine edited by Alicia Leith. *Every Girl's Magazine* was comprised of a variety of articles, fiction, and poetry. Serialized stories included Isabella Fyvie Mayo's "Aunt Winifred's Friends" and regular features included "Busy Brains and Useful Fingers," which provided information about hobbies for girls such as landscape painting, brass work, and floriculture. Like the *Girl's Own Paper*, it concerned itself with girls' health and included articles like "Gymnastics and the Swedish System of Exercises" and "Tricycles and Tricycling for Ladies."

Atalanta succeeded *Every Girl's Magazine* in 1887 and remained in print until 1898. L.T. Meade, a popular writer for girls, joined Leith as co-editor. Leith retired after the first year, and was replaced by John C. Staples until the magazine was incorporated with Alexander Balfour Symington's *Victorian Magazine* (1891–92).[7] From its auspicious beginning, the magazine's tone changed substantially with the departure of Meade in 1892. The later years include more contributions by men and its shifting attitude towards girls is signalled by a series entitled "Occupations for Gentlewomen," covering occupations like lace work and embroidery, in contrast to "Employment for Girls" under Meade's editorship. An 1896/7 series of "Letters to a Debutante" on topics such as "On Being Presented," "On the Management of a Dress Allowance," and "On the Advisability of Friendships with Men" also suggests that the magazine was attempting to broaden its readership beyond its scholarly readers. To be fair, however, the changing tone of the magazine is subtle. The same issue in which the first "Letters to a Debutante" appears also includes an illustrated article on "Women Students at Oxford" (Carr 43).

Nonetheless, in its early years, the magazine firmly established its support for girls' education, while also depicting a feminine ideal of virtue and womanliness. The *Church Quarterly Review* praised the first volume of "this exceedingly attractive magazine ... which has blossomed out into new and brilliant life under the editorship of one of our most popular writers for children" ("*Atalanta*" 500). The reviewer continues, "No girl can read these papers, or enter the lists to compete for one or other of the scholarships and prizes offered to readers of *Atalanta* in so many various branches of art and literature, without feeling stimulated to acquire

---

[7] Symington was a writer as well, producing a number of works under the pseudonym of "Cecil Grey." His serialized novel, "The Course of True Love," appeared in the 1894/5 volume of *Atalanta*. Although his earliest novel was *Glenathole* (1889), most of his work was published after the turn of the century, including *For Crown and Covenant* (1902), *A Manse Rose* (1906), and *Our Modern Life: From the Unpopular Point of View* (1910).

fresh knowledge" (501). Edward Salmon also reviewed it favourably: "The popularity of the new magazine is not surprising. It has secured the highest literary and artistic talent" (*Juvenile Literature* 196–7).

Likely because of Meade's reputation in literary circles, she was able to attract a number of well-known contributors. In the first year alone, these include fiction by H. Rider Haggard, Mary Molesworth, and Grant Allen, poetry by Christina Rossetti, book reviews by Edward Salmon, and informative articles like "Girls Who Won Success" by Sarah Tytler. Historical and natural sciences topics such as volcanos, frogs, and "Men of Ancient Days" are addressed in nonfiction articles. A series on employment for girls—discussing nursing, medicine, shorthand, and typing—reflects the ideas and concerns of the woman's movement and are written by contributors who were familiar with, or working in, these occupations. An article on working in a pharmacy, for example, was written by pharmaceutical chemist, Isabella S. Clarke-Keer, and Edith Huntley, M.D., provides an article on medical careers.

The scholarly focus includes a regular series, "The Atalanta Scholarship and Reading Union," on well-known literary figures written by respected contributors: Andrew Lang writes about Sir Walter Scott, Charlotte Yonge on John Keble, Anne Thackeray on Jane Austen, and Mrs. L.B. Walford on Elizabeth Gaskell, to name but a few. Readers subscribed to the Scholarship and Reading Union and were encouraged to write a 500-word essay each month in response to one or more "Scholarship Competition Questions." For example, following Thackeray's discussion of Austen, subscribers have a choice of three questions:

1. What do you conceive to have been the limits of Jane Austen's genius?

2. Discuss the delineation of character in *Emma*.

3. What is a Novel of Manners? (Thackeray 231)

These questions are designed to promote scholarship by encouraging *Atalanta* readers to read the novel chosen for the month (in this case *Emma*), consider its literary merits, respond at length to one or more of the questions, and submit their writing for assessment. In addition to these questions, each month includes a series of six "Search Passages," of which readers are required to identify the author and the source text. The answers are provided in the next month's issue, and the range of passages—including Francis Bacon's 1625 essay "Of Gardens," Sir Philip Sidney's "Come Sleep, O Sleep," Matthew Royden's "Astrophel," William Wordsworth's "I wandered lonely as a Cloud," Andrew Lang's "Ballads in Blue China," and William Morris's *Earthly Paradise*—demonstrate the breadth and depth of reading to which girls should aspire.

Despite *Atalanta*'s overt support for higher education, the contradiction between education and marriage is foreshadowed by the title of the periodical. A strong, athletic Greek goddess who was raised by a bear in the wild, Atalanta was determined to remain unmarried, despite being pursued by many suitors.

Eventually, Atalanta agreed to marry the first man who could beat her in a foot race. Despite Atalanta's speed and strength, Hippomenes was able to beat her by throwing three golden apples in front of her, and they were married.[8] By naming the magazine *Atalanta*, the independence and valour of its titular heroine is invoked, yet Atalanta's adventures suggest that the domain of virginity "is a place merely to pass through. It is a place of transition" (Bonnefoy 96). The space that Atalanta occupies as an unmarried, independent woman is a transitional space, not one that can be maintained. Likewise, the girl readers of *Atalanta* cannot expect to remain forever in the virginal space of scholarly endeavour. Although education is desirable and necessary, marriage remains the ultimate goal. Like Atalanta, girls must accept the eventuality of marriage.

Education and marriage thus exist within the pages of *Atalanta* in an uneasy alliance. The initial issue in October 1887 reinforces the ambiguous message of the title. It opens with a full-page illustration of a well-dressed girl playing piano, a traditional female accomplishment [Figure 5.1]. On the accompanying page is a poem entitled "Atalanta" by Sir Edwin Arnold, a well-known poet and journalist.[9] Atalanta's race with Hippomenes is part of life:

> Yet scorn not, if, before your feet,
>   The golden fruit of Life shall roll,
> Truth, duty, loving service sweet,
>   To stoop to grasp them! So, the soul
> Runs slower in the race, by these;
> But wins them—and Hippomenes! (l. 19–24)

As in the *Monthly Packet*, the golden apples of truth, duty, and service are the "fruits of Life" (l. 20). By grasping this fruit, a girl "wins" the man and a life worth living, even if she runs more slowly. Arnold privileges feminine duties over Atalanta's physical prowess and wishes to convince the girl reader that these "fruits of Life" are everything she should hope for.

Yet the magazine's support, albeit qualified, for girls' education appears elsewhere in the magazine. The April 1893 issue opens with an illustration by Gordon Browne entitled "A Girton Girl" [Figure 5.2], and under the title is the quotation "The guise that fits my brave girl-student best" (466). A girl in a long dress covered by scholarly robes sits at a table as she intently studies a book propped up against other volumes. Her room is spacious and well-appointed,

---

[8]   The versions of the myth vary. The two lovers were happy until they were turned into lions, either for forgetting to thank Aphrodite (who gave the apples to Hippomenes) or for indiscretions in Zeus's temple.

[9]   Edwin Arnold published *The Light of Asia* (1879), a verse poem of the life and teachings of Siddhartha Gautama, the founder of Buddhism. It proved immensely popular with numerous editions and translations. Arnold was also the editor of the *Daily Telegraph* from 1873 to 1889 and was a serious contender to become the poet laureate after Tennyson's death in 1892.

OLD SONGS.

Fig. 5.1   Old Songs, *Atalanta*, 1887

A GIRTON GIRL.

" The guise that fits my brave girl-student best."

Fig. 5.2   A Girton Girl, *Atalanta*, 1892

with flowers and a tablecloth on the table, framed pictures on the walls, and light streaming in the window above a window seat. On the facing page is a poem by Sir Noel Paton, a poet and historical painter, also entitled "A Girton Girl." The narrator describes her:

> … In her college room—
>> White-curtained, husht—alone among her books,
>> Beside her open casement that o'erlooks
> Fair English meads and chestnuts all a-bloom;
>
> One palm upon the serious forehead prest,
>> Lips parted, eyes bent on a well-worn tome,
>> Rich with the thought of Greece, the lore of Rome—
> The guise that fits my brave girl-student best! (l. 29–36)

This Girton Girl is studying the classics, a traditionally male subject. At the same time, however, Paton's tone is somewhat ambiguous. Like the magazine more broadly, Paton supports women's higher education yet also worries that this girl may end up alone. A girl in 1893 must be "brave" (l. 36) to obtain a higher education. The poem and the illustration position scholarly achievement as a solitary activity and place women scholars in a separate space away from either the bustle of domesticity or the vivacity of public life. A girl who studies at Girton College is choosing a life incompatible with marriage, reflecting a tension between *Atalanta*'s positive portrayal of the educated girl and the fear that this girl will not marry and fulfil her traditional role as a wife and mother.

Atalanta's ambiguity towards higher education is also found elsewhere in the periodical press. The satirical magazine *Punch* describes a similar response in 1875, in a poem entitled "Nursery Rhymes for the Times" where Sally, a scholarly girl, is contrasted to her sister Fanny, who has a lover and a home. Sally, the poem concludes, is "learned" (l. 11) but "lonely" (l. 12). Constance Rover notes that *Punch*'s attitude towards the higher education of women, "like that of the general public, continued to be ambivalent" (69). These two examples reflect similar concerns about women scholars and their position in society: a woman could be educated or she could marry, but not both. A woman who chooses education instead of marriage challenges existing beliefs about femininity and masculinity, yet the emphasis on her "loneliness" is intended to remind potential girl students of the sacrifices they will have to make.

Atalanta and the Feminine Ideal

The pages of *Atalanta* demonstrate how girls can be intelligent and feminine, yet the magazine is not always successful in managing the tensions between these two ideals. Women had been attending Girton College and other women's colleges for almost 20 years when *Atalanta* first appeared, yet it continued to struggle with how to promote higher education for women while also supporting marriage and maternity. *Atalanta* addresses this changing feminine ideal through its informational articles about higher education for girls. Curiously, the first discussion of education in 1889 comes from Charlotte Yonge. Despite Yonge's lack of support for education outside the home, her contribution highlights the quality of contributors to the magazine under Meade's editorship. In "Our Grandmother's Education," Yonge argues that the grandmothers of the girl readers were trained for "great perseverance and power of application, much intelligence, and thoroughness. There was also much more refinement of word and even of manner than at present is thought needful, together with far more respect to elders" (165). Yonge's concern about refinement is reminiscent of her letter to Davies 20 years earlier refusing support for Hitchin College. Yonge remembers the education of the past with fondness, as she does in the *Monthly Packet*, and highlights the tension between the nostalgic feminine ideal of the past and the reality of the need for girls' mental culture.

In contrast, in "Schools in the Past," Dorothea Beale rejects this nostalgic view of education and suggests that girls' education has undergone a fundamental shift since girls are now educated to think for themselves. In "Schools of Today," she describes the benefits of a modern education, including a "more vigorous" (311) and inspiring intellectual life, new and improved school buildings, appropriately sized desks and chairs, a large gymnasium, and rationalized dress better suited to school activities. Beale appeals for a "mental gymnastic" to be established alongside the changing physical norms for girls, which I discussed in Chapter 4. No longer expected to sit quietly inside, the educated girl in *Atalanta* is physically and intellectually capable, competing in traditionally male subjects: Greek and Latin, mathematics, and science. Moreover, her study of the typical "accomplishments" of the past, like music, singing, and drawing, is because she intends to use them professionally. Beale asserts that women have the right to reject the enforced idleness of the past:

> The once fashionable, but miserable doctrine, common in my youth, that a woman who had money or a place in society ought to live an idle life, on pain of losing caste, is almost obsolete, since the daughters of Cabinet-ministers and bishops and judges have thought it an honour to join the body of working women. (317)

Beale notes that the idleness that formerly signified wealth and class is giving way to an ethic of work for girls of all classes. Moreover, she gives agency to women when she suggests they have a right to choose something other than an idle life.

The forceful pro-education sentiments expressed by Beale are reinforced elsewhere in *Atalanta*. In "Oxford and Cambridge Colleges for Women," Eva Knatchbull-Hugessen, herself a Newnham student from 1883 to 1886, writes that a girl's mind "is just as much in need of development as [a boy's]; she has just as many rough corners to be rubbed away in free intercourse with equals; she is equally capable of profiting by the stimulus of advanced work and varied companionship" (421). Not only does Knatchbull-Hugessen reinforce earlier rhetoric about girls' education, but she also provides essential information about women's colleges so that girls can make informed decisions about where to pursue an advanced education. The magazine provides moral support to girls considering further education through the intelligent and encouraging rhetoric of Beale and Knatchbull-Hugessen, as well as the more practical information upon which to base a college decision. This material suggests a model of femininity where education is the norm. Although Knatchbull-Hugessen does not describe daily college life, there are other articles that do so, including "A Letter from Cambridge" (1892/3), "Girton College" by L.T. Meade (1893/4), and "Women Students at Oxford" (1896/7). Through these types of articles, *Atalanta* presents a feminine subject freed from the confines of the home, but safely ensconced within the college dorm.

Against Education

Despite *Atalanta*'s support for higher education, the magazine remained uneasy about how this shifting feminine ideal could meet traditional expectations about marriage and motherhood. In October 1889, Meade introduced "The Brown Owl" series, which closely resembles an editorial in format and tone although it was not written by Meade. Instead, in the first year, a different author contributed each month, often someone who had already published in the magazine.[10] The subjects included the benefits of good society by L.B. Walford, the need for a regular occupation as a "backbone of the day's routine" (113) by Sarah Tytler, and an article by Alfred J. Church which calls on girls to "preserve the tradition" of the humanities in England.[11] Church, a Professor of Latin at the University College of London, explains that girls should be allowed to study math and science if they wish:

> I do not wish to shut them out from any kind of learning or research. If a girl feels that she has a vocation to science, be it the science of medicine, with its practical bearing on human life, or any of what I may call the theoretic sciences, let her follow it by all means. ... [E]ach science will be advanced by the special gifts of feminine intelligence; and I am all for giving women, under such conditions as good sense may dictate, every facility for following their bent. What I mean is this, that if men abandon, as it seems likely they will, the great humanistic traditions, women will keep them up. (213)

---

[10] Mrs. Molesworth, for instance, published a serial story in the first year of the magazine, and later that same year contributed an article on "Coming Out" to "The Brown Owl."

[11] Lucy Bethia Walford contributed articles and stories to the *Monthly Packet*, the *Girl's Own Paper*, and *Hearth and Home*, as well as *Atalanta*. She authored more than 40 novels. "Sarah Tytler," the pseudonym of Henrietta Keddie, was a prodigious novelist, often producing two novels per year. She also contributed articles and fiction to a variety of periodicals, including *Good Words for the Young* and the *Girl's Own Paper*. Charlotte Yonge recommends Tytler's novels on a number of occasions in the *Monthly Packet*.

Church suggests that female scholars are interested in the classics, and the humanities more generally, because men are abandoning them. The New Woman thus is not particularly "new" after all, as she studies subjects increasingly abandoned by men. Church fears that men will become the weaker sex because they are studying science instead of the "strengthening discipline" (213) of the humanities and, as a consequence, women will become physically and mentally stronger. While Church supports girls' higher education, his comments reflect a prevailing concern in *Atalanta* about how these changes will affect the femininity of girlhood. Unusually, however, he also suggests the potentially demasculinizing influence of these changes.

Atalanta also gave opposing positions, likely intended to be provocative, a voice in "The Brown Owl." One such contribution is Professor Robert Kennaway Douglas's rejection of higher education for women. Douglas, an historian and scholar of Asia, was the keeper of Oriental Printed Books and Manuscripts at the British Museum and also collaborated with Meade on some short stories in the 1890s. In the March 1890 "Forgotten Graces," Douglas calls the higher education movement a "hobbyhorse" (459) that forces girls to be educated to the same standard as boys, regardless of whether girls have the interest or aptitude. He regards "with alarm the tendency which the present general system involves of substituting masculinely scholastic subjects of study for the graces, refinements, and arts which are proper to women" (460). Douglas echoes Maudsley's argument that education will defeminize girls and reaffirms a traditional feminine ideal. The object of female education, he writes, "should ... be to prepare women for the employment of those high and purifying influences which Nature has so peculiarly fitted them to exercise" (460). The feminine girl is seen as "natural," and all unfeminine graces, like education, are unnatural. Moreover, the girl who develops her intellect does so at the expense of the feminine accomplishments, which may explain "why the percentage of marriages is less than it was formerly" (460). Douglas highlights the threatening possibilities of educated women who choose not to marry. This idea was reinforced in many New Woman novels, such as Grant Allen's *The Woman Who Did* (1895), in which Girton Girl Herminia Barton chooses to live in a free union rather than marry.

To the educated readers of *Atalanta*, this anti-education rhetoric was inflammatory. At the end of Douglas's provocative article, a footnote invites discussion by the 20th of the next month. The June issue contains a brief note from Meade indicating that the subject "has been taken up with much warmth and spirit by many readers of *Atalanta*, and so strong are the views expressed that Professor Douglas has kindly promised to reply to them in a second Paper, which will appear in July" (461). Tantalizingly, Meade notes that "[e]xtracts from some of the letters are printed" (586), but unfortunately those extracts appeared in the supplement to the monthly issue, and have not been preserved. However, in Douglas's July rebuttal, he reiterates that his "present object is to enter a plea for a return to common sense, and the adoption of such a system of education and culture as will most truly develop the genuine woman" (643). Certain types of education will ensure his feminine ideal, and some education is necessary as long as it is appropriately feminine. History, biography, travel, modern languages, poetry, geography, literature, and some mathematics are necessary for a girl to be "learned in gracious household ways" (644). The modern girl, then, requires a solid education, although the obvious omissions include the classics and the sciences. This education, however, should not be obtained at a public institution because "the push, the rivalry, and the cram of the University career," is "ruinous" to the creation of a "truly womanly instinct" (644). For Douglas, public education is inconsistent with the feminine graces.

Readers Respond

The readers of *Atalanta* were similarly invested in the educational ideologies of the magazine. Two responses to Douglas appearing in "The Brown Owl" (rather than the more usual "Letter-Bag") highlight the uncertain reception of the changes to girls' education. In the first response, C.G. Luard, a former student of Lady Margaret Hall, Oxford, and later the Lady Superintendent of Queen's College School and principal of Whitelands Training College, argues that the system is intended to test one's "own knowledge by the highest recognised standard" (767) rather than competing against fellow students.[12] She reiterates the communal aspects of public education and rejects the claim that higher education ruins a girl's health by referring to Mrs. Henry Sidgwick's "elaborate investigations," which prove that college girls' health has "not suffered" (767).[13] Finally, she explains that universities require many of the subjects that Douglas feels are necessary for a woman's education, such as history, literature, and modern languages, yet these college girls "do not altogether forget the more graceful and softer side of life" (768). There is "music, singing, acting, dancing, needle-work, and other innocent and distinctly feminine forms of frivolity with which we temper our sterner studies" (768). Luard is personally acquainted with girls who have obtained high standings in Classics, Mathematics, and Philosophy, and who are still able to "enter a room" or "hand a cup of tea with ease and grace" (768). Thus, the "'truly womanly instinct' is ... sufficiently strong to resist those supposed evil tendencies" (768), which are encouraged by advanced education and scholarly pursuits.

Luard never questions the validity of the feminine ideal. Instead, she asserts that women who pursue higher education will continue to embody the ideal even as they undermine it through their actions. Paradoxically, even as girls felt the need to advance their own education and demand equal standing with men, they also argued that they were equally feminine as girls of the past. This suggests the continued power of the traditional feminine ideal in the 1890s. Even a college-

---

[12] Luard published *The Journal of Clarissa Trant* in 1925 based on the twenty-eight volumes of ancestor Clarissa Trant's diaries.

[13] This refers to Eleanor Sidgwick's investigation of girls' health, *Health Statistics of Women Students of Cambridge and Oxford and of Their Sisters* (1890). Sidgwick was married to Henry Sidgwick, who founded Newnham College, a women's college, at Cambridge. She was principal of Newnham from 1891 to 1910.

educated woman like Luard reaffirms an image of femininity that includes serving tea and entering a room with grace. Moreover, she does not specifically address the issue of women competing with men. Her own example, and that of her friends, serves to rebut Douglas's assertion that women are incapable of reaching the same "lofty heights" of intellect as men. By ignoring the idea that women are incapable, she expands the definition of the feminine ideal to include education and rejects the notion that scholarly women are unfeminine.

In contrast, the second response to Douglas's article reinforces a more conservative view of girls' education. "NOT an Indignant One" agrees with Douglas that examinations for girls tend to "cramp the mind and narrow the sympathies" (768) and change the focus from genuine knowledge to mere book learning. "NOT an Indignant One's" ideal woman is "strong-minded, but truly feminine; clever, but not of necessity intensely learned; firm, yet gentle; practised in all those virtues which may fit her to be the complement of man, for, whatever women themselves may say, it was for that end and no other that we were created" (768). This conservative, religious perspective reflects the instability of the feminine ideal. As more girls were educated and entering the workforce, a feminine ideal of moral superiority, beauty, and grace was both familiar and comforting. Yet, through the publication of her letter in *Atalanta*, "NOT an Indignant One" enters the public domain in a visible and vocal fashion that complicates her position. Her letter is a vital contribution to the "crucial site" (Beetham *Magazine* 118) of the periodical as a forum for the debate about gender and sexuality.

The challenge of incorporating education into the traditional feminine ideal often appears in *Atalanta* and elsewhere in the periodical press. In 1890, Cambridge women were so successful in their studies that *Punch* called it "The Ladies Year" and praised the achievements of Philippa Fawcett (of Newnham College), who placed "above the [male] senior wrangler" in the Mathematical Tripos and Margaret Alford (of Girton College), who placed first in the Classical Tripos:

> Come, hands, take your lyres and most carefully tune 'em,
> For Girton in glory now pairs off with Newnham.
> Miss Fawcett the latter with victory wreathed,
> And now, ere the males from their marvel are breathed,
> Miss Margaret Alford, the niece of the Dean,
> As a Classical First for the former is seen.
> Let Girton toast Newnham, and Newnham pledge Girton
> And—let male competitors put a brisk 'spurt' on,
> Lest when modern Minerva adds learning to grace,
> Young Apollo should find himself out of the race. (309)

Punch congratulates the women, yet also displays some anxiety that male scholars might find themselves "out of the race." This echoes Church's comment that men might become the "weaker sex" as women increasingly study the humanities while men pursue more scientific subjects. The instability of the feminine ideal is matched by similar concerns about masculinity.

Fiction in *Atalanta*

Fiction in *Atalanta* and elsewhere was troubled by these educated Girton Girls. Parodied in venues like *Punch*, and critiqued in fictional representations of the New Woman, the Girton Girl was a troublesome and troubling representation of the changing nature of girlhood. Smart and educated, trained for employment beyond the domestic sphere, she challenged the traditional feminine ideal as she demanded acceptance in the public domain. In her history of Girton College, M.C. Bradbrook finds the image of the Girton Girl in the periodical press inconsistent with the lived histories of Girton scholars, and she reminds readers to "never trust the image, trust the live encounter" (117). Sally Ledger concurs with this assessment, arguing that the New Woman, and by implication the Girton Girl, "was predominantly a journalistic phenomenon, a product of discourse" (3). The Girton Girl was a textual construction as much as she was a real person. Moreover, as a construct, she was the embodiment of anxieties about the implications of women studying alongside men, in a public space, beyond family control. She was frequently refigured throughout the 1880s and '90s to meet the changing anxieties about gender, sexuality, and women's rights. Joyce Pedersen describes the *fin-de-siècle* girl as:

> more self-disciplined and forward-looking, carefully cultivating her three 'faculties'—intellectual, physical, and social—and neatly balancing her obligations to herself, her family, and society. Her aspirations seem quite in accordance with the norms of achievement, universalism, specificity, and independence which ... the structural properties of public school and collegiate life fostered. (84)

Pederson identifies one single girl, as if girlhood at the *fin de siècle* was a unifying experience, yet Angelique Richardson and Chris Willis suggest that the New Woman "was not one figure, but several" (13). Likewise, many *fin-de-siècle* girls embodied different solutions to anxieties associated with gender and sexuality.

One example of this process of textual fabrication appears in Annie Edwarde's *A Girton Girl* (1886). This story capitalizes on the public phenomenon of the Girton Girl, despite having little to do with Girton College or women's education. In this story, essentially a romance, the intelligent Marjorie hires Geoffrey Arbuthnot, a Cambridge scholar, to tutor her so she can attend Girton College. They soon fall in love, but a misdelivered letter causes them to separate. A year later, Marjorie arrives in Cambridge, "still uncommitted to the future, to run a last forlorn chance of meeting the man she loved" (469). When they are eventually reunited, Geoffrey asks,

> "Can you give up everything for me? ... Your dream for years has been Girton. Do you desire still to become a Girton student, or—?"
> "I desire that you shall guide me," was the prompt answer. "I need no other life, no other wisdom, no other ambition than yours." (485)

Love conquers Marjorie's dreams of education and independence, and she immediately subordinates her desires. Like the "Girl of the Period," which became a commodity to be bought and sold, this novel demonstrates how a symbol like the Girton Girl could be manipulated to achieve commercial objectives.

This ambivalence towards women's higher education is also found in *Atalanta*'s fiction. Only two stories unequivocally support the educated girl. In "The Girton Girl" by Edith Nesbit, a novelist, poet, and short story writer, the "handsome and learned" Laura Wentworth has achieved "something wonderful" (755) at Girton and has decided not to marry.[14] In all other ways, she has "a natural girl's tastes" for riding, singing, dancing, tennis, boating, and shooting, yet she can also "construe one of the hardest bits of Aeschylus" (755). Laura's outspoken denunciations of marriage are tested when she meets Charles Peke. Only Laura, a strong swimmer, can save Charles when he almost drowns. When the two lovers return a year later to be married, Laura rejects a compliment on her bravery: "It was not brave; it was selfish—because I loved him—and Love is the power that moves the world" (759).

Although Laura is a highly educated Girton girl, she also has a number of other talents and skills, including the feminine accomplishments of singing and dancing, and physical capability. She is both intellectually and physically gifted, yet she reflects a traditional feminine ideal of the past. Her explicit stance against marriage—she claims it is akin to selling oneself into slavery—is her only variation from the feminine ideal. Yet the story concludes with Laura's marriage because she now believes that love will restore equal power relations between men and women. Nesbit's ideal of girlhood integrates education and femininity and constructs a new *fin-de-siècle* girl who is smart and strong but who can still marry. Moreover, Laura's physical and mental strength enables her heroism. Her friend Lavinia's betrayal suggests that less educated girls are disloyal and may not marry. The narrative is unclear about Laura's occupations after her marriage, indicative of an overarching problem with fictional accounts of educated girls. As Sally Mitchell remarks, girls' culture at the end of the century "described a new life of schools, sports, independence, and training for a profession [where] a girl's outlook was no longer limited to the ideas and models available in her own family and neighborhood" (4). Even in an openly supportive girls' magazine like *Atalanta*, the future of an educated girl is unclear since the marital trope remains an integral part of the fiction.

The same uncertainty about how education can be incorporated into the feminine ideal appears in "Maxwell Gray's" serial story, "Sweethearts and Friends" (1897).[15] The pro-educational stance and the support for women's rights are even

---

[14]   Nesbit is best known for her fantasy novels, *Five Children and It* (1902), *The Phoenix and the Carpet* (1904), and *The Story of the Amulet* (1906), all of which were first serialized in *Strand Magazine*.

[15]   "Maxwell Gray" was the pseudonym of novelist Mary Gleed Tuttiett. She published *The Silence of Dean Maitland* (1886) and was a frequent contributor to *Atalanta*, including the serialized story "A Costly Freak," "On the Development of Character in Fiction," and "Occupations for Gentlewomen: Literature."

more overt in this story than in "A Girton Girl." To the dismay of her family, Amy Langton decides to study medicine. Her mother does not understand how the feminine ideal has changed; she wishes Amy "would give up thinking" and wonders, "What good can possibly come to a girl who thinks? We never thought of thinking when I was young" (436). Amy is a troubling element within the Langton family because she refuses to fit within their feminine ideal and instead studies anatomy in her quest to become a doctor. In contrast, male family friend Vivian Lester declares that the ideal woman "is a being—whose weakness is her strength, in whom feeling replaces intellect, meekness replaces power—who should be a rest to her husband by her freedom from toil, a strength to him by the appeal of her weakness, a joy to him by her freedom from sorrow" (439). Lester draws upon the crumbling mid-Victorian middle-class notion that because a woman is not an active participant in the public world, she is freed from the sorrows of the world and can create a calm, peaceful domestic space to which a man can retreat. Although Amy responds derisively to this characterization of an ideal woman, she is concerned that her education might prevent her marriage. Her teacher assures her that "[k]nowing Greek will not unfit a girl to be a wife ... [H]alf the misery of life comes from wives knowing nothing that interests husbands" (442). This exchange highlights the uncertainty about the impact of girls' education and echoes Douglas's comment that "the more women are like men the less they are liked by men" (643). Nonetheless, in this serial story, the educated girl rejects the opposition of marriage and education and believes than an educated woman will make a more attractive wife.

Not only is Amy educated, but she also has maternal tendencies. She is prompted to become a doctor by "a desire to heal, and a motherliness" (443). She is not averse to marriage and refuses to promise not to marry. Amy is a new kind of girl; she feels education is important and believes that equality between men and women is possible. In this case, Lester's traditional views on women, including "the charms of seclusion, meekness, and dependence, the beauty of wifely and motherly virtues ... and the loneliness of professional women's lives" (446), are the impediment to their marriage, for Amy refuses to marry someone who does not agree she is an equal.

When Lester encounters Amy 5 years later, she has completed her medical studies and is caring for a group of invalids. These invalids show the reader what might have happened to Amy if she had not pursued her dream to become a doctor. Louisa is dying, technically of consumption, but really because of the strain and monotony of her prior occupation as an "overworked, worried governess" (498). A governess, of course, often worked under poor conditions for little pay, yet such work was often the only suitable occupation available to a middle-class woman. For Louisa, "the repose of wholesome study came too late" (498). The other invalid is Amy's sister Grace, a member of a Sisterhood despite having no vocation for religious life. Grace found the emptiness of a "frivolous, aimless girl-life" intolerable and makes a poor decision based on a limited set of options available to her. The "severity, monotony and tyranny" of life in a Sisterhood is killing her, and her eyes are haunting: "hungry restless eyes they were, the prison cells of a struggling soul" (494). This story emphasizes the importance of knowledge and skills for a girl's future, a dominant theme in *Atalanta*. Without a proper education, a girl has few choices except marriage, which may not be likely.

In a vehement defence of her education and her role as a doctor, Amy uses the discourses of degeneration to explain how middle-class women become deformed and stunted if they lack access to proper education. In *Degeneration* (1895), for instance, Max Nordau refers to the markers of degeneracy as "deformities" and "multiple and stunted growths" (16). Amy is a confident, healthy, capable young woman who employs similar rhetoric as she explains the importance of education:

> Think ... of the degraded, stunted, wasted lives of innumerable middle-class women, who cannot possibly marry, purely because there are not enough men to marry them. Think of the immense difficulties and obstacles that a few women have surmounted in the task of opening up new lines of usefulness to these women and removing the stigma from female erudition and labour! Picture the great mass of hopeless, superfluous spinsters 'withering on the stalk!' Think of the complex tangle of misery and vice resulting from wretched marriages, from the union of men and women without one taste or aim in common ... consider if this is a time for women to snatch at personal happiness, when they have gone as far, suffered as much, and made others to suffer as much as I have. (668)

The reality of middle-class women's lives is at odds with the traditional feminine ideal of marriage. Women often needed to work because they would not marry. Moreover, unmarried women suffer because they have no useful purpose and the domestic sphere cannot sustain the demands of their intelligence and capability.

The ambiguities and uncertainties of life for educated women are also true in this story. As a doctor, Amy demonstrates the possibilities offered by education, yet her work life is not entirely satisfying: "She was very tired, the romance of daring an unusual life in the teeth of opposition had evaporated with the novelty of it, leaving a barren stretch of grey, uninviting duty behind. Life seemed nothing but perpetual labour, all illusions and loveliness crushed beneath the grim monotony of work" (666). Her work is no longer a joy; thus the "brave girl-student" of Paton's poem must have courage to persevere in a field infrequently occupied by women, where the work is lonely and tiring. The collegiality emphasized in the school experience has disappeared under the pressures of working alone in a predominantly male field. The climax of the story occurs when Amy saves Lester from a burning building. Like Laura in "A Girton Girl," Amy is the capable hero who saves her male lover. Amy embodies a new feminine ideal combining education, feminine graces, and healthy vigour. This feminine ideal is so attractive that Lester is finally persuaded of Amy's equality, and she agrees to marry him. Unlike the Nesbit story, where Laura's future as a wife remains intentionally obscure, Lester promises Amy that she will not have to change to become his wife. This relationship of equality and respect is unusual in the fiction of the period and especially in *Atalanta*. The womanly woman and the scholarly woman finally coexist in a single figure. Yet, despite this strong and rather unconventional ending, the story's conclusion of marriage is significant. The many destabilizing forces embodied by Amy are contained within the traditional form of marriage.

The ideal of education and femininity is less positively portrayed in other *Atalanta* fiction, which reinforces the difficulties of adapting the traditional feminine ideal to include education. In Mary Molesworth's serial story, "White Turrets," for example, Winifred becomes so absorbed by education and useful employment that she fails to recognize her domestic responsibilities. A novelist and prolific children's writer, Molesworth wrote over 100 books, many of which were concerned with social status. As Mary Sebag-Montefiore notes, Molesworth's novels often "spell out a work message of caution and restraint" (375). In "White Turrets," the protagonist Winifred is particularly threatening because she refuses to accept that her family duties must outweigh her personal desire for satisfactory work, and this destabilizing influence is contained only when she acknowledges that her presence on the family estate is vital to the health and welfare of the family. Winifred embodies the difficulties of adapting the feminine ideal to include education and employment. She is demonstrably in the wrong, and later suitably chastized, when she deceives a charity agency into believing she needs paid employment, which ought to be given to those who need it to survive. A family friend reminds Winifred of her responsibilities as a woman and as a daughter to her home, because home is

> the place we are born into—in a very special sense woman's own kingdom. Outside interests should radiate from and revolve round home—that is the ideal. When home has to be given up it should be done regretfully, as a sad necessity, whereas the wish to escape from it is, I fear, in many cases now-a-days, the great motive. (795)

Her sister Celia presents a more positive incorporation of education into the feminine ideal of girlhood. Studying to become an artist, Celia's career is a more suitably feminine accomplishment. She pursues it with the support of her family and eventually marries. In contrast, Winifred has no prospect of a romantic relationship. She denounces marriage because it makes a woman either a "plaything" or a "slave" (534). Instead, the narrator notes that Celia receives from Winifred "lists of appallingly clever books on eminently practical subjects, all directly or indirectly connected with the management on the best possible lines of a large estate" (798). Winifred's cleverness is acknowledged, but contained within her responsibilities on the family estate. Female agency and education are to be celebrated within appropriately feminine limits.

Similarly, marriage and employment are incompatible in Mary Fraser's "One Woman's Destiny" (1898). Eleanor Forsyth rejects an offer of marriage from Donald Macpherson because she does not intend to marry: "I did well at Newnham, very well indeed, better than all the women and almost all the men: and what is the use of it all if I marry?" (625). This educated Newnham girl articulates the longstanding incompatibility, even at the end of the century, between education and marriage. When Emily Davies introduced the idea in 1866 that girls should be educated irrespective of their future occupations, the possibility emerged that girls might seek work other than marriage and maternity. Thirty years later, how and where these educated women fit in British society remains unclear. If they marry, they give up the possibilities offered by education, and vice versa. What, then, is to be done with these educated women? Only Amy Langton holds out for both work and love. Eleanor cannot see how married life can be compatible with her desire to work.

The promise of education gives way to the reality, and necessity, of working for a living. Seven years later, Eleanor is lonely and laments "all these years of work to be so utterly alone!" (625). She is a teacher, stuck in a "dull academic round, varied by duller holidays," with little hope for relief from the never-ending drudgery, for it "had come to a fight for her daily bread for Eleanor Forsyth, bracketed fourth wrangler" (625). She encounters Donald while walking down the Strand. "[T]his big bronzed Colonial" (625) has made his millions in Kimberley diamonds and is still in love with Eleanor. When he asks her again to marry him, she is ashamed: "What had she to bring in return for all that he could offer? Neither youth nor beauty was hers now" (626). She is worn down by her life of work, but she dares not reject this precious offer of love and friendship, and later feels "strangely peaceful. Thankful, not so much that drudgery with her was at an end, that care had departed from her path, but that love had come into her life, and, taking her by the hand, gave her a promise of happiness such as she had never known" (626). Her education, then, has only fitted her for loneliness, toil, and the loss of her beauty (a key characteristic of the feminine ideal, as I discussed in the previous chapter). Quite explicitly, education is placed in opposition to love; she can have education, even if it ultimately proves unfulfilling, or love, but not both. In *Atalanta*'s fiction, the support for education is muted, if not negated, by the possibility of spinsterhood. The feminine ideal is not sufficiently adaptable to incorporate the instabilities signalled by education. The college-educated girl is too threatening, as she seeks an independent life, to be included within traditional expectations of marriage. In the end, even a Newnham girl will choose love over work. Marriage, more than work or education, is the true source of happiness.

Other fiction in *Atalanta* betrays the same anxieties about how society is supposed to function if girls no longer remain at home. Girls are either contained within the home or demonstrate that the experiences outside the home are less positive than they had anticipated. Sexuality is especially problematic in the opposition between education and marriage. There are implicit contradictions in the sexualized Girton girl, who was often portrayed (particularly in periodicals like *Punch*) as masculine and asexual, while elsewhere she advocated free love and moral decadence. Elaine Showalter explains that "[s]exual difference was … one of the threatened borders" of the *fin de siècle*, and sexuality "one of the areas in which anarchy seemed imminent" (4). In *Atalanta*, however, sexuality remains stable, with the heterosexual rhetoric continuing throughout the magazine's run. Between October 1895 and September 1896, for example, three stories show young women to be fickle and self-centered in comparison to their steady, stalwart male lovers. In each case, the young couple unites in love and marriage, and like Laura in "A Girton Girl," each girl recognizes that love paves the way for happiness. In "A Race for a Sweetheart," for example, heterosexual love is integrated into a story of national identity. The Canadian girl Rosette is both impulsive, a trait coming from her French father, and conscientious, a trait coming from her English mother. When she refuses a warning about thin ice and almost drowns, her English friend Ralph saves her after his French rival Pierre abandons her to her fate. Similarly in "A Guard's Last Run," the working-class Adam has seemingly lost Bessie to a London suitor. Repentant, she returns to Adam when he is almost killed trying to ascertain whether the London suitor will make Bessie happy. Finally, in "The Girl at the Dower House," Rhea breaks off her engagement with Augustus and then gratefully welcomes his return because she hasn't been "happy one single day without you" (Giberne 370).

Nonetheless, the models of femininity in the fiction are quite different from the educated girls who appear elsewhere in *Atalanta*'s pages. Margaret Beetham has noted about the women's magazine *Queen* that "[f]avourable comments on higher education … remained isolated from the other models of femininity in its pages" (*Magazine* 137). Readers had to ask themselves how these contradictory depictions of femininity "related to each other and to their own experience in the materiality of their lives" (*Magazine* 137). Similarly, *Atalanta*'s readers had to decode the conflicting models of femininity appearing in the magazine. A feminine ideal of marriage frequently appears in its fiction, and even those stories that include educated girls are constrained by this heterosexual framework. At the same time, *Atalanta* also engaged with and supported progressive ideas of education, work, and gender. Its move towards more fashion articles and less pro-education fiction and nonfiction towards the end of its run may be a symptom of its changing ideological framework as well as its inability to navigate the complicated territory of education and gender in the final years of the century. In the earliest days of the magazine, for example, "The Brown Owl" section included a variety of contributions (and contributors) discussing topics ranging from cooking, cycling, and suffrage. In 1897/8, however, "The Brown Owl" dealt exclusively with "The World of Fashion." At a time when women were making increasingly substantial contributions to public life in England, *Atalanta*'s failure to respond to and encourage these contributions reflects how complicated the construction of girlhood could be. In the next chapter, I will demonstrate a further facet of this complicated girlhood as I explore how the tensions between marriage and reproductive choice are contained within the figure of the virtuous yet knowledgeable girl at the *fin de siècle*.

Chapter 6
The Marrying Girl:
Social Purity and Marriage in
the *Young Woman* (1892–1915)

Although the *Young Woman* (1892–1915) seems to support a traditional feminine ideal of marriage and children, the magazine adjusts this ideal by engaging with the ideas of social purists to assert a new conception of marriage that includes a single sexual standard. In articles by noted New Woman novelists like Sarah Grand (whose novel *The Heavenly Twins* moved conversations about sexual experience into the drawing room) and women's rights activists like Florence Fenwick Miller, a more progressive model of femininity encourages girls to seek options beyond marriage while also emphasizing the importance of marriage and maternity. Yet the magazine also includes depictions of conservative femininity, like those of Eliza Lynn Linton and John Ruskin. Thus the girl found in the *Young Woman* represents a unique figure within girls' periodicals as the magazine encourages girls to marry but shapes its discussions of marriage to reflect the biological determinism of feminist eugenicists. The marrying girl responds to New Woman concerns about marriage, asserts new possibilities for marriage based on sexual and moral equality, and expands notions of girlhood by insisting that men be held to similar standards as women. This girl rejects the idea that only women can and should be held to an absolute standard of purity.

Although the representations of femininity within the magazine may seem contradictory, they are part of the magazine's sophisticated strategy to encourage girls to marry, after obtaining the necessary and appropriate knowledge regarding the sexual histories of their suitors. The young woman in the magazine eagerly anticipates her marriage and understands her responsibility to select the best husband. Alongside a traditional feminine ideal of duty, purity, and charity, the *Young Woman* also includes a variety of informational articles, editorials, and fictional stories about the New Woman, thereby opening a space for the redefinition of the feminine ideal. These two apparently contrasting depictions of femininity are reconciled through the employment of social purity rhetoric. The importance of educating young women to select the best reproductive partner emphasizes the female function of choice. A young woman's choice of who and when to marry is paramount, and a variety of contributors discuss these issues at length in the *Young Woman*.

The formal launch of the social purity movement is often attributed to W.T. Stead's sensational depictions of prostitution in his "Maiden Tribute of Modern

Babylon," appearing in the July 1885 *Pall Mall Gazette*.[1] However, the origins of the movement emerged from the campaign to repeal the Contagious Diseases Acts, which legislated the inspection and incarceration of prostitutes who were suspected of having syphilis. Stead's articles and the repeal campaign demonstrate the controversial and somewhat ambiguous representations of sexually active women and highlight the double sexual standard that permitted men unlimited sexual activity while condemning the same behaviour in women. Sue Morgan notes that the 1880s and '90s marked the rise of the purity movement, "a loose national network of powerful religious lobby-groups that sought to reinforce Christian norms of sexuality, marriage and family life through a series of demands for enhanced moral legislation issued from the pulpit and the press" ("Wild Oats" 151–2). The movement employed traditional religious ideology to position women as the chaste centre of the home. It also used contemporary scientific discourses about gender and sex differences to assert women's moral and spiritual superiority to men and to encourage men to reach the same standard as women.

The publication of Charles Darwin's *On the Origin of Species* (1859) and *The Descent of Man and Selection in Relation to Sex* (1871) introduced religious doubt and a scientific explanation for sex differences into the mainstream debate over the "Woman Question." In *On the Origin of the Species*, which was primarily a biological work, Darwin argues that a species' adaptation to its environment gradually improved as the characteristics best fitted for survival were passed on to the next generation. In *The Descent of Man*, which was primarily a work of anthropology, Darwin adds the principle of sexual selection, arguing that males compete not just for food and space, but also for mates. While the competition occurs between males, the females have the important role of selecting their reproductive partners. These ideas about sexual difference were "readily absorbed into the popular debate" (King 31) about women's roles as a variety of activists asserted that a woman's natural and inevitable role as wife and mother was justified by the evolutionary imperative to preserve the race from degeneration and disease. These ideas are central to the rhetoric of purity employed in the *Young Woman* to encourage girls to demand and obtain good information before selecting a husband. Yet, by the end of the century, the Christian construction of moral and chaste womanhood came under increasing attack as a result of advances in medicine and natural science. Paradoxically, the rise of science, both as a profession and a discourse, helped to "shore up traditional ideas about gender" as scientists attempted to describe "what women objectively were—a verdict from which there was no appeal, for scientific claims to objectivity [tended] to carry greater weight than the more overtly ideological claims of religion or literature" (King 12). Scientific investigation was seen as a more legitimate means of knowing about the world than religious theology.

---

[1]   Stead launched an investigation into white slavery in London, which ultimately forced the government to raise the age of sexual consent to 16.

Consequently, New Woman writers used the discourse of science to advance their cause for female agency. They "combined concepts from evolutionary theory and science with conceptions of religion" and "posited women as the agents of change" (Bland 48). Women became the keepers of the moral and spiritual sanctity of the home because of their biological superiority. Lyn Pykett writes that

> [p]articularly in the latter part of the century, scientific discourse figured women's resistance to their conventional social roles as contrary to the laws of nature, and as threatening the health and continuance of the race. New Woman writers boldly transposed the terms of this discourse, making their male characters serve as both the symptoms of a diseased society and as the carriers of actual disease. 'Proper' (i.e., socially sanctioned) masculine behaviour, not improper femininity, was thus represented as the main threat to the future of the race. (*The "Improper" Feminine* 155)

A key component of the discussion by New Woman writers was how questions of marriage, reproductive choice, and maternity were intertwined to leverage the shifting nature of femininity and womanliness at the *fin de siècle*. As Talia Schaffer has noted, "in the process of rejecting, affirming, decrying, or defining the 'New Woman', writers were able to enunciate where they stood on various issues" ("Nothing" 49). With women increasingly seen as the gatekeepers of the family and the race, some New Women writers seized control of purity debates to critique the double sexual standard made explicit through the Contagious Diseases Acts and to insist that men be held to the same standard of purity as women. Jane Lewis explains that "[a]s the moral guardians of the home [women] were considered to bear responsibility for male sexual behaviour and for imparting a high moral standard of behaviour to society as a whole" (123).[2] The *Young Woman* uses this feminine ideal of moral and sexual purity to encourage its girl readers to demand better behaviour from their suitors.

The influence of the social purity campaign is apparent through the magazine's focus on selecting a spouse, demanding a single sexual standard for men and women, and discussing the qualities of an ideal husband. First appearing in 1892, the *Young Woman* stresses the importance of the feminine ideal, but reshapes the traditional feminine ideal to satisfy "late nineteenth-century British fears of racial decline and imperial loss" (Richardson 9). Angelique Richardson argues compellingly that *fin-de-siècle* eugenic feminists felt that "sex and society were biologically determined, but that change might be induced through biological rather than social means" (35). Thus "feminism might work *with* rather than against nature, intervening in the process of biological evolution in order to alter biological destiny" (35). Some, though by no means all, aspects of this eugenic feminist thought can be found in the *Young Woman*, where a young woman is held

---

2   Lesley Hall's "Hauling Down the Double Standard: Feminism, Social Purity and Sexual Science in Late Nineteenth-Century Britain" (2004) has an excellent overview of the recent scholarship on social purity and a single sexual standard.

responsible for her own future through her selection of an appropriate husband and father for her children. The ideal of girlhood developed in the *Young Woman* incorporates Darwinist ideas of reproductive choice into the feminine ideal of marriage and maternity. Like the attempts to refine the feminine ideal in other girls' periodicals, a similar tension exists in this magazine between the traditional ideal of the past and the realities of girls' lives. In this case, the need to adapt the ideal of girlhood to include knowledge and reproductive choice arises from a fear of the consequences of an ill-informed decision.

The *Young Woman*

The *Young Woman* was founded and edited by novelist and clergyman Frederick A. Atkins and was intended as a companion magazine to his *Young Man* (1887–1919).[3] Atkins writes in an introductory letter, "To Our Readers," that "[w]e wish to produce a journal that shall prove interesting and useful to the great body of young women who read and think and take a genuine interest in social and Christian effort" (24). The magazine establishes its ideal readership of "young women," suggesting girls finished with the schoolroom who are educated, thoughtful, and "genuinely" interested in charitable efforts. The Christian ethos is remarkably overt in contrast to other *fin-de-siècle* girls' periodicals like *Atalanta* and the *Girl's Realm*, where religion tends to be much more muted. A series like "Young Women of the Bible," for example, highlights the Christian nature of the magazine. As I discussed in Chapter 2, the influence and positioning of religion in the periodical press, especially in girls' magazines, became increasingly challenging as the twentieth century approached. The *Young Woman*'s religiosity emphasizes the moral and spiritual superiority of women that is employed by the New Woman writers in the magazine to attack the double sexual standard and insist on proper education for girls.

According to Rosemary Van Arsdel, the *Young Woman* "enjoyed a large circulation from the first issue, October 1892, which was reprinted three times for a sale of 80,000 copies" (173). It received a favourable review from *Myra's Journal*, where it was noted that "the new venture ... has not only a sturdiness of purpose, but has many well-known contributors ... .The motto of the little magazine—'The sweetest lives are those to duty wed'—is a beacon towards which our wives and daughters may safely steer" ("*The Young Woman*" 5). A comment in the last number of the first volume suggests that the original demand subsided to approximately 50,000 monthly subscribers. Atkins urges every reader "to help us by securing at least one new subscriber" so that "we shall start our second volume with a circulation of 100,000" ("To Our Readers: The Arrangements" 376). Circulation

---

[3]   Atkins was author of books like *Moral Muscle, and How to Use It: A Chat with Young Men* (1891) and *Life Worth While: Talks with Young Men* (1911). He also pursued his liberal Christian philosophy in a weekly magazine, *The New Age: A Weekly Record of Culture, Social Service, and Literary Life.*

numbers remained healthy by encouraging young women to read the magazine aimed at young men and vice versa. Unlike the *Girl's Own Paper*, which was founded in the hopes of minimizing these cross-gender reading habits, the *Young Woman* felt that a mixed-gender readership was acceptable. The Correspondence editor, Mrs. Esler, thanks "Exegesis" for her letter: "I am glad to know you like *The Young Man* also; it has many women readers, and *The Young Woman* has many men readers, that is all right and as it ought to be" ("Answers" 79).

The contents of the *Young Woman* reinforce the perception that it was intended as a literary or scholarly journal. Each 36-page number contains few illustrations, except for photographic portraits of influential women working in the public domain. Regular features include "My Monthly Chat with the Girls" as well as nonfiction articles on careers for girls, women's work around the world, and a number of "character sketches" on social and cultural figures like Margaret Oliphant, Frances E. Willard, and Princess May. The Countess of Aberdeen, Florence Fenwick Miller, and Josephine Butler are some of the prominent celebrities and activists who are interviewed, and their interests reflect the *Young Woman*'s desire to attract a wide range of readers who were involved in the issues of the day.[4] The variety of women included in the *Young Woman* emphasizes the success women had achieved in public arenas in the 1890s. In W.J. Dawson's "My Study Diary," he describes the origins and intentions of the magazine and alludes to "the growing power of women in journalism" (31). He writes, "It is our aim to make this a real woman's journal, … by opening its columns to all the foremost writers of our day, and particularly to those women who are best qualified to address women" (31). The magazine appealed to a progressive audience with topical articles on "Young Women and Journalism," "Nursing as a Profession for Women," and "The Laws which affect Women." Fiction, which typically takes up between four and eight pages, includes serialized novels like L.T. Meade's "Aunt Cassandra" and Margaret Oliphant's "A House in Bloomsbury," but the majority of each number deals with women's issues and female public figures. By 1896, each issue was 40

---

[4] Frances Willard, for example, was an American suffragette and social activist who framed her desire for suffrage in domestic terms. Margaret Oliphant, of course, was a popular domestic novelist and frequent contributor to *Blackwood's Edinburgh Magazine*. Princess May became Queen Mary, consort of George V, when Edward VII died in 1910. Isabel Maria Marjoribanks became the Countess of Aberdeen when she married Sir John Campbell Hamilton-Gordon in 1877. An energetic philanthropist, she was elected president of the International Congress of Women, which worked for the improvement of the social and economic position of women and the promotion of peace. Florence Fenwick Miller was a journalist, contributing to journals such as *Fraser's Magazine*, *Lett's Illustrated Household Magazine*, *Belgravia*, *Lady's Pictorial*, *Women's World*, and *The Echo*. She was a regular columnist for the *Illustrated London News* from 1886 to 1918. As Barbara Onslow explains, she "was equally well-known as a feminist activist as she was a columnist" ("Preaching" 90). Between 1895 and 1899, she was editor and proprietor of the *Woman's Signal*. Josephine Butler, a women's rights activist, campaigned tirelessly against the Contagious Diseases Acts.

pages, and fiction occupied a much greater percentage, up to 50 percent, generally across three or more stories. These later numbers also have more illustrations. Yet these issues remain focused on female public figures, including lengthy profiles of six to eight pages on celebrities like author Jane Barlow and the Duchess of Fife.

Confirming the Feminine Ideal

Alongside these progressive articles, however, the *Young Woman* presents conflicting images of young womanhood and highlights the tension between the feminine ideal of the past and the changing conditions of girlhood at the end of the century. In addition to discussions of marriage that reflect feminist eugenicist concerns about a sexual double standard, a strongly conservative feminine ideal also appears. From its first issue, the *Young Woman* depicts the young woman as a wife. This wifely role is interwoven with ideals of femininity and the domestic sphere, an image of the New Woman consistent with those appearing in the women's press in the early 1890s. Michelle Tusan explains how the New Woman "was represented in these pages as a reasonable and thoughtful woman who had only the best interests of the British state at heart … . Her interest in politics and social justice … [was] depicted as an extension of her domestic duties" (170). These duties are emphasized through the epigraph of the *Young Woman*: "The sweetest lives are those to duty wed," a line from Elizabeth Barrett Browning's poem "The Sweetest Lives." This epigraph, which appears monthly between 1892 and 1896, endorses a life of charity, service, and marriage, especially given the highly suggestive "wed." Moreover, the poem, which is printed in full in the first issue, also describes the happiness of "a child's kiss" (l. 8). As the natural consequence of marriage, children contribute to a woman's happy and productive life. The regular appearance of this epigraph reinforces the ideal of marriage and children for readers of the *Young Woman*.

This ideal is frequently reinforced, particularly in the magazine's early years. In a November 1892 article on "The Ideal Woman," for example, Dawson refers to Wordsworth's "She was a phantom of delight." Like Yonge in the *Monthly Packet*, clergyman and author Dawson also uses this poem to extol service and the domestic sphere as the two main facets of the ideal woman.[5] Dawson imagines the qualities he wishes to see in the girls of today, including

> the glow of virginal grace in their faces, innocence, untroubled calm, unsuspicious virtue, the fearless glances of a balanced mind: they work for no pay save the reward of love, for it is the household which is their sphere, and to keep that bright, fresh, happy, is their sufficing ambition. It is an alluring picture, impossible to some, but for most girls possible enough. (41)

---

[5]   Dawson also contributed to the *Young Man*. His 1896 series on "The Gospel According to the Novelists" included a paper on Robert Louis Stevenson. He published a number of novels, essays, and poetry collections, including *The Quest of a Simple Life* (1903), *Poems and Lyrics* (1893), and *The Making of Manhood* (1894).

Dawson's depiction of the ideal middle-class woman is somewhat nostalgic at a time when women were increasingly entering the workforce and were less likely to marry. Jane Lewis notes that between 1871 and 1911 the steadily increasing imbalance of the sex ratio meant that many women never married.[6] Although Dawson acknowledges that some women must work outside the home, "it is in the household and beside the hearthstone that woman finds her true environment. No woman need complain of a narrow lot who is the mistress of a household" (41). He ignores the lengthy campaign for better education and the reality that many girls may never marry. Instead, he promotes the superior morality and virtue of the ideal woman and reasserts her domestic role. Moreover, Dawson highlights the longevity of this feminine ideal with a Proverb:

> The price of the virtuous woman is far above rubies: strength and dignity are her clothing: she openeth her mouth with wisdom, and the law of kindness is on her tongue: she looketh well to the ways of her household, and eateth not the bread of idleness: favour is deceitful and beauty is vain, but a woman that feareth the Lord, she shall be praised. (Prov 31:10–30)

Dawson depicts an innocent, virginal, and virtuous girl who does not look beyond the home for fulfillment. He reinforces a feminine ideal of love, wisdom, and charity, and implicitly suggests that a girl who rejects this ideal is unnatural and unchristian.

This feminine ideal is similarly developed and reinforced in the magazine through frequent references to Ruskin's model of femininity. First presented in the 1864 Manchester lecture, "Of Queen's Gardens," and later published as part of *Sesame and Lilies*, Ruskin discusses woman's "queenly power" (69), which is the power "to heal, to redeem, to guide, and to guard" (88). His ideal is predicated on the ideology of separate spheres, where women occupy the moral and spiritual center of the home. Men and women are complementary, for "[e]ach has what the other has not: each completes the other, and is completed by the other: they are in nothing alike" (77). While the man is "the doer, the creator, the discoverer, the defender," the woman uses her power "for rule, not battle, and her intellect is not for invention or creation, but for sweet ordering, arrangement, and decision" (77). This conservative message is employed in the *Young Woman* to highlight the differences between men and women, which are seen as fundamental, innate, and natural, and which presage the Darwinian rhetoric of sexual difference that would appear after the publication of *The Descent of Man*. Yet, as we will see, the magazine's narrative becomes increasingly complicated as it is entwined with contradictory narratives about the New Woman and the need for reproductive choice.

Nonetheless, the feminine ideal articulated by Ruskin appears frequently in the pages of the magazine. In "Ruskin's Ideal Woman," for example, Dawson

---

[6]   See Lewis's *Women in England, 1870–1950: Sexual Divisions and Social Change* (1984) for further details, especially Chapter 1, "Patterns of Marriage and Motherhood."

explores the relevance of this ideal for *Young Woman* readers. He writes that "[t]o the more ardent and inconsiderate spirits in the modern revolt of woman, all this may seem somewhat antiquated philosophy nowadays" (374). Although this ideal may be perceived as old fashioned, Dawson believes it still has value for the modern girl. In addition to Dawson's endorsement of "true womanhood" (376), quotations from "Of Queen's Gardens" appear elsewhere in the *Young Woman*. The placement of these quotations at the bottom of a page might suggest that they are insignificant, intended only to fill space that would otherwise have been blank. Yet the frequent references to Ruskin are a reflection of his cultural authority in late-Victorian England. Ruskin was, after all, a respected critic who had written extensively on art, myth, and social and political economy. These references to "Of Queen's Gardens" are significant not only because they uphold a traditional model of femininity, but also because that model is employed with an almost casual ease in the pages of the magazine.

Ruskin's feminine ideal of moral virtue functions almost as a synecdoche for the complex ideologies operating and being contested at the *fin de siècle*. Angelique Richardson points out that "[w]omen had long been associated with moral virtue in evangelical and medical discourse" (45) but, by the end of the century, the ideological underpinnings of gender were being reshaped by medical discourses about the role of the female body, which asserted that female virtue was determined and ensured by biology. Thus a woman's moral "duty" became her biological "instinct" (Richardson 46), an idea that was employed elsewhere in the *Young Woman* when writers like Sarah Grand argued for the improvement of a young woman's education so she could make the best possible decision about a husband.

The New Woman Disrupts the Feminine Ideal

The appearance of the New Woman in the *Young Woman* presents an important contrast to the traditional feminine ideal. In the first "Monthly Chat" in November 1892, Correspondence editor Erminda Rentoul Esler remarks that "*The Young Woman* is intended to be the companion of girls who think, and therefore it aims at saying not the thing that is hackneyed but the thing that is true" (62).[7] *Young Woman* readers are sufficiently intelligent to recognize the truth, and the need to be knowledgeable about prospective suitors is not "hackneyed" journalism but fact. They are encouraged to become self-sustaining, which reflects the *fin-de-siècle* feminist strategy of "personal autonomy" (Bland 125). Esler writes that "[y]our duty is to cultivate your powers and your individuality to the best of

---

[7]   Although Atkins was editor, Esler's participation as Correspondence editor provided regular monthly communication between the magazine and its readers. Esler was a novelist, publishing her first novel, *Almost a Pauper: A Tale of Trial and Triumph*, in 1888. She also contributed "Some Village Chronicles" and "A Tardy Wooing" to the *Woman's Signal* in 1894.

your ability; to become an independent, happy, self-sufficing—as distinguished from self-sufficient—human creature, and never to contemplate yourself as a mere appendage to any problematical man" (62). She also rejects the idea that marriage is a girl's destiny: "Think for yourselves, see for yourselves, and form your characters on the best models you know. For each woman there is a useful sphere in life open" (62). Rather than sentimentalizing the beauty of a marriage that may not occur, each girl is encouraged to decide for herself what she wishes to do with her life. The traditional ideal of marriage and family as the center of a woman's life is replaced in the "Chat" by a celebration of the unmarried woman.

Esler addresses the changing circumstances of girls and young women, and her "Monthly Chat" is the first of many such articles to appear in the *Young Woman*. She writes that she is trying to think of "the actual girl as she is, and the conditions under which she lives, and will try to make the latter not theoretically but actually good for her" (64). Her discussion of "The New Woman" (as part of her monthly column "Between Ourselves") appears in December 1894, providing the first direct reference to the New Woman.[8] Formally endorsing the latest incarnation of girlhood, this article presents an alternative to the traditional feminine ideal that appears elsewhere in the magazine. The New Woman is an idea whose time has come:

> Circumstances became favourable, old disabilities were removed after much opposition and divers bitter struggles, and it was whispered in the ear of woman that she might thenceforward have opinions of her own, and might express them if occasion arose, that she might study seriously any subject that interested her, that she might use her brain and body legitimately, and that if she owned or earned anything she might justly retain or dispose of it uncontrolled. When this thought penetrated her mind, her faith in herself and her possibilities awoke, and behold, the birth of the New Woman! (106)

Referring to recent advances in women's education and property rights, Esler calls her story a fairy tale but also suggests that the New Woman is a real woman. Yet the New Woman is also an "unfortunate creature" (106) to whom all sorts

---

[8]   The New Woman became a ubiquitous icon after she was popularized in the mainstream periodical press by Sarah Grand and Ouida in 1894. Talia Schaffer concludes that the "real war may well have been a war of words—that the New Woman's literary status was the most challenging aspect of her identity" ("Nothing" 47). Michelle Tusan has demonstrated that the New Woman first appeared in August 1893 in the feminist *Woman's Herald* as a "fictional icon to represent the political woman of the coming century" (169). Tusan differentiates between the New Woman appearing in the women's press and the mannish, overly sexualized figure appearing in novels and the mainstream periodical press. Even before that, however, the figure of the New Woman appeared in the periodical press in various guises as a "deviant" woman who was, over the years, "redundant," "odd," "wild," and "revolting" (Beetham *Magazine* 115). Ann Ardis explains that the naming of the New Woman was an "attempt to restabilise all of the social hierarchies" (28) that this figure disrupted.

of extreme qualities have been attached. Esler supports the desires of the New Woman for independence and freedom and presents a contrasting feminine ideal to the Ruskinian model appearing elsewhere in the magazine. The traditional model of femininity is presented beside a modern incarnation, revealing the extent to which the *Young Woman* engages with different perspectives of girlhood to create its own unique young woman who supports the idea of marriage, yet also reflects New Woman concerns.

Esler wants her readers to emulate actual, real women rather than the New Woman who is merely a "non-existent type" (107) created by the periodical press. In their "Introduction" to *The New Woman in Fiction and In Fact* (2002), Angelique Richardson and Chris Willis note that

> Journalists and cartoonists played a significant part in establishing the cultural status of the New Woman. Smoking, rational dress and bicycling provided cartoonists and satirists with easy targets and through such powerful visual iconography the New Woman became firmly established as a cultural stereotype. (13)

As a cultural icon, the New Woman was created in, and through, the periodical press and she was easily commodified and critiqued. In the *Young Woman*, however, contributors engaged with the New Woman both as a real woman and as a "type" whose origins must be exploded. In an 1895 two-part series entitled "The 'Old' Woman and the 'New,'" Hulda Friederichs argues that "the odious, loud creature who appears as the New type on the stage, in the caricaturist's work, and in the cheap sensational novel" cannot be considered "the real New Woman" (203). Unlike these caricatures, which deserve laughter, the real New Woman "has to be reckoned with as an important factor in the life of to-day" (203).

A journalist who began her career with the *Pall Mall Gazette* in 1883 and specialized in women's rights and social realist journalism, Friederichs places the New Woman alongside women of the past in order to develop a new feminine ideal. She puts the "Old" Woman "under the microscope" and observes that "three words are stamped all over her brain and her heart ... Conceal, Restrict, Simulate" (203). The girl of the past hides her true nature, is restricted in the activities she is permitted to perform, and must simulate the feminine ideal of "submission" to embody the "ideal type of womanhood" (204). Although there have always been occasional women who were "New and not Old," the New Woman has finally "appeared *en masse*," and "she has come to stay" (273). By suggesting that the historical feminine ideal was created through subterfuge and unnatural behaviour, Friederichs describes the girl of the present as natural and truthful and paves the way for the girl who will not submit to a bad husband but will demand good information and qualified advisers as she decides on a husband.

Like Esler's discussion of the New Woman, Friederichs is reacting to the uncomplimentary depictions of the New Woman in the press and describing a new kind of young woman who disrupts the traditional feminine ideal. In disrupting an ideal appearing elsewhere in the *Young Woman*, she creates a space for the new girl. Yet she reassures her readers that the New Woman retains those feminine qualities that "have always made her the centre of the home circle, the being towards which men turn in times of pain, anxiety, and trouble; the helper of the helpless, the healer of the wounds of life, the faithful, loyal friend, the interpreter of all that is most tender, graceful, true, and fair" (275). The New Woman "can be all this and more, with the more chances of success, the more she is allowed to develop her mental faculties; the less she is dependent for her daily bread and for her pleasures, on man, her former master, but now her fellow-worker, her friend, her equal" (275). Friederichs's New Woman is a paragon of femininity and a model of new relations between men and women because she is man's equal. Yet, "[i]t does not follow by any means that because the sexes are thus brought together on equal terms, that marrying and giving in marriage will have no place in the programmes of future periods" (275). In the *Young Woman*, marriage remains an important facet of girlhood, but the traditional feminine ideal is expanding to include equality.

Friederichs's New Woman retains her feminine graces, yet she is also man's equal and his partner in marriage. She disavows some of the more radical positions towards marriage, such as New Woman novelist Mona Caird's endorsement of free union. The New Woman is "the Old Woman made perfect" (276), seeking opportunities for education, employment, and love while maintaining her position as the moral and spiritual center of the home. The New Woman extends the traditional role, and she will be a better marriage partner and mother if she has a suitable education and employment. Friederichs adeptly negotiates the position of the New Woman; she is man's equal but is also morally superior. This paradox is not resolved, suggesting uneasiness about the role of the New Woman and the extent to which the magazine could support her more radical tendencies. In the *Young Woman*, this paradox is usefully employed to empower women as agents of change as they insist on a single sexual standard.

A different intersection of tensions appears in religious novelist Grace Stebbing's 1896 short story, "The New Woman."[9] Religion is positioned in opposition to femininity and New Womanhood to present a unique New Woman who values religion above independence and achievement. Laura MacWhiter, a devout Newnham girl, hopes to become the Senior Wrangler, but a friend's illness prompts her to relinquish her academic aspirations and take up nursing. When her friend questions how she can be a New Woman if she gives up her dreams, Laura responds that "[t]he 'New Woman' should be the embodiment of charity, of perfect love" (410). Stebbing radically redefines the New Woman by making Laura the "embodiment of charity" whose religious beliefs are privileged over

---

[9]   Stebbing published a number of novels, beginning with *Walter Benn, and How He Stepped Out of the Gutter* in 1877. She also contributed to a variety of children's periodicals, including *Goods Things for the Young of All Ages*, *Kind Words*, *Young England*, and the *Girl's Own Paper.*

education. Stebbing's New Womanhood is defined by religion instead of academic achievement, thereby constraining the radical potential of the New Woman.

The New Woman in the *Young Woman* is unquestionably ambiguous. The traditional feminine ideal has been redefined to meet the needs of a progressive readership and to satisfy demands that young women have an important role to play in the future of the British race. Moreover, the mix of genres and contributors in the magazine permitted inconsistencies in its approach towards the New Woman. These inconsistencies are perhaps inevitable in a magazine like the *Young Woman*, which was using the traditional feminine ideal while also responding to the need for agency among the young women who were the guardians of the moral sanctity of the family and the nation. Yet the *Young Woman* adopts a sophisticated strategy by merging marriage and the New Woman in its presentations of girlhood to reflect contemporary concerns about social purity and to depict a unique figure at the *fin de siècle*.

"The Ideal Husband"

Marriage is an important subject in the *Young Woman* because one of the key elements of *fin-de-siècle* feminine agency arises from Darwinist thought that the female's choice of reproductive partner strongly influences which genetic traits are passed on to the offspring. Moreover, the discussion in the magazine is part of a larger conversation elsewhere in the periodical press about the role of marriage in a girl's life. It raises the specter of the New Woman, a figure who provoked much of the *fin-de-siècle* controversy about the institution of marriage. Lyn Pykett has observed that the developing debate on the Marriage Question was "clearly an important component of the New Woman writing" (*Improper* 144), which "does not simply attack marriage, but rather renders it problematic" (*Improper* 147). The wholesale rejection of marriage was not part of the campaign of most New Woman writers. Instead, these writers challenged ideas about the marital union. In Mona Caird's famous 1888 essay on "Marriage," for example, she argues that "the present form of marriage ... is a vexatious failure" (79) because of the unequal power relations between husband and wife. When the *Daily Telegraph* posed the similar question, "Is marriage a failure?", it received an overwhelming 27,000 replies, underlining the importance of the discussion at the *fin de siècle*.[10]

---

[10]   In John M. Robson's *Marriage or Celibacy? The* Daily Telegraph *on a Victorian Dilemma* (1995), he analyzes and contextualizes the phenomenon of the responses to the *Daily Telegraph*. He pays particular attention to the "close relations among the issues that concerned the editors and readers of the *Daily Telegraph*, namely, prostitution, its causes and cures; ideal and practical marriage, its joys, duties, and costs; and emigration, its promises and dangers" (3). Although these responses occurred in the 1860s, the connection to the ongoing "encounters" in the *Young Woman* is notable and suggests the extent to which the debate remained topical in the 1890s.

Marriage was increasingly seen as a site of contested relations between men and women. In the *Young Woman*, this tension is resolved by endorsing marriage as the preferred solution for girls, yet also recognizing that girls must be better educated and more knowledgeable so that they can make better decisions. Ella Hepworth Dixon, a journalist and New Woman novelist who was best known for her 1895 novel *The Story of a Modern Woman*, presented her explanation in the periodical press about "Why Women Are Ceasing to Marry." She writes that

> [f]ormerly, girls married in order to gain their social liberty; now, they more often remain single to bring about that desirable consummation. If young and pleasing women are permitted by public opinion to go to college, to live alone, to travel, to have a profession, to belong to a club, to give parties, to read and discuss whatsoever seems good to them, and to go to theatres without masculine escort, they have most of the privileges—and several others thrown in—for which the girl of twenty or thirty years ago was ready to barter herself to the first suitor who offered himself and the shelter of his name. (86)

The increasingly liberated lives of *fin-de-siècle* girls are signaled by Dixon's assertion that a girl no longer needs a husband because she has many more freedoms than ever before. These young women threatened traditional marital norms, and many people feared the repercussions for the future of the British race if they also rejected the idea of motherhood. Sally Ledger argues that "one of the defining features of the dominant discourse on the New Woman at the *fin de siècle* was the supposition that the New Woman posed a threat to the institution of marriage" (*New Woman* 11). In the *Young Woman*, however, marriage is not threatened by the New Woman, nor is it a "failure" or an unhappy alternative to unmarried life. Instead, marriage is the appropriate choice for most young women provided they have enough information about their suitors to make a knowledgeable decision. The new girl in the *Young Woman* is more conventional than the New Woman depicted elsewhere in the periodical press. She marries, yet she demonstrates her affinity with the woman's movement because she is determined to be fully informed. The magazine is thus able to reconcile two apparently competitive forces through the figure of the girl.

From its earliest issues, the *Young Woman* endorses marriage but also encourages young women to make good choices about their reproductive partners. In the Rev. Edward John Hardy's "On the Choice of a Husband," he stresses the importance of choice, suggesting a degree of agency in selecting a marriage partner and reinforcing the social purity campaign's desire for a single sexual standard.[11] Angelique Richardson explains that social purists were "reinvesting women with the agency of selection on the grounds that only they were sufficiently race aware to make responsible sexual choices. Resisting male passion, women, as the bearers

---

[11]   The Reverend Edward John Hardy wrote on the subject of the everyday religious life, including *How to be Happy Though Married* (1885), *The Five Talents of Women* (1888), and *Concerning Marriage* (1901).

of moral biology, would initiate the replacement of romantic love by rational eugenic love—conscious sexual selection" (56). The social purists provide the impetus for better education for girls so that they can select an equally virtuous partner as a rational reproductive choice. Although Hardy's article asserts that "a refined girl will not take the initiative" to ask someone to marry her, the girl still has the "negative but very responsible duty of refusing those who are ineligible" (10). Also in the first issue is "Don't Marry Him!", which cautions against marriage to a man of dubious character. A man who is "sowing a few wild oats just now" is to be avoided because "what is sown before marriage is reaped after marriage" (42). This is likely an oblique reference to sexually transmitted diseases, which had become an important topic of conversation and debate among some New Women. Grand's *Heavenly Twins*, for instance, describes the consequences of syphilis for wives and children. The subtext of disease is never overtly discussed in the *Young Woman*, yet it provides the impetus for the rationalization of the competing forces of marriage and the feminism of the New Woman.

The widespread problem of sexually transmitted diseases was well known in England from the 1850s.[12] As I briefly discussed in Chapter 3, the Contagious Diseases Act of 1864 allowed for the compulsory medical inspection and incarceration of prostitutes and was extended to further garrison and naval towns in 1866 and 1869. The Acts became a symbol of female oppression because they allowed women to be forcibly examined and incarcerated in order to preserve the health of men while simultaneously "protecting male rights to enjoy promiscuous intercourse with impunity" (Hall *Sex* 23). Finally repealed in 1886 through the force of middle-class women activists and social reformers, particularly Josephine Butler, their elimination was part of the social purity movement aimed at transforming society by replacing the inequitable double sexual standard with a "higher, single, moral standard" (Hall *Sex* 32). The successful implementation of a single moral standard depended on girls being adequately informed of the consequences of making a poor choice for a husband. Often ill prepared for marriage and sexually ignorant, girls needed more information and better advisers if they were to make good choices for their future.

Sexual education was crucial factor associated with the campaign to improve girls' knowledge about their prospective partners. Traditional attitudes towards femininity linked sexuality with virtue. Girls were kept ignorant of both male and female sexuality in order to keep them pure. Meanwhile, social purists felt that discourses of sexuality must be placed in the public domain since, as Frank Mort points out, "[e]nforced silence was no guarantee of innocence or security" (115). The social purists argued that "women needed to be educated about human

---

[12]   Lesley Hall notes that venereal diseases were a "considerable problem" (*Sex* 22) in mid-Victorian Britain, and a Royal Commission in 1860 identified that 394 of 1000 soldiers were hospitalized for venereal disease, equal to the total of those hospitalized for tuberculosis, infections, and fevers. This was "several times greater than that for the Navy, and compared very unfavourably with other European nations" (Hall *Sex* 22).

physiology and sexuality, both for their own protection, and also to equip them, as mothers, for the task of teaching their children" (Bland 83). This opinion was contrary to official arguments, "which opposed ... public discussion on the grounds that this would only draw attention to sex and incite immorality" (Mort 114).

Early articles in the *Young Woman* remain reasonably oblique about the consequences of poor choices for the British nation and for the young women themselves, but they encourage young women to obtain appropriate knowledge about the men who wish to wed them. Grand makes similar comments in "The Modern Girl," which appeared in the June 1894 number of *North American Review*:

> It is no longer possible, even if it were desirable, to protect the modern girl, in the old acceptation of the word. What we are aiming at is to make the world a safe and pleasant place for her to live in, and it is found best to arm her with information that she may know her enemies when she meets them, and be able to protect herself—from herself as well as from her enemies. (711)

Obtaining and assessing the validity of information are key components of Grand's campaign to ensure that the modern girl is not forced into a marriage or a career for which she is unsuited. Grand reminds her readers that "[i]t is not her parents' prospects that are at stake, but her own, and the happiness of her whole life depends upon the early choice of a career suited to her constitution, taste, and abilities" ("The Modern Girl" 713). In Grand's comments and in the two early *Young Woman* articles, choosing the right husband is an important facet of a girl's life. An article written by a member of the clergy in 1897 encourages girls to "look before you leap" and explains that a girl is justified in breaking off an engagement if she "finds out such things about her lover ... which make it impossible for her ... ever to respect him" (H.R. Haweis 257). The number and variety of articles and contributors in the *Young Woman* suggests the topicality and the importance of encouraging girls to demand better information before making life-altering decisions.

Nonetheless, marriage remains an important imperative within the *Young Woman*. The act of choosing a husband is foregrounded in these discussions of marriage. In a series entitled "The Ideal Husband," for example, a masculine ideal is discussed and debated, and girls are given the responsibility for deciding whether their suitors meet that ideal. Moreover, this discussion also places women in the position of moral superiority. By employing the discourses of Christianity to establish their spiritual and moral superiority over men, women could demand that their prospective husbands be equally pure. Sue Morgan writes that

> [b]y drawing upon dominant Victorian ideologies of women as the spiritual and moral superiors of men, purity women reappropriated Christian categories of female virtue and pious motherhood forging a highly successful coalition between religious expectations of male self-restraint and feminist demands for the elimination of the sexual double standard. ("Wild Oats" 155)

Beginning in October 1894 and continuing for almost a year, the "ideal husband" is described by contributors to the *Young Woman*, all of whom were notable writers and journalists, including writer and activist Lady Jeune, Eliza Lynn Linton, novelist John Strange Winter, journalist, activist, and public lecturer Florence Fenwick Miller, and Isabella Fyvie Mayo.[13] Oscar Wilde may have been influenced by this discussion, since his play, "The Ideal Husband," was first performed in January 1895. Although Wilde mocks the possibility of the ideal, the contributors to the *Young Woman* suggest that a masculine ideal is not only possible but also important because it encourages men to adopt a higher standard of behaviour.[14]

In the discussion of "The Ideal Husband," the contributors—with the exception of Linton—reinforce equality and friendship between husband and wife. John Strange Winter, for example, suggests that the ideal husband will "choose a girl for her personal qualities before all else" and "will marry for love" (119). Having made a good choice, the ideal husband will "from the very first make his wife his friend, his chum, his other half. He will keep no secrets from her" (119). Lady Jeune perceives this equality somewhat differently. She argues that the arrival of the New Woman has resulted in the creation of the new man (and ideal husband). The new woman is determined to "share the man's life in every sense of the word" (23) and "men are not to be permitted greater liberty and indulgence than women" (23), yet Jeune wonders how a single moral standard can be achieved. Unlike the other contributors, who suggest that the ideal husband already exists, Jeune's ideal has not yet appeared. Instead, women must encourage the manifestation of this ideal, "not by preaching, abuse, or vituperation, but by making their own example … and by the subtle influence they possess" (23). Jeune emphasizes that women's moral and spiritual influence must be exerted to create the ideal marriage partner, highlighting the challenges encountered by the New Woman. The "ideal husband" who would treat his wife with honesty and equality may not yet exist, and the marrying girl must use her moral and spiritual influence to guide him towards virtuous behaviour equal to her own.

The series on the "Ideal Husband" demonstrates the difficulties of refining the feminine ideal to include sexual knowledge when the kind of knowledge and how it should be used remains contentious. Isabella Fyvie Mayo contradicts Lady

---

[13]   Susan Elizabeth Mary Constantine Stanley married Francis Henry Jeune and became Lady Jeune and afterward Lady St Helier. She was known for her service to the poor and for her critique of "London Society," which appeared in the *North American Review* in 1892. "John Strange Winter" was one of the pseudonyms of Henrietta Stannard, an author and journalist who wrote a number of novels featuring British soldiers. She also wrote children's fiction and serialized fiction. She was interested in women's rights, dress reform, and animal rights. Isabella Fyvie Mayo was a frequent contributor to the *Girl's Own Paper* and *Routledge's Every Girl's Annual*. She published novels under her own name and under the pseudonym "Edward Garrett."

[14]   The series was sufficiently popular that Atkins arranged to have the articles reprinted in a "charming booklet" ("Ideal Husband" 411) at 1s. each, with a first edition of 5000 copies.

Jeune, warning young women and young men to "choose the future partner of life for what he or she is, and not for what it is hoped that he or she may become under 'influence' or 'management'" ("Ideal Husband" 194). Not only is this strategy unlikely to be successful, secretly planning to remould one's partner is also unfair. Mayo is concerned that "the solemn responsibility of a woman's own choice in matters matrimonial actually seems more in danger of being forgotten in this epoch of the 'New Woman'" (194) than it was in the past. The modern young women of today, swayed by "flimsy romance" (195), wilfully close their eyes and ears to the evidence that would allow them to make better choices. Ultimately, men will not change, and a young woman should never consider marrying a man whose chastity is in doubt. Likewise, a young woman should not consider marrying a man who has such doubts about her. Instead, with a common standard of moral and sexual purity, husband and wife can both move forward with confidence in married life. Even Eliza Lynn Linton asserts the need for "equal rights" in marriage for men and women, albeit with "the necessity of one supreme head, one authoritative voice when grave occasion demands an absolute and final decision" ("Ideal Husband" 56). She does not explain how equal rights can be reconciled with this autocracy.

Each contributor brings a unique perspective about how marriage can be incorporated within the new feminine ideal being developed in the *Young Woman*. In contrast to Linton, Fenwick Miller asserts that the ideal marriage "is not a relation of master and subject; nor one in which a godlike being, with infallible judgments and overmastering moral superiorities, lives with a weaker brain and lower moral character, to which he dictates rules and actions" ("Ideal Husband" 163). She suggests equality is the proper basis for marriage and describes "a friendship in which the tastes and powers are sufficiently on a level for constant companionship in ease and comfort and yet in which each has certain points of superiority" (163). The strengths of each partner, combined with friendship, "the sex relation and the joint affection for the children" (163) will make for a happy and healthy relationship. However, the ideal husband "must be absolutely faithful to his marriage vow" (164). Likely a reference to the potentially devastating consequences of sexually transmitted diseases like syphilis, Fenwick Miller declares that "equal morality of husband and wife is essential to honourable wedlock and to married happiness" (164) because a dishonoured wedding vow breaks a marriage, which "can never be ideal afterwards" (164).

The role of the ideal wife—a key factor in the development of the ideal marriage—is mentioned only casually by one contributor. Annie Boyd Carpenter suggests that "an 'ideal husband' is not possible without also an ideal wife" (388).[15] The lack of discussion about the ideal wife is owing to the fact that men's sexual and moral purity was considerably more controversial and problematic than

---

[15]   Annie Boyd Carpenter (daughter of the publisher W.W. Gardner) was married to William Boyd Carpenter, the bishop of Ripon. She contributed an article on women's work within the Church of England to *Woman's Mission: A Series of Congress Papers on the Philanthropic Work of Women* (1893), edited by Baroness Burdett-Coutts. She was also the President of the Central Conference of Women Workers.

women's, especially for the readership of this magazine. The implicit assumption here, as elsewhere in girls' periodicals, is that girls and young women are virtuous and pure. A girl's role as the moral and spiritual center of the home remains unquestioned. The "problem" of marriage and marital relations resides with the husband. He has historically had the license to be sexually promiscuous, while girls have never had such opportunities. Josephine Butler comments that "[w]e never hear it carelessly or complacently asserted of a young woman that '*she* is only sowing her wild oats'" (8). Moreover, the most significant implication of identifying and describing the "ideal husband" is the underlying discussion about sexuality in a girl's periodical, an uncommon venue in the nineteenth century. Frank Mort explains that the first step for purists was "to speak out about sex. The aim was to confront the conspiracy of silence and shame which surrounded the subject and create a climate where immorality could be tackled seriously" (114). This discussion of the ideal husband, then, allows contributors to address the problem of male sexuality, the implications for young women, and the solution of a single sexual standard.

"On the Choice of a Husband"

The articulation and definition of the "ideal husband" is part of a wider strategy in the *Young Woman* to define a new relationship of equality between men and women, while continuing to reinforce a traditional feminine ideal of purity and marriage. At the same time, social purists were agitating for changes to the education and preparation of girls as they became adults. By challenging attitudes that claimed sexual immorality was "beyond the parameters of civilized discourse" (Morgan "Wild Oats" 159), the double sexual standard could be openly addressed and used as the basis of discussions about female choice and responsibility in marriage. Social purists and eugenic feminists endorsed the common belief regarding "the unhealthy tendency of men to promiscuity and vice, and the natural instinct of women to virtue" to emphasize "the importance of female choice of a reproductive partner, replacing male passion with rational female selection" (Richardson 49). In the *Young Woman*, this "natural instinct" of purity and virtue is integral to the feminine ideal that is employed to encourage girls to gain the knowledge necessary to choose the best partner.

The notion of an ideal husband provides the basis for an 1898 article, "On the Choice of a Husband." Author Sarah Grand insists that a girl be well informed about her husband and his character, part of her ongoing campaign that supported marriage but contested the sexual double standard of the era.[16] Grand was best known for the publication of *The Heavenly Twins*, which became a sensational bestseller and was the first of what came to be called "New Woman" novels that

---

[16] "Sarah Grand" is the pseudonym of Frances McFall (née Clarke). She published her first book, *Two Dear Little Feet*, in 1873. This was followed much later by *Ideala: A Study from Life* (1888), *The Heavenly Twins* (1893), and *The Beth Book* (1897).

dealt frankly with sexuality and contemporary issues of women's rights. As Janet Beer and Ann Heilmann explain, Grand felt that "to deny girls access to vital sexual knowledge amounted to criminal negligence, for, far from protecting girls from corrupting influences, it made them vulnerable to abuse by depriving them of the insight to make informed decisions" (186). Certainly Grand's contributions to both the *Young Woman* and the *Young Man* are significant because of her status as a New Woman novelist and a social purist.

In the same month that Grand's article appears in the *Young Woman*, she also contributed a corresponding article "On the Choice of a Wife" in the *Young Man*. Readers of the *Young Woman* were encouraged to read the other article for it is "as interesting to young women as it is to young men" (Atkins "Sarah Grand" 9). Atkins was evidently attempting to leverage Grand's celebrity status by having her contribute both articles in the same month. The provocative question of choosing a suitable husband or wife is designed to attract new readers and encourage casual readers to subscribe, while also sensationalizing the discussion of marriage and choice, a key characteristic of successful periodicals at the *fin de siècle*.

Although Grand is not as explicit about the potential hazards of an ill-informed decision as she is in *The Heavenly Twins*, her rhetoric remains striking. She argues that "such information as a girl has been able to obtain on the subject of marriage has for the most part been admirably calculated to mislead her" ("Husband" 1). A girl is often led to "her own destruction" (1) when she relies on this misinformation and her own feelings to guide her. A girl has "a right to demand of those in authority over her the knowledge requisite to enable her to choose a husband properly when the time comes" (1). A girl can become the "victim" of well-meaning relations who wish to see her married but who inadvertently cause her "destruction" (1). Grand asserts the imperfection of marriage and also declares that marriage is "no longer the only career" (3) available to a girl. Thus a girl "can take time to make her choice, and time to be sure of herself as well" (3). Unlike the Rev. Hardy, who employs Darwinian rhetoric to negate the girl's agency and limit her responsibility to the rejection of inappropriate suitors, Grand's girl seeks information, takes time to be sure of her choice, and acknowledges that she has options other than marriage. Sarah Grand's article is significant not only because of her standing as a major New Woman novelist and feminist, but also because of her message. The Ruskinian model of femininity employed elsewhere in the magazine becomes a site of interrogation when someone with Grand's cultural authority offers a different, and more contemporary, model. Importantly, however, Grand does not reject marriage as an acceptable choice for girls; instead she suggests that girls have the right and the duty to demand better information so they can make better choices.

In both articles, Grand laments the "stupid system of separating young people when they should be growing up together" ("Wife" 325) because young people need to know themselves and each other to develop a better understanding of relations between the sexes and choose the best spouse. Somewhat inconsistently, Grand declares that "the *girl* is beginning to be better educated on the subject than the *young man*; she has better advisers, and she has higher ideals" ("Wife" 325). In contrast, young men are the "chief sinners" within the marriage because they lack "ideals" (325) about the institution. For them, marriage is "but a superior kind of prostitution" (325) and they are "apt to regard the wife as a temporary pleasure, but a permanent encumbrance" (326). This rhetoric echoes the discussion of the *demi-monde* in Linton's attack on the "Girl of the Period," which I discussed in Chapter 3. Moreover, Grand's argument reinforces the idea that many contributors to the *Young Woman* found it unnecessary to reinforce the feminine ideal of purity and morality because it was integral to *fin-de-siècle* definitions of middle-class girlhood. Girls' adherence to this ideal is, in fact, a source of danger to them; without the knowledge and confidence to ask tough questions about the sexual history of their suitors, they risk endangering their own lives and those of their unborn children.

In contrast to the "classical" feminine ideal of the past, Grand's "modern girl" has the right to demand information and make her own choice about a husband. Untroubled by "rudimentary" emotions, the modern girl is more complex, advanced, and subtle, yet she is still "good" because she is pure, chaste, and moral. Thus, the young man who seeks a "good wife must begin by being worthy of one" (Grand "Wife" 327). If he can claim purity, chastity, and morality to the same degree as a young woman, then the young couple will be well suited. In "On the Choice of a Wife," Grand adroitly shifts her focus from the qualities of a wife to the qualities required of a young man if he wishes to obtain a good wife. A woman must be properly advised and willing to seek out information on a potential husband, but a man must have high ideals for himself and for the institution of marriage. Implicit in both articles is that women remain pure and morally superior. Somewhat paradoxically, knowledge of the seamier side of life will facilitate the selection of a proper husband and will allow women to maintain their superiority. The feminine ideal of the *Young Woman* incorporates moral and sexual purity with marriage, yet it differs from the ideal of the past by insisting that a husband be held to the same standards as the wife. This overtly reformulates the marrying girl because, for the first time, she has both the right and the responsibility to demand an equally virtuous partner.

Perhaps owing to Grand's articles, the November 1898 correspondence section reflects a similar concern with moral purity. Esler is "convinced that clear and forcible teaching on questions affecting that special section of virtuous living which we usually term morality is becoming more and more a need of the present day" ("Answers" 79). As novels and plays break "all barriers of reserve, ... lapses from virtue" are becoming "an everyday occurrence" (79). Grand's determination that young women and girls should be knowledgeable differs intriguingly from Esler's belief that exposure to this knowledge leads to moral laxity. Esler uses similar racial rhetoric to assert that women's virtue "is an instinct of the human race, far more pronounced among savages and nomads than among the dwellers in cities—surely a grievous indictment of the effects of what we call civilisation" (79). Feminine instinct to morality and virtue is corrupted by exposure to the city, to immoral literature and drama, and to morally lax men and women. Grand would certainly have disagreed with this position. Despite a strong endorsement of this refined feminine ideal, the magazine nonetheless reflects some inconsistencies in its approach to the marrying girl. Although girls are more moral and pure than their prospective suitors, they can be tainted by exposure to vice and moral laxity.

Although the focus on marriage is a dominant concern in the *Young Woman*, other possibilities are also present. Emma Liggins demonstrates persuasively that the magazine "is more accepting of the female bachelor" because "certain series and articles are addressed to readers who are single, working and potentially living outside the family home, and, what is more significant, not necessarily accepting marriage as their next life stage" (230). While this is indeed the case, I find the ideology reinforcing the institution of marriage to be even more pervasive, especially through the appearance of two articles, "On the Choice of a Wife" and "On the Choice of a Husband," by an author who is so closely identified with the New Woman movement. I attribute considerable significance to these articles *because* they are authored by Sarah Grand. The same articles by someone who was less well known in *fin-de-siècle* England would less notable. Moreover, while I have no way of knowing whether Grand approached Atkins with the idea for the articles or vice versa, the decision to include two Grand articles in the same month represents a strategic decision by Atkins to leverage both the topical material and Grand's notoriety to maximum effect. Most importantly, the inclusion of a Grand article in both the *Young Woman* and the *Young Man* reinforces the message of a single moral standard.

The magazine is also interested in determining the age at which girls could be expected to have the appropriate knowledge to make a suitable choice. A series beginning in February 1899 discusses the ideal age for a girl to marry. Grand considers it "a sign of progress" ("At What Age" 161) that the question should be asked at all, since it suggests a reconsideration of the role of marriage in a girl's life. Whereas the girl was formerly "an instrument to be used for the furtherance of ambitious schemes" (161) and her training was designed to keep her ignorant, "the whole tendency of the modern system of education for girls is to prolong their girlhood" (162). An extended girlhood allows the modern girl to become properly educated and to develop her own ideas about how her life will be directed because "she knows that a woman's life is no longer considered a failure simply because she does not marry" (163). Sally Mitchell notes that this "transitional period" in a girl's life "authorized a change in outlook" (3). Grand signals this change when she suggests that a girl be given time after exiting the schoolroom to decide whether to marry and, if so, to whom and when.

In response to Grand's article, some of the same contributors who discussed the ideal husband also present their opinions. According to Isabella Fyvie Mayo, for example, the education of a girl who is considering marriage must include financial management. Only then can a girl be "competent to judge for herself of the character and past history of the man she marries" ("At What Age" 164). Knowledge remains a critical component of the feminine ideal since it enables a girl to make the best choice for her future.

Maternity in the *Young Woman*

Alongside a focus on marriage and knowledge, the *Young Woman* also promoted the idea of motherhood. In Sarah Grand's final contribution to the *Young Woman* in 1899, she emphasizes the important and natural maternal role. In "Should Married Women Follow Professions?" Grand criticizes women who are not happy in their roles as wives and mothers and sees the need for a profession for married women only in cases where money is "sorely wanted" (258). A woman's home and children should be her most important responsibility, and a woman "is neglectful of her best interests who goes out to the world to work when she can get a nice man to do the work for her" (259). If she is fortunate enough to have children, "they must be her primary consideration" (257). While there are some "abnormal" (257) women who have no aptitude for motherhood, these women are the exception; thus maternity is presented as natural and normal. Nonetheless, although Grand considers these childless women "failures" (257), they should be entitled to try something else, such as law, literature, medicine, or art.

Grand defines marriage and motherhood as a woman's duty to her country. Sally Ledger explains that, in the context of British imperialism and questions of eugenics, "the repeated assertion that the New Woman rejected motherhood has a profound political significance at the *fin de siècle*: such a rejection was regarded by some not merely as a rebellious whim but as a threat to the English 'race'" (18). Within the *Young Woman*, however, maternity is natural and the most important work a woman can undertake. The stereotypical New Woman may have been against marriage and maternity, but the feminine ideal in the *Young Woman* reflected feminist and social purity concerns while supporting marriage and motherhood.

Although these articles discussing the best age to marry contain few references to maternity, Katharine Tynan and Annie Boyd Carpenter both refer to the responsibilities and rewards of motherhood.[17] Indeed, although the contributors did not often refer to the consequences of marriage (indicating that the discomfort in talking about sex had not been fully overcome), maternity is nonetheless an important subtext for these conversations. While the contributors acknowledge that not all young women will marry, marriage and motherhood remain imperative and desirable. Lyn Pykett explains that "[m]otherhood is represented not as a mere lapsing back into the traditional role of the womanly woman, but as a freely chosen and newly defined feminine role—that of the reinvigorator or saviour of the race by means of the woman's sexual selection of a non-degenerate male" (*Improper* 149). The traditional feminine ideal of maternity is reclaimed in the *Young Woman* to save the race by encouraging young women to select the best father for their future children.

---

[17]   Katharine Tynan, an Irish poet and novelist, was the major provider for her family, producing 94 novels and 27 poetry collections as well as a variety of anthologies, biographies, and histories.

Florence Fenwick Miller's "The Twentieth-Century Wife and Mother" is an example of this reclamation of the maternal role. Although she discusses alternative occupations for women elsewhere in the *Young Woman*, in this article she claims that "[n]o matter how many careers and occupations may be thrown open to women, there is little doubt that the average ordinary girl will always regard marriage and maternity as the profession most to be desired" (18). Marriage and motherhood are defined as a woman's "instinctive ... profession, her bread-winning business" (18). Moreover, domestic work within one's own home is more favourable to the constitution of women who might need to rest. As I demonstrated in Chapter 4, women's poor health was often interpreted as a reflection of a natural physiological weakness, and Fenwick Miller accounts for that weakness by reinforcing domestic ideology that situates women within the home. Although domestic work is more desirable, Fenwick Miller acknowledges that "the tendency of the twentieth-century wife and mother is towards working outside the home for a definite wage" (18). Wives and mothers should remain at home because this improves "family happiness" and "the mother's constant care is precious to the children" (19). The improved education helps girls to become better mothers because "the modern woman is applying her enlarged mind very anxiously to her maternal duties; there never was a time in which mothers more carefully sought to study the best means for child-nurture, mental and bodily" (20). Anxieties about the degeneration of the race inflect Fenwick Miller's rhetoric about motherhood, in which she balances the competing demands of family and employment by presenting family responsibilities as natural. She refocuses the feminine ideal to reflect contemporary ideas of national responsibility, racial improvement, and civic duty. This strong rhetoric about maternity is uncommon in other girls' periodicals, suggesting a slightly older intended readership for the *Young Woman*. Yet even in the *Young Woman*, this language is somewhat unusual since girls' periodicals tended to ignore the implications of marriage. In the context of the *Young Woman*'s feminine ideal, however, Grand and Fenwick Miller extend the notion of responsible choice to include its consequences for children and the nation.

The first 11 years of the *Young Woman*, from 1892 to 1903, are notable for their deft consideration of the shifting roles of girls and women in British society. Articles reinforcing traditional expectations of moral and spiritual purity are placed alongside articles encouraging girls to obtain proper information to make informed marriage choices. There is, nonetheless, a strongly modern bent to the magazine as it attempted to maintain its relevance to its contemporary readers, as the inclusion of articles by women's rights activists and New Woman novelists demonstrates. After 1903, however, there are no extant copies of the *Young Woman* until the magazine reappears in 1915 as the *Young Man and Woman*.[18] The newly merged

---

[18] Mitchell's *Newspaper Press Directory and Advertisers' Guide* confirms that the *Young Woman* was published between 1904 and 1915. In 1920, the title became *The British Man and Woman*, but this title lasted only six months, ending in June 1920.

magazine under the editorship of the Rev. Walter Wynn encourages young men and women to read the magazine, "whether you are married or single, whether you are engaged or otherwise" (1).[19] Owning that he feels the recent years of the *Young Man* "belonged to a past era," Wynn wants to create an "up-to-date magazine that will make good reading" (1) for both sexes. Wynn encourages "all the courting couples, and the young married couples" to buy the new journal and declares his belief that "marriage, the home, and the family idea of life" are the "three roots of a sound national tree" (2). The New Woman and social purity rhetoric of the *Young Woman* is preempted by articles like "The Mothers of Famous Men" and poems like Mary Hodgkinson's "Married Life," which support traditional feminine roles. Whether the intervening years of the *Young Woman* also saw a shift in the rhetoric of the feminine ideal is unknown, but in its first decade it was committed to a single moral standard and to improving education so girls could make intelligent decisions about their reproductive partners to improve the British "race." In the next chapter, I shall attempt to fill the gap left by the missing years of the *Young Woman* by turning to the distinctly modern *Girl's Realm* and exploring the social, economic, and political circumstances of girlhood in the first decade of the twentieth century.

---

[19]   The Rev. Walter Wynn was a confirmed spiritualist who wrote a number of religious and prophetic works, including *The Apostle Paul's Reply to Lord Halifax* (1899) and *The Secrets of Success in Life* (1914).

Chapter 7

The Modern Girl:
Heroic Adventures in
the *Girl's Realm* (1898–1915)

Beginning in 1898, the *Girl's Realm* was keenly interested in developing a readership that was both contemporary and modern. The changed circumstances of girls' lives combined with the availability of a wide variety of reading material meant that a new entrant into the field of girls' publishing had to be unique. Although the magazine's editors were determined to remain apolitical, they nonetheless used current events to create an ethos of bravery and heroism for its girl readers. The Boer War, the dawn of the twentieth century, the women's suffrage campaign, and the rise of adventure fiction for girls were some of the influences that appeared in the *Girl's Realm*. Unlike the other girls' periodicals I have discussed, the *Girl's Realm* is significantly less constrained by nineteenth-century ideas of femininity. Instead, the magazine uses current events to fashion girlhood as a time of bravery and courage. The girls in its pages are educated and feminine, yet the *Girl's Realm* focuses on girl heroes. Involved in adventures both at home and abroad, girls are capable and confident when they need to be. Alongside adventure stories set in the Colonies are equally thrilling stories of bravery closer to home, and non-fiction articles encourage girls to seek opportunities beyond the domestic sphere. The "girl's realm" of the title encompasses the feminine ideal, but also includes an equally important heroic ideal, signalling a shift in thinking about girls and their "realm" as they moved into areas that were traditionally considered male. Furthermore, "realm" suggests imperialism, as the magazine also claims the imperial realm for its girl readers. Importantly, however, owing in part to wider social and cultural shifts in English society alongside changes to the market for girls' periodicals, in its final years the magazine began to retreat from its heroic ideal and emphasized a return to domesticity.

Nonetheless, the magazine's policy of responding to major events in the public sphere was a key strategy in conveying the expanding girls' realm and its modernity. This responsiveness suggests that readers were interested in timely features and representations of femininity that resisted the mid-Victorian feminine ideal of duty, charity, and service. Between 1898 and 1915, when the magazine merged with *Woman at Home*, the circumstances of British life changed rapidly, thereby influencing the content and direction of the magazine. The Second Boer war, for example, inspired the girl's adventure story and supported the idea of girls as heroes, even if they were generally defending their families and their homes. This tradition was strengthened by the inclusion of stories by Bessie Marchant—a writer of adventure fiction for girls—between 1910 and 1912. These stories signalled an important shift in representations of girlhood to include heroism in both domestic and foreign realms. Local heroism was also encouraged through both nonfiction articles and fiction about girls' courageous acts. At the same time, the militant suffrage campaign of the first decade of the twentieth century was increasingly viewed with disdain in the pages of the *Girl's Realm*, despite acknowledging the legitimacy of the suffragettes' goals. The militant actions of the suffragettes transcended the appropriate bounds of femininity, yet the need to grant women suffrage was relatively unopposed. This chapter, then, will argue that the feminine ideal of the nineteenth century expanded prior to World War I to include bravery and heroism, provided this behaviour remained decorous. The ideal was substantially expanded, even as it remained constrained by marriage and duty.

Although some of the other magazines I have discussed, like the *Young Woman* and the *Girl's Own Paper*, continued well into the twentieth century, the *Girl's Realm* publication coincides closely with the Edwardian period. It provides a unique opportunity to examine the manifestation of the social and political contexts immediately prior to and during King Edward's reign in the pages of a girls' magazine. Prince Albert ascended the throne as King Edward VII after Victoria's death in 1901, and his reign was marked by increasing economic disparity between the rich and the poor, but also by an increasingly mobile population, brought about by the availability of motorized vehicles.[1] The Edwardian era is often said to extend to the advent of the First World War and is consequently marked by military conflicts at both ends since Edward inherited the Second Boer War, begun in 1899. The most significant political conflict of the period was undoubtedly the campaign for women's suffrage, which brought to a head the question of women's rights and responsibilities within Britain. Improved opportunities for education and employment led to more women living independently. This period was also the "high point of British emigration to the Empire" (Crow 70), which meant fewer women married, instead emigrating to the Colonies. Combined with the critical scrutiny of the institution of marriage instigated by the New Woman novelists of the 1890s, "The changing status of women in British society at the time constituted nothing less than a social revolution, and it served as a major energizing and complicating force in Edwardian fiction" (Miller 3). This "social revolution" helps to explain the unique heroines of the *Girl's Realm*. The *Girl's Realm* often veers from its officially apolitical stance to comment on the behaviour of women in the public arena, such as its support for women involved in the siege of Ladysmith or its condemnation of some radical suffragette activities.

Moreover, unlike the modest, domestically-inclined, feminine ideal of the *Girl's Own Paper*, heroic girls in exotic settings in the *Girl's Realm* are adaptations of the strength and bravery found in boys' adventure fiction that first appeared

---

[1]   See Paul Thompson's *The Edwardians: The Remaking of British Society* (1992) for a comprehensive assessment of the significant social changes marking the early twentieth century.

in mid-nineteenth-century novels by Frederick Marryat, W.H.G. Kingston, and later George Henty. The prevalence of girl heroes from the inception of the *Girl's Realm* is particularly striking. Moreover, these heroines are not always engaged in imperialist ventures. Equally as often, especially in the early years of the magazine, the girls have their adventures in Britain. Regardless of their location, these heroines signal the changing roles of girls at the dawn of the twentieth century.

The Modernity of the *Girl's Realm*

The *Girl's Realm* established itself as a thoroughly modern publication from its inception. A 2 November 1901 review of "Christmas Books" in the *Times* emphasizes the freshness of the *Girl's Realm*, describing it as "decidedly more lively" than the "unexceptionable" (16) *Girl's Own Paper*. One feature that the reviewer commends is the "number of stories by well-known writers" that are "mostly crisp and short, which in our opinion should be preferable to slow and lengthy serials" (16). *The Girl's Realm* is extensively illustrated—the first volume proclaims its "upwards of 1200 illustrations"—and contains short stories, some extended serialized fiction, and numerous informational articles about girl heroines and successful girls in the real world. For example, the regular feature, "What Girls Are Doing," chronicles girls' successes in the public sphere. Contributors include Rosa Carey, Evelyn Everett-Green, Charlotte Yonge, Rosa Campbell Praed, Katherine Tynan, L.T. Meade, Frances Hodgson Burnett, Agnes Giberne, and Evelyn Sharp. Priced at 6d., it is seemingly targeted at a middle-class readership. Diana Dixon argues that the *Girl's Realm* did not contain "material that would interest girls working in non-professional occupations. Indeed, [it] explicitly stated that it catered for the better-class women and described itself as a high-class monthly" (139). According to Drotner, however, the magazine was "not consciously excluding the working class" (121) as it attempted to interest both working-class and lower middle-class markets.

The reviews of the *Girl's Realm* suggest that the magazine was positioning itself as uniquely modern. On 17 November 1898, the *Daily News* declared that articles like editor Alice Corkran's "Chat with a Girl of the Period" testified to the "modern spirit" (6) of the new magazine. The *Belfast News-Letter* similarly announced that the *Girl's Realm* would be "an up-to-date high-class magazine, made bright, amusing, interesting, and instructive" ("Literary Gossip" 3). This notice from Belfast must surely have been based on advertising sent out by the publishers Hutchinson and Co., since the magazine's first issue did not appear until mid-October and this announcement appeared on 7 September 1898. Positioning the magazine as modern and "up-to-date" was consequently part of a unique marketing strategy. Unlike other girls' periodicals, which attempt to depict girlhood as an extension of a traditional feminine ideal, the *Girl's Realm* is less concerned with expanding the ideal. Instead, girlhood is seen as a modern experience distinct from ideals of the past.

The *Girl's Realm* was intended as a companion magazine to the *Lady's Realm*, which was also published by Hutchinson and Co.[2] In a *Daily News* advertisement, the publisher heralded its new girls' magazine as "The First of Its Kind," calling it a "high-class monthly" aimed at "young gentlewomen" (3) everywhere. This "magazine de luxe" would be read by 500,000 girls and it contained "everything of interest to girlhood" (3). At least some of the marketing was aimed at girls' mothers, suggesting that mothers still had a strong influence over their daughters' reading. Kate Flint points out in her comprehensive study of women readers between 1837 and 1914 that "[t]hroughout the period, it was widely assumed that a girl's mother was the best person to give advice" (83) on the choice of reading material. One such advertisement appeared in the *Daily News,* claiming "[e]very mother should see the new number of the most wonderful magazine for girls ever published" ("Every Mother" 6). The magazine hoped to attract girl readers by appealing to their mothers, displaying a somewhat curious contradiction between the magazine's avowed modernity and the attempt to attract its modern girl readers by directing advertising to their mothers. Although the girl reader is modern, she can still be located within the maternal sphere of influence and is guided by parental authority.

The title of the magazine encourages readers to consider the boundaries of girlhood and how girls' traditional domestic roles are expanding. The "girl's realm" evokes a space traditionally inhabited by middle-class girls: the domestic and the feminine. At the same time, the magazine creates a new realm for girls beyond the domestic sphere, redefining the "girl's realm" to include both the traditional realm of the past and the modern world. In the Honourable Cicely Henniker's poetic 1899 "Dedication to the Readers of 'The Girl's Realm,'" the realm for "maidens of this happy latter time" includes both Love and Art. Although the narrator of the poem encourages girl readers to embrace the "wider, sunnier clime" of the "kingdom" (l. 5) of the present, she also reminds them not to forget "that other realm you own—/A realm where woman's queen, and reigns alone" (l. 19–20). The feminine, spiritual realm is the kingdom of "Love" (l. 24), "whose blue skies/ Are heaven to man, through one sweet woman's eyes" (l. 21–2). The narrator reminds her readers of their responsibilities towards others and argues that the two "twin-kingdoms" (l. 25) must reign together in a girl's soul so that "soul, mind, spirit, all, shall blend" (l. 28). Only achievements in both realms can make a girl's life "a part/Of God's great perfect whole" (l. 26–7). Although the girl's realm can include achievements in art and literature, a girl must also remember her marital and maternal responsibilities.

As "A Dedication" suggests, the magazine offers balanced representations of girlhood to obtain and retain subscribers, yet it also signals from the first issue that the girls in the *Girl's Realm* are different from the girls of the past. In the inaugural "Chat with the Girl of the Period," editor Alice Corkran marks this shift by apologizing to her girl readers for giving them a name "that recalls an attack made by a woman of brilliant talents on the girls of more than a quarter-of-a-

---

2   Both magazines ceased publication in 1915.

century ago" (216).[3] Corkran opposes Linton's infamous position on "The Girl of the Period" (discussed in Chapter 3), arguing that there never was or will be a "girl of the period. Every period has its girls and you are the girls of yours" (216). She compares the ideal girl reader of the *Girl's Realm* to girls of the past: "The modern girl is weary of this ideal of ladyhood. She is a creature of the open air; she wants to be stirring. ... She glories in being a sportswoman, and in every form of physical culture. The result is, that she has not the appeal of feminine dependence in her deportment" (216). Not only is she physically capable (a necessary quality for all potential heroines), but she is "tired of living in a doll's house, and married or unmarried, she will never take a back seat" (216). This reference to a doll's house evokes Ibsen's 1879 play of the same name, in which Nora rejects the constraints of a domestic life.

In previous chapters, I have shown how girlhood is often constructed through nostalgic references to a feminine ideal of the past. At the end of the nineteenth century, the girl in the *Girl's Realm* throws off the constraints of the past, and demands an active, independent life. This girl insists that "she has as much right to a good education as have her brothers," and this education will assist her in becoming "as good a housekeeper, and better, for having her judgment and her taste cultivated" (Corkran "Chat" 216). She will also be "as good a wife, and better, for being her husband's comrade and chum" (216). As in the *Young Woman*, the girl in the *Girl's Realm* is her husband's equal, able to lead a professional life, while also upholding her role as a wife and mother. Girls brought up to think affirmatively and creatively about the future are "more essentially feminine" (216) than the girls of the past and they remain modest, courageous, truthful, and unselfish. Moreover, Corkran's "girl of the Period" is a "'fine fellow,' breezy, plucky, quick to enjoy, and ready to stand by her sex" (216). Corkran admires her girl readers and her reference to "sex loyalty" foreshadows the women's suffrage rhetoric of the next decade, where women of all classes joined together to agitate for votes for women on equal terms as men. Corkran writes that "[t]here is forming an *esprit de corps* among girls which delights me" (216) and that has been sadly lacking among girls of the past.

The magazine supports the modernity of the twentieth-century girl. The anxiety and tension that often accompanied shifts in the feminine ideal elsewhere in the girls' periodical press (such as the shift to include health in the *Girl's Own Paper* and education in *Atalanta*) are significantly muted in the *Girl's Realm*. Instead, the modern girl is portrayed enthusiastically. In the 1901 illustration, "Going Out to Meet the New Century" [Figure 7.1], for example, a young woman drives a

---

3   Corkran was a novelist, publishing her first novel *Bessie Lang* in 1876. She edited the children's magazine *Bairns' Annual* from 1885–1890. She wrote domestic fiction for girls such as *Margery Merton's Girlhood* (1888) and a variation on Carroll's *Alice's Adventures in Wonderland* called *Down the Snow Stairs; Or, From Good-Night to Good-Morning* (1887). She published occasional articles in others girls' magazines including *Atalanta* and *Every Girl's Annual*.

GOING OUT TO MEET THE NEW CENTURY.

From an original drawing by ALFRED PEARSE.

Fig. 7.1   Going Out to Meet the New Century, *Girl's Realm*, 1901

motorcar, while a man in the back seat apprehensively holds onto his hat. Finely dressed, the woman driver calmly looks forward to meeting "the new century." The image suggests that the twentieth century will be the woman's century and that she is ready for whatever may come. In addition, it reflects the magazine's repositioning of femininity by inverting traditional gender roles and placing the modern girl in a position of control. It also highlights the heroism of the modern girl in the pages of the *Girl's Realm* as she bravely faces the new experiences of the next century.

The courage with which the woman faces the twentieth century is emblematic of the bravery with which all girls in the *Girl's Realm* face their futures. Not content to be dependent, uneducated, or unemployed, the girl of the *Girl's Realm* is determined and courageous, a theme developed by Corkran in the first years of the magazine. In another "Chat with the Girl of the Period," she describes the purpose of the twentieth-century woman to be "essentially brave" (432), a sentiment that is emphasized in the readers' correspondence with the magazine. "Susie" writes, for example,

> I think I am a modern girl … I can't imagine anything more awful than being a girl of the time of Jane Austen's novels, who is always fainting or crying, and not able to do anything jolly. Yet I don't think I only want to have a 'good time.' … My great ambition is to do something really useful in my life and then let the good time come out of that. (432)

Susie rejects a feminine ideal that insists on helplessness. The modern girl is capable, active, useful, and superior to the weak, dependent girls of the past.

Unlike some magazines that attempted to gain readerships with girls *and* their mothers, the *Girl's Realm* is aimed at a modern, young audience and is unconcerned about the possibility of alienating previous generations of girls. Instead, the girls of the past are set aside in favour of the new girl of the new century, although the magazine does acknowledge that these "girls of the period" might be controversial. In Phil Eprutt's 1902 illustration, "A Shocked Ancestral Audience" [Figure 7.2], three girls play field hockey. One girl has either fallen or been knocked to the ground, a second stretches across her to reach the ball, and a third watches from behind. These hockey players are suitably dressed for their game: ankle-length skirts, blouses rolled up to the elbow, and sturdy shoes. In the background, a series of ghostly figures look upon the girls with horrified expressions. These figures are dressed in period dress and represent, among others, an Elizabethan woman, a medieval knight, and a Victorian man and woman. Ably assisted by the caption, the intent of the illustration is clear: men and women of the past would be horrified by the activities of modern girls, yet the shock of the ancients is represented comically. These girls, and presumably the readers of the *Girl's Realm*, are unconcerned with the response their actions generate. In presenting girls in a distinctly modern fashion, the magazine demonstrates its unique offering. Its portrayal of girlhood distinguishes it from other girls' magazines at the turn of the century. In contrast to the religious girl in the *Monthly Packet*, for example, the *Girl's Realm* is not hampered either by expectations

A SHOCKED ANCESTRAL AUDIENCE.

Fig. 7.2   A Shocked Ancestral Audience, *Girl's Realm*, 1902

of older readers or by a conservative religious ideal. Neither does the magazine reflect the tension of maintaining virtue and purity in the feminine ideal while also expanding it to include new dimensions like health in the *Girl's Own Paper* or education in *Atalanta*. Furthermore, these girls demonstrate their courage when they transcend traditional expectations of feminine behaviour and demand to be accepted on their own terms as twentieth-century girls.

Heroines in the *Girl's Realm*

Courage and modernity are explicitly linked in the *Girl's Realm* through the heroic activities of modern girls. Prior to the first issue of the magazine, a *Daily News* reporter writes that "[g]irl heroines, with and without Humane Society medals, will form a most interesting topic in the first or following numbers. Not the British girl only, but the foreigner also, is to be the theme" ("Art and Letters" 6). Girls can be heroes even if they do not receive official acknowledgement through awards or medals. In its advance advertising, the magazine sets readers' expectations for a different kind of girl than the girl of the past. Not only is the girl of the *Girl's Realm* heroic, but she is also interested in girls from the far reaches of the world. The magazine establishes a definition of girlhood that is international, cooperative, and inclusive.

Corkran herself chronicles the bravery exhibited by English girls in "Girl Heroines" in the first issue. She describes a Roll of Honour drawn up for the Victorian Era Exhibition, which lists several hundred women and young girls who, during Queen Victoria's reign, "rendered signal services" (65) to others. This 1897 Exhibition was part of the celebration of the Queen's reign marked by her Diamond Jubilee and included sections on fine arts, women's work, drama and music, science, economics, and commerce.[4] Tellingly, Corkran notes that each heroine whose name is listed "had received some medal or badge of honour" (65). Female heroism can result in public acknowledgement and will be recognized in the press through periodicals like the *Girl's Realm*. Corkran describes some of these girls' adventures—like Grace Darling, who "faced death" to rescue the survivors of a shipwreck—and laments the lack of space that limits her ability to recount "many more deeds of heroism done by girls … but enough has been said to show that in the girls of to-day, still burns the spirit that found its highest expression in the martyr and warrior soul of the Maid of Orleans, and of other noble and saintly virgins of long ago" (68).[5] Using Joan of Arc, an icon of courage,

---

[4]   The *Times* reviews the Exhibition as "a creditable and, to some extent, a successful attempt to present to the public some of the salient features of the work and amusements of the people during the last 60 years" ("Victorian Era Exhibition" 5).

[5]   With her father, Grace Darling rowed out to rescue the survivors of the shipwrecked *Forfarshire* in 1838. She is, as Hugh Cunningham notes, "defined purely by her heroism" (2). Cunningham's *Grace Darling: Victorian Heroine* (2007) examines the history of Darling's fame.

persistence, and martyrdom, as an example of heroism allows Corkran to encourage girls to be courageous outside their normal "realm" of the domestic, but she also extols heroism in the traditional domestic space.[6] Later that same year, novelist and journalist Maud Rawson proposes a series entitled "What Girls Are Doing," focusing on the intellectual, industrial, and social progress of girls.[7] Chronicling the achievements of girls everywhere, this feature is dedicated "[t]o every girl, then, who has shown special valour in the overcoming of technical difficulties and won distinction thereby, as well as to those who have endured risks for brave ends" (530). She encourages girls to also consider the heroic possibilities of their daily lives: "To be heroic it is not at all necessary to deal solely with issues of life and death. There is as much valour in the daily routine that leads to success at a high school, or a school of music or painting, as there is in facing a whole battery of artillery" (530). Corkran and her contributors position heroism as a possibility for all girls, regardless of their circumstances. Not only available to the physically courageous, heroism is possible in England and abroad.

Heroism is, moreover, a quality that can unite girls from around the world. An "international social sisterhood" is "at the basis of this journal" (Rawson 530), and Corkran encourages contributions from all her readers in an attempt to depict a girlhood unconstrained by national boundaries and part of a common experience, especially the shared experience of reading the *Girl's Realm*. At the end of the first volume, she announces special arrangements for "our readers in the Colonies" so that "all daughters of Greater Britain may take effective share in our competitions" ("Chat" 1272). Through the pages of the *Girl's Realm*, an ethos of heroism is formulated for all girl readers throughout the English-speaking world. This ethos is reinforced through articles that encourage British girls to think about their "sisters" in the Colonies, like "A Daughter of Greater Britain: The Australian Girl" by Australian-born Rosa Campbell Praed and "The Canadian Girl: Her Home and School Life, Her Sports, Occupations and Amusements" by Canadian journalist Jean Graham.[8] These articles tend to highlight the exotic nature of these "daughters" of Great Britain, yet they also encourage girl readers, wherever they may be, to see girlhood as a shared experience.

The reader of the *Girl's Realm* was not exclusively British born and bred. Many girl readers lived throughout the British Empire and may have had little

---

6   George Bernard Shaw uses Joan of Arc in his 1923 play, *Saint Joan*, to engage with questions raised by the New Woman.

7   Rawson also contributed articles like "Women Under Victoria" and "Where To Go and What To See" to *Hearth and Home*. Her first novel was *A Lady of the Regency* (1900), and it was followed in quick succession by almost a novel a year until 1917.

8   Praed was born and married in Australia before moving with her husband to England. Her first novel, *An Australian Heroine*, was published in 1880 and she published almost 50 books during her lifetime. Her literary reputation was based largely on her Australian novels, including *Policy and Passion* (1881), *The Head Station* (1885), and *Outlaw and Lawmaker* (1893). Jean Graham was the women's editor of *Saturday Night* and later became the editor of *Canadian Home Journal*.

direct contact with the British feminine ideal, except through their reading. In one of her "Chats," Corkran refers to readers "from Johannesburg, from Melbourne, and other districts of Australia, from Canada, from New Orleans, from Jamaica" (1272). In an article commemorating Corkran, her biographer Blanche Warre-Cornish describes how Corkran "felt the pulse of girlhood, not only in England, but wherever English is read in our Empire" (851). The appropriateness and effectiveness of imperialism thus underpins much of the magazine. Girls were an integral part of the British Empire at the turn of the century, an idea (and an ideal) that became even clearer with the appearance of girls' adventure fiction in the later years of the magazine.

The culture of female heroism is apparent in the early numbers of the magazine, which include stories extolling female courage in the face of immense odds. For instance, in "Frank Aubrey's" 1899 short story, "Saved by a Cat: A True Story of Adventure," a girl prepares to sacrifice herself to a venomous snake in order to save a young child she is tending, only to be saved by a brave cat.[9] A series by Evelyn Everett-Green, "True Stories of Girl Heroines" (1898–1901), traces brave women through history, including Catherine the Rose, Inez Arroya, and Elsje Van Houwening.[10] These girl heroines come from all nations and all walks of life, and the stories insist that women are capable of acting heroically. These young women are remarkable for their strength and courage in the face of danger, yet they clearly understand the possible consequences. In the story about Catherine the Rose, for example, Everett-Green writes that: "These girls were not undertaking the task in ignorance of its perils. They had seen enough of wounds and death. They knew what they were facing" (490). Catherine encourages other women to help build the fort's defenses because "I am not a weak woman ... I am a strong woman, and so are you" (488). Moreover, women do not wish to be congratulated for defending their homes like men: "You must not praise me; why should not women do their duty to the cause of freedom as well as men?" (491). The results of an 1899 survey of readers' favourite features demonstrate that these stories were appreciated and enjoyed by the readers of the *Girl's Realm*. "True Stories of Girl Heroines" ranked first among the 16 to 21 age group and second among the under-16 age group ("Result" 293), highlighting the popularity of this material among its readers.

These true stories are supplemented by the focus on fictional girl heroes. Bravery and modernity are intertwined in Hannah Lynch's short story, "A Girl's

---

[9]   "Frank Aubrey" was the pseudonym of Francis Henry Atkins. He published juvenile science fiction like *The Deviltree of El Dorado: A Romance of British Guiana* (1896) and *A Queen of Atlantis: A Romance of the Caribbean Sea* (1899) in the vein of Jules Verne.

[10]   Everett-Green wrote almost 350 novels, initially for children and particularly boys, but later for slightly older girls. Among these novels are about 50 historical tales. The fictionalized tales she included in the *Girl's Realm* all focus on the true stories of strong heroic girls. Catherine the Rose, for example, was instrumental in defending a fort during the Dutch War of Independence (1568–1648). Elsje Van Houwening, a maid, helped her master Hugo Grotius escape imprisonment for defending free will in Calvinist Holland. These stories were published in a single volume in 1901.

Ride on an Engine."[11] Appearing in 1900, the story chronicles 16-year-old Ella Morgan's frantic trip to Jersey to say farewell to her dying mother. The story is framed by a domestic setting. We are first introduced to Ella as she spends a month with her wealthy grandmother in Sussex; this visit to England is the basis of "very big hopes" (465) of a family reconciliation. The story concludes with Ella's return to Jersey "in time to bid her mother a last farewell" (469). In between these domestic scenes, however, Ella travels without her grandmother's knowledge or approval and makes unusual arrangements to travel on a train engine when she misses the scheduled train.

By riding on the engine, Ella engages with the modernity of industrial life in a thoroughly new way. In Nicholas Daly's analysis of technology and modernity, he describes how industrial modernity "is predicated on the intellectual separation of people and machines," and how modernity "obsessively replays the meeting of the two" (2). The railway is "both an agent and icon of modernization" (Daly 20) and was "assumed to have the capacity to produce modern, nervous, and accelerated bodies" (Daly 7). Ella's lack of experience with many modern technologies is highlighted by her unfamiliarity with a telegram, yet she bravely travels through the night and encounters a mode of transport that is both unfamiliar and overwhelming. The engine is a "red-eyed monster" that "plunged ... into the darkness" and "raced with an incredible rush" to inspire the "idea of untameable velocity" (467). Ella is overwhelmed by the experience:

> the appalling roar of steam shook her entire system with brutal, elemental force. She ceased to be a thinking creature, and became merely a bag of nerves in that thunder of unfamiliar sound. Sensation and sight were so acutely merged into one, and indivisible, that she could make no distinction between what she was seeing and what she was feeling. (467)

Sight and sensation are indecipherable in this encounter with modern transportation, and Ella cannot retain her reason and rationality. Instead, she is "dazzled" (468) by the hellish experience. The engine's furnace has a "terrific, mesmeric power" which gives her "the vertigo of the abyss, and seemed to draw her with the haunting and deadly eloquence of peril" (468). She loses her own identity when the landscape through which she travels, "like her own personality, had crumbled out of existence upon waves of horrid smoke" (468). She has traveled through both time and space on her journey, and the two dimensions have become confused: Ella "would have been puzzled to say if she had been a century or a minute on the wings of steam" (468).

Although Ella has travelled by train before, her unique experience of riding the engine highlights her modernity, since she is not safely contained within one of the

---

[11]   Hannah Lynch, a novelist and journalist, was born in Dublin but spent much of her life in France. Her first novel, *Through Troubled Waters*, was published in 1885, and she contributed frequently to the periodical press, writing for *Macmillan's Magazine*, *Fortnightly Review*, *Blackwood's Magazine*, and *The Academy*.

travelling carriages. This journey is only possible with the assistance of working-class men who go out of their way to help her, and without whom the trip would have been impossible. The stationmaster comments that young ladies have "taken to the bicycle, but they've wisely left us the engine" (467), emphasizing Ella's unusual journey. She has entered a male domain and this exposure to masculine spaces frightens Ella but, as she reminds the stationmaster, she is strong and brave. Moreover, Ella's actions are justified because she is fulfilling her duty to her mother. She only succumbs to the experience once she is on the ferry to Jersey and her engine ride is over.

On another level, this engine journey is a carefully coded sexual experience that is unusual in the fiction appearing in girls' magazines. Daly notes that "[t]he jolts of the railway were also thought to produce a specifically sexual response" (43). This story can be read to represent Ella's loss of virginity, where the darkness of the night enables her experience of the masculine because the train "appeared to threaten not just to shake up the individual body, but to erode the social barriers between the sexes in a way that was both tantalizing and frightening" (Daly 44). Ella waits for the engine to leave the station, "every nerve of her body was thrilling to be off" (467), and her loss of self during the journey, as well as the confusion of time and space, suggests the engine ride is orgasmic. It liberates her from the social constraints of femininity. When the lights of the Southampton station appear and the engine slows down, it belches forth "a volley of steam that spluttered downward, and drenched Ella's head and arms in warm moisture" (468). This journey is thus a loss of innocence, but the experience Ella gains is positive because without her bravery and strength she would not have arrived in time to say a final farewell to her mother. Modernity and sexuality are linked to enable a young woman to achieve her goals, but Ella's aim to be reunited with her mother is significant. Her sexual experience is framed on both ends by the domestic, yet this story nonetheless demonstrates the power of the modern to potentially liberate young women from nineteenth-century feminine ideals about sexuality. Modernity offers possibilities of freedom that nineteenth-century girls had not encountered.

War in the Girl's Realm

The strong theme of heroism in the *Girl's Realm* is reinforced through discussions of the conflict in South Africa. Unlike the *Girl's Own Paper* or the *Young Woman*, two magazines in which there was little acknowledgement of the Second Boer War, the *Girl's Realm* incorporates some realities of the conflict into its discussion of heroism. Women are important contributors to the war effort, although their heroism tends to function realistically within domestic or care-giving roles. The magazine's portrayal of this war is particularly relevant because of how it is presented elsewhere in the periodical press, where a debate soon emerged about Britain's roles and responsibilities as a colonial power. In the pages of the *Girl's Realm*, the war effort was mobilized to incorporate girlhood within a culture of bravery, sacrifice, and duty.

The Second Boer War was fought between the British Empire and the Boer republics of the Orange Free State and the Transvaal. The smaller Boer force was substantially outnumbered and the British assumed that the war would be over quickly. However, John Peck notes that "technically and strategically it was a new kind of war, moving beyond the era of the cavalry charge" (166). Daly likewise calls it "Britain's first experience of industrialized warfare" (8). New weapons were accurate over long distances, and the Boer guerrilla tactics meant that they were often invisible to the British forces; these new strategies and technologies meant that the experience of the war was significantly different from military campaigns of the past. Steve Attridge writes that "the Boer War was a pendulum that swung not only between centuries, but between national assurance and introspection, between Victorian certainties and the doubts and vicissitudes of modernity, between a national character that knew exactly who it was and one which was confused" (1). A peace agreement was signed on 31 May 1902, creating a federated British South Africa in which British and Boer shared power over non-whites. The difficulty of achieving a victory provoked a serious inquiry into the state of the British military and its preparedness for war:

> The Boers never had more than 40000 men in the field. The British numbered 450000 at the height of the war; 7792 British were killed in action and 13250 from disease. The Boers lost 6000 men, while 26370 women and children died in concentration camps. The official figure of 14154 blacks dying in camps is now known to be wrong. It was over 20000. (Attridge 3)

Most controversial during the British military campaign was the incarceration of Boer women and children in concentration camps, which provoked bipartisan disapproval in the British press and raised questions about women's roles in wartime.[12]

The periodical press played an important role in the public perception of the Boer War. This war had an "unprecedented visual presence" (Daly 62) in Britain, in part because the development of new technologies, like film and the user-

---

[12]   The British commanders felt that if Boer women were left on their farms, they would provide food and other assistance to the Boer guerrilla fighters. They developed a policy of burning farms and corralling women and children in concentration camps, but found themselves ill-equipped to handle the logistical problems on the African front of housing and feeding enormous numbers of people and the ideological problems on the home front of incarcerating white women and children. Although a first-hand report by Emily Hobhouse on the conditions in the camps, first published in the *Manchester Guardian*, helped change the terms of the debate from political to bipartisan, the resulting discussion in the press made it clear that "[w]hite womanhood ... was not as strong a signifier as *English* womanhood" (Krebs 65). While the incarceration of white Boer women was increasingly criticized, especially because of the logistical difficulties that resulted in extremely poor living conditions, the outrage in the British press was not as extreme as it would have been if the women had been English. The construction of femininity in England was more clearly connected to nationality than to race.

friendly Kodak camera, allowed for more images to be captured with greater rapidity than ever before. The war was thus accompanied by "a mountain of print and pictures such as the world had never seen" (Attridge 3), making it one of the "first modern media wars" (Daly 62). The siege of Ladysmith received particular attention in the *Girl's Realm*. As the main British military supply base in Natal, Ladysmith was a key military target besieged by Boer forces for 118 days from 2 November 1899 to 28 February 1900, thereby subjecting the men, women, and children of the town to wartime privations. The *Girl's Realm* used examples of Ladysmith's heroic women to guide girls towards an ideal of girlhood that supported the war effort and encouraged them to be brave, either at home in England or abroad.

In one of Corkran's monthly "Chats" in 1900, for instance, she uses the example of the Boer War to persuade the girl reader "that the best service to be rendered to her country, and to her kind, [is] to go on being a girl; that girls have quite as distinct a *role*, and are quite as useful in this life, as are men" (455). Although some people may feel that girls are "useless" in this time of war, British girls are also fighting by their example, by their pluck, and "by helping to bring up the children rightly" (455). Not only can girls "fight" on the domestic front, but the experience also has the potential to be transformative, for "the war will have made a woman of many a girl" (455). The domestic battleground thus becomes a space for gaining maturity and experience, and allowing girls to demonstrate their bravery to their military fathers. The besieged populations of Ladysmith, Kimberley, and Mafeking include girls who are "bravely playing their part" (455). Moreover, "in spite of the want of all the thousand-and-one amenities of life that are dear especially to womankind, these brave girls keep up a good heart" (455). Girls who can remain cheerful in the face of terrors and privations "deserve to be called heroines" (455). This aspirational model encourages girls to believe that their contributions during wartime are vital. Girlhood in the *Girl's Realm* is being redefined to acknowledge the realities and sacrifices of war and to encourage girls to be brave. Yet while encouraging heroism in girls, the magazine remains both cautious and conservative in its depictions of these heroic aspects of girlhood. Although its references to the Boer War are unusual in girls' periodicals, the *Girl's Realm* carefully frames heroic behaviour within the realistic boundaries of femininity. Despite its modern outlook, it presents an image of girlhood consistent with contemporary expectations.

Nonetheless, the *Girl's Realm* defines the bravery of modern girls as noteworthy. Writing a history of girls is particularly important because these stories are often excluded from "official" histories. In another 1900 "Chat," Corkran declares that girls can be useful in times of war:

> Girls are no use in times of national distress, you said, but I knew it was otherwise. I knew that they had a part to play, and that when the history of this war comes to be written, it will be found that the girls in the beleaguered cities and at home had acted not only with calm and with courage, but that they had helped to nurse the sick and to uphold the spirits of those around them. (833)

Corkran self-reflexively refers to the writing of "the history of this war," since she herself is producing this history through the inclusion of multiple articles about the women and girls involved in the conflict. For example, journalist Harry Steele Morrison's tribute to "The Conduct of Girls in the War" is based on testimony from Lady Randolph Churchill, who worked on the hospital ship "Maine," and General Sir George White, commander during the siege of Ladysmith. White wonders "whether our people at home were hearing of the great services of girls, and I believe now that they have not known of them" (Morrison 804). White's contribution to this article, then, is his attempt to bring girls' war activities to the attention of the general public. He writes that "I do not know of any startling feats of heroism such as have sometimes happened in the past, but I do know of many patriotic girls in Ladysmith who were very brave and did all in their power to make our men comfortable while we were shut in" (Morrison 804). The mundane activities of caring for children and keeping up spirits indicate that "the women were as brave as the men" (Morrison 804). White even equates the bravery of girls' nursing and care giving with the fighting men of the front: "They have been real heroines, just as brave as the men who have fought in battle" (Morrison 805).

Like Corkran, White suggests that girls can be heroic in whatever situations they encounter. Lady Randolph Churchill is similarly enthusiastic about girls' wartime activities because "[t]hey do indeed deserve a very great deal of credit" (Morrison 805). Churchill's time spent aboard the hospital ship "Maine" means she is less aware of girls' activities at the front, but she instead speaks of the work "our British girls" have done at home, through the "substantial contributions towards the expenses of the 'Maine' from girls' schools, and … the many letters of interest and sympathy which have been sent me by girls from all over the kingdom" (Morrison 805). The opportunities for girls to demonstrate their bravery and their support for the war are manifold. A girl anywhere in the Empire can support the troops in Africa financially or through sympathetic correspondence, and all contributions are appreciated. The girl of the *Girl's Realm* is heroic, yet her contributions remain distinctly feminine.

The fictional stories about the war appearing in the *Girl's Realm* likewise encourage girls to develop the feminine qualities of patience and encouragement. Unlike Joan of Arc, who actively fights for her cause, in Lady Troubridge's "None But the Brave," Peggy inspires her soldier friend Jock to great acts of bravery.[13] She accuses him of cowardice and only after she reads in the *Daily Telegraph* of his "plucky" action to ride through the Boer lines, "simply to rejoin his regiment" (797), does Peggy realize her "great mistake" (797) of questioning the courage of a British soldier. When Jock returns home, wounded but safe, Peggy is properly apologetic and ashamed. Jock forgives her and claims that her harsh words "helped" (799) him. Their eventual marriage is a foregone conclusion, yet this

---

[13]   Novelist Lady Laura Troubridge published her first novel, *Paul's Stepmother, and One Other Story* in 1897. Her second novel, *The Woman Thou Gavest*, appeared in 1906 and was followed by almost annual publications until the late 1930s.

happy ending is possible only because Peggy is able to recognize Jock's heroism and beg forgiveness for doubting him. A girl's faith and love can inspire average soldiers to great acts of bravery, and a girl who doubts must be proven wrong, because the British Army does not include cowards. Likewise, there can be no happy ending for a girl who fails to recognize the valour and honour of England's soldiers. Wartime is carefully positioned in the *Girl's Realm* to reflect two somewhat contradictory positions where girls are encouraged to be brave through articles that describe heroic adventures while also being reminded that courage can involve the patience of waiting while their lovers go off to war.

In Agnes Giberne's 1900 "For England's Sake," the ultimate sacrifice for a girl is the loss of a loved one.[14] Maud falls in love with Lennox, a soldier, but worries that he will not return from North India. He assures her that "[n]othing can keep me from you, my darling. Except duty" (848) and death. When Maud quails at his dangerous job, Lennox tells her she must be brave: "You are going to marry a soldier, and that is part of a soldier's life. If danger or hurt should come, I know your first thought will be that it is for England's sake" (848). Female bravery is reinforced through Lennox's reminder that Maud's womanly duty is to support him and England. Lennox expects no less of Maud than he would expect of his fellow soldiers, and he has no doubt about her courage. When she finds Lennox's name on the War Office death lists, "Maud did not cry or faint. Though so slight-looking, she was of tough fibre" and later tells her mother that "it was for England's sake!" (850). She understands the sacrifice Lennox made for his country, and bravely withstands her own personal loss. Although this story is set in India, the timing of its appearance suggests that it should be read as a message about the Boer conflict, especially in light of the high casualty rates. It may also be intended to evoke the British sacrifices in 1857. The ideal of girlhood in the pages of the magazine, then, positions active bravery alongside a feminine ideal of patience and support.

Despite the magazine's explicit support of wartime bravery, Corkran is clearly happy to mark its end in 1902. In a "Chat" published just after the peace agreement was signed, she rejoices that there will be:

> No more hacking and wounding, no more fear to open the paper in the morning, no more trembling of heart as we look down the columns, sick with fear, lest we should detect some loved name among those of the sufferers; and if we do not, to know that there is no name set down the sight of which does not bring sorrow to some household, some heart-break to wife or mother, daughter or sister. (851)

Even as Corkran acknowledges the fear and sorrow associated with the war, she also supports the imperialist cause, remarking that "more children are added to the great family of which our country is the mother" (851). Now that the war

---

[14]   Giberne published many of her earlier publications under her initials A.G. but with *The Curate's Home* (1869) she began publishing under her own name. She contributed serialized fiction to the *Girl's Own Paper* and *Atalanta* and articles on astronomy and geology to the *Monthly Packet*.

is over, Boer and British become a united family under the maternal guidance of England. However, Corkran reminds her girl readers of the responsibilities associated with this new governance because "England has a solemn duty to perform and … England's daughters must be ready to help her to perform it" (851). As girls of England and daughters of the Empire, they must assume their responsibilities over these new members of the Empire while holding firm to their feminine qualities of "charity and patience" (851). As we will see, this tension between courage and femininity also appears in other areas of the *Girl's Realm*. In discussions of women's suffrage, for instance, the vote is presented as appropriate and necessary, yet women's behaviour as they seek this right of citizenship is the subject of inquiry and anxiety.

Votes for Women

In the increasingly militant campaign for women's suffrage of the 1900s and early 1910s, women moved beyond an essentially passive form of feminine bravery into active engagement with politics and public demonstration. The *Girl's Realm* is generally supportive of the agitation for women's rights through its fiction and informational articles, but it nonetheless viewed the unfeminine behaviour of the more strident activists with some discomfort.[15] Various suffrage societies were united in 1897 with the formation of the National Union of Women's Suffrage Societies (NUWSS), whose aim was to improve social conditions for women through constitutional means. Frustrated by the NUWSS' lack of progress, a group of women led by Emmeline Pankhurst left in 1903 to form the Women's Social and Political Union (WSPU). The WSPU energized the women's suffrage campaign as it embarked on a militant campaign to attract publicity and transform the political system of male privilege. Questioning, heckling, and outright disruption were all tactics pursued by the WSPU at political meetings.[16] This campaign continued

---

[15] Most histories of the women's suffrage campaign in England begin in 1867 with the presentation to Parliament of a petition signed by 1,499 women asking for the vote. Josephine Butler's campaign against the Contagious Diseases Acts is also seen as a formative moment in defining women's political rights. Efforts continued until the end of the century in the form of additional bills introduced in Parliament and petitions signed by thousands. The granting of women's suffrage in New Zealand in 1893 and in South Australia in 1894 was inspiring, but at the beginning of the twentieth century the cause in Britain, as in America, was languishing (Crow 80).

[16] In 1905, Christabel Pankhurst and Annie Kenney were arrested at a public political meeting for demanding the introduction of legislation that would enfranchise women on equal terms with men. As Jon Lawrence notes in an insightful analysis of the WSPU, the women's rebellion lay

in their determination to force a 'women's issue' into the arena of (male) party politics, in their refusal to relent when [Liberal politician Sir Edward] Grey declined to answer, and, of course, in being women 'who dared to intrude … into a man's meeting.' Intrude, that is, not by their presence, which as we have seen was

despite the fact that the women who disrupted these kinds of public meetings "were frequently subjected to considerable violence both by party stewards and by members of the audience" (Lawrence 212). The violence was often overtly sexual, highlighting the threatening nature of this "unwomanly" behaviour.[17]

The readers of the *Girl's Realm* demanded a forum to discuss and debate the public activities of suffragettes despite Corkran's attempts to keep the magazine apolitical.[18] In a "Chat" in 1904, for example, Corkran acknowledges "Margaret's" dismay at a *North American Review* article by a woman rejecting female suffrage, but writes that "I am not concerned with woman's claims for the suffrage, because *The Girl's Realm* is not a political publication" (692).[19] In 1908, however, Corkran cedes to the desires of her readers, who have sent so many letters on "the great, the burning, question of the franchise for women that I must depart from my general rule of ignoring political questions, and answer some" (525). Instead of treating the political aspects of the question, however, Corkran argues that of greater importance "than the consideration of its justice or injustice is the consideration of the spirit in which we conduct our enquiry" (525). How a woman conducts herself is more relevant than whether she deserves the vote. The alignment of changes to the feminine ideal with decorum and modesty is a common concern in the girls' periodicals in this study. In the *Girl's Own Paper*, for example, the great

---

unremarkable, but by their insistence on being treated as full participants in the theatre of public politics. (208)

In addition to the disruption of public meetings, the WSPU demanded meetings with the Prime Minister and became increasingly violent and troublesome as they destroyed property. As the campaign continued, women under arrest resorted to hunger strikes to make their demands known and were then subject to forced feeding. By the time the militant campaign ceased with the advent of World War I, over 1000 women had been arrested and the leaders of the WSPU were either in jail or in exile. The WSPU and the NUWSS agreed to halt all campaigns so they could redirect their efforts to supporting the war and, in 1918, the NUWSS brokered an agreement where women over 30 who were householders or the wives of householders were enfranchised. Although this gave 6 million out of a possible 11 million adult women the right to vote, it was still seen by some as an abandonment of its "long-held principle of sex equality" (Kent 221) where votes were granted for women on the same basis as they were, or should be, granted to men. It was only in 1928 that women were granted voting rights on equal terms.

[17] In many ways, the militant activities of the suffragettes can be seen to have complicated an enfranchisement campaign that "had long been seen as a means of changing wider social and political culture—hence the early links between suffragists and the 'social purity' movement, and the widespread determination, among 'militants' and 'constitutionalists' alike, to end double standards in sexual morality" (Lawrence 223).

[18] Although S.H. Leeder, an historian, took over as editor in 1903, Alice Corkran continued to write the monthly "My Chat with the Girl of the Period" until she finally ceased her connection with the magazine in 1911, likely owing to poor health.

[19] "Woman's Assumption of Sex Superiority" by Annie Nathan Meyer appeared in January 1904 in *North American Review*. Meyer declares, "I fail to see in women any evidence of the character that is needed in our public life" (107) and argues that women do not deserve the vote.

strides in girls' health were met with acceptance but also concerns that girls might become less feminine. The same fears are implicit in Corkran's description of the suffrage campaign. She worries that militant campaigners are (or are perceived to be) increasingly unfeminine because of their indecorous behaviour.

In fact, Corkran almost suggests that a woman's right to enfranchisement is a given. Many of her correspondents raise the question of whether "Is it right or wrong to keep women from the vote—to stop their voices being heard on the great national questions?" (525). Corkran replies that they "have a right to ask this" and only wonders whether they have the right "to ask it in a rowdy manner even if this rowdiness contributes to give publicity to your demands" (525). Corkran disapproves of the militant suffragette campaign because "[t]he dignity of woman is at stake in the manner in which this battle for the franchise is conducted, and everything seems to me secondary to this" (525). She observes of the campaign: "Their object is to increase the dignity of women by securing for them the right of speech in the government of the country, yet are they not imperilling that dignity by showing lack of self-control and gentleness?" (525). Corkran highlights the challenges of conducting a campaign in which the behaviour of the female agitators is perceived to be unfeminine.

Three correspondents' responses in April 1908 demonstrate the range of positions occupied by readers of the *Girl's Realm*. "Nellie" is pro-suffrage by whatever means are necessary. She writes that "[t]he suffragettes, if they did nothing else, have drawn attention, and they deserve the respect and consideration of all women and the great gratitude of many of them" (525). In contrast, "Hilda" is opposed to women having the vote because "I am sure man was intended to do the business of life. I often feel quite unhappy at the noise women are making. There seem to be so few earnest, quiet women" (525). "Georgina" presents a third perspective, one with which Corkran is most sympathetic:

> Women ought to have suffrage. I do not understand how there can be a doubt about it. Those that are fitted for it by their fortunes, by their education, by their great care for humanity, why should they not have the means of expressing their opinion upon the questions affecting the nation? But I think their appeal to the consciences of men ought to be enough. They ought to hold meetings and expose their views, appealing to women for support, but they ought not to join in the noisy outcry that is now going on. (525)

While Corkran supports women's suffrage, she does so only through "Georgina's" perspective, which adopts a traditionally feminine position by appealing to men to do the right thing. As with the discussions of bravery in wartime, the most appropriate behaviour for modern girls is to support men in their efforts. This perspective reflects the broader position of the *Girl's Realm* to encourage both heroism and modernity, but only insofar as these qualities can be incorporated within a feminine ideal of modesty and decorum.

Perhaps because of the vehemence of the debate, Corkran leaves the issue of suffrage to each girl's conscience. She explains that

I have dwelt upon this question of the franchise because it is one that occupies much of your thought, and it is difficult to ignore it. I believe the time is coming when all women will have to take a decision, and I should wish you, my dear girls, to be prepared to declare yourselves one way or the other. Only I do hope that, above all things you will consider the necessity of keeping up the womanly ideal of dignity and gentleness. Men should feel, at any rate, whatever they may think of your claims, that you are waging the war in a manner that is worthy of the cause you have at heart. (525–6)

She envisions a time when girls will have to take a stand on suffrage and hopes to encourage them to behave in ways that are more womanly than the current militant campaign. In effect, Corkran endorses the nonmilitant NUWSS suffragists, although she is careful to refer to them in general terms. Nonetheless, she supports women's suffrage and can see no reason why women should not have a say in the great national debates of the day. Girls in the *Girl's Realm* are encouraged to inform themselves about the issues so that they can make decisions for themselves about their voting rights, yet Corkran guides them towards a political group whose stance regarding militant activities most closely represents her own.

In the following month, Corkran includes a letter from "Utopia," who writes in response to the April letters and declares that the WSPU suffragettes have finally "roused the country from a state of quiet to one of burning zeal" (685). "Utopia" compares the reception of John Stuart Mill's introduction of a Franchise Bill amendment in 1867 to the recent 1903 introduction of a private member's Women's Franchise Bill and finds that the speeches on the earlier Bill "were much more just and sympathetic towards the movement than those of last year" (685). She feels that politicians are impatient and intolerant of the suffrage campaign. Forty years of activism and attempted reform have resulted in few noticeable gains for women, and the campaign itself suffers from apathy and a lack of sympathy. Only the radical behaviour of the WSPU is able to energize a lackluster campaign for women who have been "in subjection too long, and now that they demand bare justice, they are not answered except with promises" (686). The demand for women's suffrage is a long overdue question of justice.

In the spring of 1909, Corkran again discusses women's suffrage, although she still wishes to remain apolitical:

The woman question has assumed an immense importance; it is a question of the day. I get from you a number of letters on the subject. I have long resisted noticing them, for I am wishful that my Chat should have no controversial spirit. Yet I cannot leave them unanswered longer, when you ask me to give you my opinion and ask your fellow-readers to give theirs. (527)

The girl readers are insisting on being heard. Moreover, their letters demonstrate their understanding of the debate and their fierce belief in the validity of their demand for equal political rights. "Hilda" quotes a passage from Charlotte Brontë's *Jane Eyre* (1847) that she and her friends selected as a suitable motto for women's suffrage while at an afternoon tea party:

> It is in vain to say human beings ought to be satisfied with tranquillity: they must have action; and they will make it if they cannot find it. Nobody knows how many rebellions besides political rebellions ferment in the masses of life which people earth. Women are supposed to be very calm generally; but women feel just as men feel; they need exercise for their faculties, and a field for their efforts, as much as their brothers do; they suffer from too rigid a restraint, too absolute a stagnation, precisely as men would suffer; and it is narrow-minded in their more privileged fellow-creatures to restrict them to making puddings and knitting stockings, to playing on the piano and embroidering bags. (Brontë 125–6)

"Hilda" and her suffragist friends were at a typically feminine function, a tea party, when they decided to look for a motto for the women's movement. The motto had to be from what "Hilda" terms the "standard authors" (527), presumably those who were well known and well respected, and she little expected to find such a suitable motto in a mid-century Brontë novel. Yet, as she explains, this passage was written by "the quiet country clergyman's daughter, instinct with genius, rebelling, at any rate in print, from the narrowness of the life women had to lead in the much-vaunted (by the anti-suffragists) time of our grandmothers" (527). "Hilda" and "Utopia" both find similarities between the situation for women at mid-century and modern circumstances, and they both believe that women should be granted the vote. Moreover, these contributions highlight the extent to which the readers of the *Girl's Realm* are engaged in the suffrage debate, although their enthusiasm for militant activity varies.

Other correspondents signal the groundswell of support for women's suffrage. "Laura" unequivocally writes, "I am entirely for [the vote], for I admit of no difference between men and women—none intellectually, I mean" (527). "Evangeline" was not initially in favour but, "Recently I have met some 'Suffragettes,' and since I have known all that they are fighting for, I have quite altered my opinion" (527). She also encourages girls from the Colonies to write in about their experiences of having the vote to help the "girls in the Mother Country" (527) make their own decision. Although a few correspondents suggest that women should not have the vote, the "Chat" generally supports suffrage. Corkran reminds her readers that "woman's plea for suffrage follows naturally the larger opportunities given her in education, in the choice of callings. It is the crown of all. It is no use telling her now that she is fitted for one thing, and for one only, and that is the care of the home" (527–8). The demand for suffrage has evolved naturally out of the improved education and opportunities available to girls, and the vote is a self-evident consequence of the changing circumstances of the late-nineteenth and early-twentieth centuries. Moreover, the tone of Corkran's comments has changed. She is no longer focused on the conduct of the suffragettes. Instead, she writes, "I was sorry to see that Helen K. Watts, one of our Guild girls, has had to suffer for her convictions. She is in prison, after the raid made on the House of Commons by the Suffragettes on Wednesday, February 24th" (528). At least some readers of the *Girl's Realm* are actively involved in the militant campaign for suffrage, and Corkran does not wish to alienate these readers or their supporters.

The "Chats" and the responses highlight the extent to which readers supported the campaign for the vote and how the magazine was forced to adapt its feminine ideal of decorum and modesty. The modern girl who reads the *Girl's Realm* is unwilling to be constrained by the feminine ideal of patience.

Nonetheless, the suffrage fiction in the *Girl's Realm* is significantly less supportive than the "Chats" and the correspondence. Although titles like "A Twentieth Century Martyr: A 'Votes for Women' Story" and "Woman's Suffrage at St. Austin's" suggest that these stories might seriously discuss the cause, they are instead used to undermine it. Maroula Joannou points out that "the figure of the suffragette is ubiquitous in the mainstream culture of twentieth-century Britain" (101), and the "tendency of much mainstream fiction written at the time of the suffragette militancy was to discredit the movement by exposing the personal defects of its supporters or exploiting the entertainment value of militancy to the full" (102). Both tendencies are present in the fiction that appears in the pages of the *Girl's Realm*. In poet and short-story writer Edna Wallace's "A Twentieth Century Martyr," for example, aspiring writer Una Trafford is frustrated by her unsuccessful attempts to break into the literary scene in London. Without fame and notoriety to place her name at the forefront of the press, she finds it difficult to get her stories published and fears she will be forced to return to her family's country home. Nearly 25, she laments that "I've never had a real adventure in my life" (779). On the street, she generously offers to mind a placard and brochures for a suffragette who is in danger of fainting from cold and exhaustion. The "little" suffragette is a "young and apparently delicate" (781) girl who is grateful to be given a respite. Although the suffragette is portrayed with dignity and compassion, Una never gains a genuine understanding of what would motivate someone to such levels of self-sacrifice. She wonders whether the girl is truly dedicated to her cause, "or was it that she was merely earning her living in the only way that offered," or perhaps "striving after cheap notoriety like the rest of the world" (781). That some women might support the cause merely because of its earning potential suggests to readers of the *Girl's Realm* that not all women are motivated by a desire for equality.

Moreover, instead of having a transformational effect upon Una, the story becomes increasingly humorous when Una is arrested for obstructing pedestrian traffic while distributing "her" pamphlets. After spending the night in jail, she is brought up before the Justices, where she "stoutly denie[s] any connection with the suffragettes" (783) and is dismissed with a caution. On her return home, she discovers her exploits have been reported in the papers, where she is described as "the well-known writer of short stories" (783). She also discovers that a popular magazine of "considerable standing" (784) has accepted her story, presumably because of her exploits as a suffragette. Being a suffragette is a mechanism by which Una gains the "cheap notoriety" she desires.

This story stands in contrast to the series of suffragette stories written by writer and suffragette Evelyn Sharp. She was active in the WPSU and was briefly imprisoned in 1911 and 1913, where she was forcibly fed. During the First World

War, she edited the women's suffrage journal, *Votes for Women*, and refused to pay taxes until she was assured of taxation with representation. Until 1908, Sharp frequently contributed fiction to the *Girl's Realm*, but her suffrage stories were published in the *Manchester Guardian* and the *Daily Chronicle* before being published in a single volume as *Rebel Women* (1910). Both suffragettes and nonsuffragettes alike welcomed Sharp's humorous accounts because they "did much to dispel the popular misconception of the suffragettes as ladies of leisure, cranks, or humourless feminists, as well as boosting the morale and self-esteem of the suffragettes" (Joannou 105). Sharp's nameless suffragettes encouraged women readers to identify with them. In contrast, Una distances herself from the suffragettes and their objectives, and never gains a genuine understanding of their objectives.

The challenges of a life dedicated to the cause are highlighted in Wallace's 1911 story, "The Cause—and Cupid." A girl wearing the suffragette colours of purple, green, and white distributes pamphlets listing the names and photos of martyrs to the suffragette cause. When a group of "rough-looking men" laugh and joke about these martyrs, she protests that "[i]t may seem funny to you that women should be imprisoned and tortured for the sake of the cause, but if only you would read the other side and try to see the unfairness" (516). When the men chase her, she is saved by an unusually well spoken cab driver who believes that women "are better in their own sphere—and that is home," while she argues that some women have "a higher ambition than that" (517). However, this woman distributes pamphlets to earn money rather than because she is committed to the cause. The man inquires,

> Do you really care whether you get the vote or not, or is it just that you have
> to earn your living somehow like the rest of us, and the excitement of this sort
> of thing appeals to you? If you had a comfortable home of your own, now,
> with someone to care for you—a husband and—and all that sort of thing—
> wouldn't you prefer it to knocking about the streets all weathers, enduring a lot
> of hardships for which you are physically unfitted? (518)

This evocation of the idea of a home, and someone to love her, brings the girl to tears, which she hides from the man. Later, over a cup of tea in her shabby rooms, he comments on "how much more charming and natural" she looks "pouring out the tea than standing at a street corner selling pamphlets" (520). The domestic space is the "natural" space for women, and her argument that working towards suffrage is her "duty" provokes his anger:

> "Duty be blowed," he exclaimed with sudden energy, "and the cause too. It's
> woman's first duty to be a good wife and mother and to leave the affairs of the
> State to the men—she hasn't time to combine the two. If only your sex would
> understand that their real strength lies in their weakness, we should hear less
> about the inequality between men and women and more of suitable and happy
> marriages." (521)

The feminine ideal of marriage and maternity supplants the need for equal representation, and the girl is easily persuaded to give up her suffragette activities in favour of domestic responsibilities. Wallace concludes that "the cause of woman's freedom lost another of its followers" (521). Because this woman is not identified by name, the reader is encouraged to think of all suffragettes as women who desire love and marriage and who would readily forsake the militant campaign if given the option. A similar story in 1910 by Irene Harrison, "A Capable Help," depicts a girl working as a housekeeper for a man and his suffragette sister. The sister is relieved of her domestic responsibilities, allowing her to dedicate herself to the cause, and the story concludes with the girl's engagement to the brother. The narrator laughs that "though I am marrying the Brother to help the Suffragettes, he absolutely refuses to let me be one!" (606). Being part of the cause is subject to male authority and control, and although a man might permit his sister to be a suffragette, his wife cannot have that freedom.

Further evidence of this shift appears in a 1911 discussion of women's suffrage. Editor S.H. Leeder solicited articles from well-known proponents of each side of the suffrage debate.[20] Including two opposing positions on suffrage was consistent with journalism practices from as early as the 1860s, which sought to sell more magazines by being provocative and encouraging controversy, as I discussed in Chapter 3. In "The Case Against Woman Suffrage," Ethel Harrison argues that the ideal of femininity will be compromised by suffrage. A prominent opponent of women's suffrage, Harrison served on the executive committee of Women's National Anti-Suffrage League founded in 1908. Her argument is founded on the premise that men and women have separate roles. She evokes a feminine ideal that was the subject of discussion and debate throughout much of the nineteenth century: "Woman is saved for gentler, humaner purposes; she stands, or should stand, for the ideal in life" (666). Although she agrees that "women are clever enough and good enough to be entrusted with a vote" (667), she feels that they will have to give up their feminine duties as nurturing caregivers to take up political positions. If women gain the vote, "they must lose their privilege and give up their birthright" as the keepers of the "standard of right feeling, justice, and noble conduct" (668). The feminine ideal Harrison presents is at odds with the brave modern girl elsewhere in the magazine, and she identifies the losses that she believes will accompany the move towards equal representation. Ironically, she argues that women can only maintain their position as the keepers of justice if they are disenfranchised, while in Christabel Pankhurst's paper supporting the cause, justice is at the core of the argument for giving women the vote.

In "What Woman Suffrage Means," Pankhurst argues that marital and maternal roles will be reinforced through universal suffrage. Although girls and women

---

[20]   Simon Henry Leeder is a somewhat unusual choice to head up the *Girl's Realm* after Corkran's departure. Leeder was an historian, publishing books like *The Desert Gateway: Biskra and Thereabouts* (1910), *The Veiled Mysteries of Egypt* (1912), and *Modern Sons of the Pharaohs* (1918).

have now demonstrated their capabilities, girls "are still at a discount" and are "still denied opportunities because they are women" (575). With the vote, women will have the power to help the poor and unfortunate, and will be able "to work for the prosperity and the honour of their country" (576). Pankhurst invokes imperialist rhetoric to demonstrate how women can assist with the important work of "preserving and strengthening this Empire of ours" (576). Moreover,

> Votes for women will have a very important effect upon their lives as wives and mothers. The wider life and outlook which she will have as a result of being enfranchised will make it easier for a woman to be the companion and equal of her husband, and to be the guide and teacher of her children. (576)

Like Emily Davies in her education campaign, Pankhurst argues that women will be better wives and mothers if they are given access to domains from which they have hitherto been restricted.[21] Pankhurst concludes that "[g]irls who have read their history will find no difficulty in understanding the necessity of militant methods" (577), which are a natural outcome of more than 40 years of limited success for the movement and the current political apathy. She justifies the "new methods" because they "have brought great results. They have stirred public interest so much that the Union now has branches in all parts of the country, with large central offices in London" (577). Pankhurst's article advertises for the WSPU and encourages likeminded girls and women to consider joining. Pankhurst's militant attitude is unique in the *Girl's Realm* because the dominant depiction of femininity is typically less strident. Even though the girl in the magazine supports the cause, she rarely goes to the lengths suggested by Pankhurst. Despite radically opposing views, Pankhurst and Harrison both draw on traditional feminine roles to support their positions in ways that are similar to other attempts in the girls' periodical press to either expand or, in Harrison's case, resist the expansion of the feminine ideal.

Unfortunately, no evidence of readers' responses to these position papers exists. The final reference to suffrage appears in L. Elliot's 1912 short story, "Woman's Suffrage at St. Austin's," where suffrage is firmly positioned in the "woman's realm" rather than the "girl's realm." In this school story, suffragette schoolgirls debate the anti-suffragettes but become so obsessed with the details of staging the debate that they forget to argue the point. The story ends happily when the girls for both sides share a picnic and then go to bed, "putting off the question of Woman's Suffrage till we were women" (406). In a remarkable shift from the agency and responsibility promoted by Corkran, girls' involvement in political issues is positioned as foolish and better left to adults. It may also signal the declining average age of the reader, and thus more overtly political stories were seen as inappropriate.

---

[21]   However, Davies refused to become involved in the women's rights campaigns of the 1860s because she was concerned that such involvement might tarnish her efforts at establishing a college for women at Cambridge.

Although the support for women's suffrage was less obvious after Corkran ceased writing her "Chats," the *Girl's Realm* nonetheless retained its modernity and uniqueness by addressing the issue of "Votes for Women." It could have ignored the issue entirely, but instead wrestled with conflicting notions of femininity and sought to guide girls towards conduct that the magazine felt was most becoming for young women of the early twentieth century. The rhetoric of heroism is muted in discussions of women's citizenship, but its presence in the magazine suggests that girls were justified in demanding equal voting rights. Corkran's positive comments, even as they attempted to mute the more militant aspects of the suffrage movement, suggest that the modern girls of the twentieth century had the right and the responsibility to be equal citizens. However, the *Girl's Realm* was sometimes uncertain about how suffrage could, or should, be incorporated within its ideal of the brave, modern girl. The militant campaign for suffrage threatened the foundations of the feminine ideal as women entered the male domain of politics and increasingly used masculine tactics to gain publicity. These tactics were met with unease as the magazine attempted to negotiate between traditional ideas of femininity and its girl readers' support for suffrage. Fortunately, the magazine was able to use girls' adventure fiction to depict a feminine ideal more consistent with its modernity.

Adventures in the *Girl's Realm*

The strongly capable heroine embodied in girls' adventure fiction, set both at home and abroad, is a consistent motif throughout the *Girl's Realm*, yet the girls in the Colonies appear to have significantly more freedom than their British counterparts. Jane Eldridge Miller notes that the changing status of women in British society, which was marked by increased employment and educational opportunities as well as the suffrage campaign and the scrutiny of the institution of marriage, "served as a major energizing and complicating force in Edwardian fiction" (3). Although Miller is primarily interested in asserting Edwardian novelists as distinctly "modern" writers, her argument is helpful in explaining the rise of girls' adventure fiction, which is also a feature of the period. She writes that

> Edwardian novelists derived momentum from the content of their fiction, not from any desire to alter its form. They clearly wanted to be perceived as *modern* writers, yet as participants in an extremely competitive literary market, they did not consciously choose to be *experimental* writers. It was their need to write about women in new ways, and to challenge ideas about gender and marriage, that forced them to attend to and subsequently reshape narrative form. But as a result, many Edwardian novels about women and feminism mark a significant movement away from the traditions of the nineteenth-century novel; thus I argue that these works of fiction should be considered examples of the modernism of content, an antecedent stage to the more familiar, canonized modernism of form. (7)

This "modernism of content" is marked in the *Girl's Realm* by the inclusion of girls' adventure fiction. Although this fiction does not reflect new forms of narrative, these adventurous female heroes represent an important development in girls' fiction because they present possibilities for girls that rarely appeared in the nineteenth century. In contrast to the domestic fiction that was the predominant narrative form for girls in the previous century, adventure fiction aimed specifically at girls emerges in part because of changes in the market for fiction, where "writers sought out new and more narrowly defined readerships ... by creating new characters, new points of view, and new sub-genres" (Kemp et al. xv).

Adventure fiction for girls emerged as a new genre in the twentieth century. In contrast, boys' adventure fiction had a much lengthier history.[22] The genre of girls' adventure fiction and its appearance in girls' magazines has its antecedents in imperial expansion and heroic masculinity. The "imperial romance" provides "a highly flexible locus of experimentation, distinguished by the fluidity of the form, its hybridity, and its radical as well as conservative tendencies" (Jones 408) and offers new possibilities for girls' writers. Writing girls' adventure fiction was challenging because the feminine ideology at the turn of the century included "a blend of aspirations and restraints" for readers that were difficult to incorporate into new structures:

> In practical terms, new narrative and character models, which would maintain the old values but offer a more modern standard of activity for girls, were not easy to set up. A century of writing for girls had established the norm of the

---

[22]   Boys' adventure fiction began in the 1840s, with Frederick Marryat's sea stories, which were followed in the 1850s and '60s by two immensely popular evangelical adventure writers, W.H.G. Kingston and R.M. Ballantyne, who together wrote over 270 books. Intended to appeal to boys and channel their energies into "approved directions" (Richards 4), these kinds of books were recommended by Charlotte Yonge, who writes that boys should "have heroism and nobleness kept before their eyes; and learn to despise all that is untruthful and cowardly, and to respect womanhood" (*What Books to Lend* 6). As Jeffrey Richards notes, however, the last decades of the century saw a shift in the type of boys' adventure fiction being produced:

> The evangelicalism, the commercial and cultural imperialism that characterise the work of mid-century writers like Ballantyne and Kingston gave way in the last decades of the nineteenth century to the aggressive militarism of G.A. Henty and Gordon Stables, as the evangelical impulse itself became secularised and fed into full-blown imperialism. (5)

Susan Jones uses the term "imperial romance" (406) to refer to the adventures set in the colonies which appeared in Britain between the 1880s and the 1920s and describes them as developing within a "complex political context" (406) of the fiercely competitive scramble among European nations to conquer unclaimed territory. George Alfred Henty was a popular proponent of this genre, producing over 120 books in his lifetime in addition to prolific contributions to newspapers and periodicals. Later writers like Robert Louis Stevenson, Henry Rider Haggard, Rudyard Kipling, and Joseph Conrad would draw on the boys' adventure genre but their interpretations often reflected an "ambivalent reaction to expansionist policy" (407).

> domestic tale, in which the trials of the heroine were involved with the learning
> of discipline, the internalisation of the feminine values of self-abnegation,
> obedience and subordination. This pattern could easily accommodate the
> sacrificial and inspiring aspect of the imperial lady. But no model which could
> be utilised for the representation of the sterner face of pioneering and imperialist
> motherhood had yet been established. (Bratton "British Imperialism" 197)

Reframing the feminine ideal of the past to incorporate the new expectations of
pioneering and imperialism within a fictional narrative was beset with many of the
same challenges that were operating elsewhere in the girls' periodical press. The
traditional ideal continued into the twentieth century and was not always easily
incorporated into a narrative of modernity. In Chapter 4, I demonstrated some of
the challenges involved in depicting girls as strong and capable, yet also feminine.
Similarly, the *Girl's Realm* is grappling with its girl readers' new and evolving
opportunities.

By including girls' adventure stories, Corkran and later Leeder are able to
present new narratives and new models for girls even though they were largely
aspirational. In *The New Girl*, Sally Mitchell points out that the fiction read by
girls was often at odds with the more constrained reality of their lives. In the *Girl's
Realm*, girl readers encountered female characters that were sometimes able to
move beyond the constraints of the nineteenth-century feminine ideal. In contrast,
Daphne Kutzer concludes in *Empire's Children* (2000) that children's fiction
is "highly conservative" because it presents childhood as an "ideal, innocent
kingdom" (xvi). She argues that adults, who "may be aware that a long-accepted
cultural code is crumbling," attempt to "shield children from these changes and
encourage them to continue believing in and practicing cultural beliefs and codes
that are no longer unquestioned in the adult world, perhaps in an unconscious
desire to maintain those earlier cultural codes" (xvi). I believe that the presence of
girls' adventure fiction in the *Girl's Realm* indicates less conservative possibilities.
Instead of orienting girls exclusively towards the home and their domestic
responsibilities, this fiction depicts girls who are actively engaged beyond the
domestic realm. Even if the narratives often conclude with a marriage plot,
feminine activity and action is encouraged to a degree uncommon in nineteenth-
century girls' fiction. These adventure stories present the girl as inherently modern
and brave in the face of physical danger, and they encourage behaviours that
reflect the changing conditions of girlhood.

Corkran stresses the importance of adventure fiction for girls in a 1904 "Chat":
"Every girl would be the better" if she reads "stories of adventure, of strange lands,
of wild heroic deeds" like her brother does, for "there is nothing namby-pamby
in a lad's taste" and "there should be nothing namby-pamby in a girl's books, for
there should be nothing namby-pamby in her outlook on life" (611). Adventure
stories will strengthen a girl's outlook and prepare her for the challenges of real
life. Corkran endorses adventure fiction for girls because "[t]he field of the world's
activity has greatly widened for girls, and the field of the drama of their lives has
likewise widened" (611) although "the drama of [a girl's] existence may be more

restricted than is that of her brother" (611). There is perhaps some slippage in Corkran's definition of adventure fiction for she defines the term as books that show "courage, resourcefulness, and a high devotion" and "a spirit of pluck" (611), yet she uses *Little Women* by Louisa May Alcott as an example of such fiction. Children's literature critic Jack Zipes describes Alcott as "the most significant writer of domestic fiction for the young" (2169). Corkran's "Chat" highlights the inconsistencies in definitions of girlhood at the turn of the century. Although she reflects on the need for new and different narratives to reflect the changes in the feminine ideal, she occasionally retreats to more traditional conceptions of girlhood.

The stories that appear in the *Girl's Realm* also reflect these inconsistencies, but they are nevertheless startling in contrast to the domestic fiction found in the *Monthly Packet* and *Atalanta*. One of the earliest adventure stories is Dr. Gordon Stables' "The Girl Crusoes: A Tale of the Indian Ocean," appearing in 1902.[23] This Robinsonade follows in the tradition of Daniel Defoe's *Robinson Crusoe* (1717) when the daughters of the British consul to Zanzibar, Lucy and Lottie, are shipwrecked off the coast of Zanzibar. Bored by the expatriate society in Zanzibar, Lucy expects a proposal from a British Navy Lieutenant and is also being courted, to her amusement, by the Arab Prince Sudgee. Lucy, unaware of local custom, does not realize that her "acceptance of the costly gifts would be looked upon as an encouragement to his suit" (189). For excitement, the girls, who are excellent sailors, plan and provision an expedition to a small island, demonstrating the healthy capability that Stables as "Medicus" endorses in the *Girl's Own Paper*. Yet Lottie comments that if Lucy had only been a man, "What a general you would have made" (190). Even in a magazine where bravery and modernity are part of its depiction of girlhood, gender remains a constraint on girls' lives. The girls survive a storm only to have their boat stolen. Prince Sudgee rescues them but holds them hostage because he hates the British. Lucy refuses to acknowledge his position of power and instead assumes a superior position because "English girls are not to be frightened by threats as Arabs may be" (194). The Arab is not a genuine threat to the girls. Jenny Sharpe argues in her study of Anglo-Indian fiction that "the European fear of interracial rape does not exist as long as there is a belief that colonial structures of power are firmly in place" (3). In "The Girl Crusoes," the power structures are stable and secure, and the girls' English femininity protects them.

Although the story ends conventionally with a double marriage, the girls have an exciting, exotic adventure far from their British homeland, which provides them with the opportunity to demonstrate their superiority over the colonial natives. In part, the girls' superiority is predicated on the presence of subordinate racial others who lack the authority to be threatening. Eventually, the British navy attacks Sudgee's boat and the narrator reassures the reader that "our British bluejackets

---

[23]   This story is consistent with his popular boys' adventure stories, many of which appeared in the *Boy's Own Paper.*

won at last. Don't they always?" (195). Moreover, the girls only need rescuing because of the Prince's interference. They manage the violent storm capably, do not give way to panic, and would have been able to return to Zanzibar had their boat not been stolen. Their conduct as female British subjects is unassailable, although their excursion was perhaps ill conceived. This story encourages bravery and adventure (within appropriate limits) for girls, yet also remains constrained by traditional expectations of marriage.

The real thrust of the girls' adventure stories in the *Girl's Realm* begins in 1910 with a number of stories by Bessie Marchant, who was an immensely popular novelist for girls from the 1890s. She published over 200 books during her lifetime, often producing up to five books per year, and was called "the girl's Henty" for the type of fiction she wrote. Unlike Henty, who travelled extensively, however, Marchant never left England. Six of her short stories appear in the *Girl's Realm* between 1910 and 1912, and all feature exotic settings. Although numerous authors contributed to the magazine regularly, the frequency of Marchant's contributions during this period signals the rise of girls' adventure fiction within the periodical. "Bessel's Wedding," the first of Marchant's stories to appear, is preoccupied with imperialism and female heroism. Three young women and a baby are travelling to a wedding, accompanied by Kaffir servants. When a Zulu man offers to trade some stones for three horses, the British women recognize the stones as rubies and agree to the trade knowing that they are taking advantage of the man. Bertha suggests they tell the Zulu man of the stones' value, but Tottie replies sharply, "He would not understand if I did" (128). When their wagon is attacked in the night, the "cowardly Kaffirs" (129) flee. Bertha takes the baby and escapes while the other two women, who know how to shoot, successfully defend the wagon against the Chinese raiders although they seemingly lose the rubies. Bertha and the baby are rescued by a member of the Cape Mounted Police and Bertha is "the heroine of the occasion, because she had saved the baby and the rubies also" (130).

Adventure fiction in colonial outposts offered new opportunities for girls to fulfil their imperial roles. As J.S. Bratton observes, fiction by novelists like Marchant brought together domestic and imperialist values: "The girl's proper sphere is the home; when she becomes the heroine of the adventure story, home duties become the paradigm of her conquest of the wider world" ("British Imperialism" 205). Yet, as Michelle Smith observes, Marchant's novels "are not preoccupied with maintaining British identity in foreign lands [since] they do not, in most instances, present the heroines engaging in any meaningful contact with indigenous inhabitants" (*Empire* 85). The indigenous peoples appearing in Marchant's stories may help to drive the narrative forward, but they are rarely presented as unique individuals. They function as signifiers of inferiority to which all British people are superior.

The racist overtones to Marchant's story are overt. The Kaffirs are cowardly and dishonest. The Chinese steal, murder, and burn the countryside. The Zulu are ignorant and childlike, attracted to shiny things and incapable of grasping the value of precious stones. In contrast to these figures, the British women are brave and stalwart. They defend British property and protect the innocent baby. They are not, however, all equally good. Tottie momentarily regrets haggling for the stones, acknowledging that "[i]t serves me right for being so avaricious" (130). Yet Bertha embodies feminine innocence and moral rectitude because she does not recognize the stones as rubies, and she is disturbed when Tottie swindles the Zulu man. Because she does not know how to shoot a pistol, a masculine signifier, she is given the task of escaping with the baby, thus becoming the true protector of the family. Moreover, Bertha has unintentionally saved the rubies—thereby restoring them to their rightful imperial owner—because they were accidentally stored in her cloak. Bertha's heroic qualities come from her femininity, her lack of interest in material possessions, and her lack of affinity for masculine pursuits. Surprisingly, the story does not conclude with a mention of whom she will marry and how happy they will be. Instead, it demonstrates the possibilities for female bravery in all three girls, yet the heroic portrayal of Bertha as the morally superior protector of the young establishes her as the feminine ideal of the early twentieth century. This ideal reflects the female role as the moral and spiritual center of the home; yet by locating the story in South Africa, Marchant gives her heroine the opportunity to demonstrate her bravery as well.

These adventure stories signal the challenges of incorporating bravery into a traditional culture of femininity more than the other examples of modernity that I have discussed in the *Girl's Realm*. These challenges are highlighted in a posthumously published story by G.A. Henty. In "A Soldier's Daughter" (1903), Nita and Lieutenant Henry Carter undergo a series of adventures after being captured while defending a British fort. Despite a strongly platonic relationship, in the last paragraph Henty resolves the narrative to describe Nita's transformation into a proper English lady, Carter's career success, and their engagement. Although ostensibly about a female hero, the conclusion of the story refers to Carter's future, not Nita's. Henty's story, then, sits somewhat uncomfortably in a girl's magazine. Because Nita's bravery is outside conventional feminine norms, she must go away to a boarding school run by an English lady to become properly feminine, yet her transformation is necessary if she is to gain access to the world of marriage and motherhood. Without the womanly skills of an English lady, she could not be a suitable wife. To a certain extent, her girlhood bravery is presented in opposition to her maturity. She can either be heroic or she can be a proper English wife, but she cannot be both at the same time. The extent to which the brave girl transcends the boundaries of femininity and how she can subsequently be contained is met with occasional unease in the *Girl's Realm*.

In contrast, the nonfiction articles contain none of the hesitation about girls' adventures that is found in the fiction. Capability and adaptability are at the forefront of the qualities of colonial girls. In Jean Graham's 1909 "The Canadian Girl," the text and photographs depict Canadian girls at work and at play. Graham explains that "[t]he Canadian girl has been living in comparative obscurity all these years, overshadowed by her sister in the South; but she has a sturdy individuality, which makes her no insignificant feature in the life of the community" (654). Moreover,

British readers should "make no apology for considering the characteristics of the girls in one of the youngest nations of the Empire" (654). Less cosmopolitan than American girls, Canadian girls are valuable daughters of the Empire and are healthy and hardy as they help with the farm work, canoe, play ice hockey and tennis, tramp in the woods, and snow shoe. All of the accompanying photos show girls outdoors rather than contained within domestic spaces, and Graham's description of a Canadian girl suggests that she has an important role in settling the wilds of Canada:

> There may have been beauty—there may have been grace—but it was not these which gleamed from the eyes of the girl in the gorgeous-tinted orchard, looking across the inland sea of limitless sapphire. There were confidence, hope, and a glad belief in the brightness of the world, which made her a glowing vindication of those who kindled the first hearth-fires in the great lonely Dominion. (660)

The Canadian girl is optimistic and hopeful as she anticipates her future in Canada. The heroic colonial girl is capable and brave in face of the challenges of living in exotic locations, and she has frequent opportunities to demonstrate her bravery. Instead of the uncertainty embodied in the fictional girl, the real daughter of the Empire is celebrated and supported as she faces new experiences and meets them with courage.

Closer to home, British girls are also seen outdoors, engaging with the natural world for their leisure. No longer forced to "sit still" for long periods—as Yonge describes in an article for *Macmillan's Magazine*—girls are climbing cliffs, skate sailing, and caravanning, and the *Girl's Realm* endorses all these activities.[24] Magdalen F.P. Tuck describes how "cliff-climbing in all its various aspects ... has had for me an irresistible, ever-growing fascination" (403).[25] A full-page illustration celebrates "A New Sport for Girls: Skate Sailing" [Figure 7.3] and enthusiastically describes the experience as akin to flying, "so inconceivably rapid is the speed possible on smooth ice on a windy day" (Minns 187). An article on "Caravaning for Girls: A New and Delightful Summer Pastime" supports a nomadic lifestyle "amongst beautiful scenery and constantly varying surroundings" (Crozier 785). Not only are these girls outdoors, but they are also fit and healthy, an important consideration at the turn of the century, when the health and welfare of children was becoming increasingly important, especially after a number of soldiers enlisting for the Boer War were disqualified based on their fitness. The shift in the feminine ideal to include health was increasingly important if girls wished to explore new occupations and leisure activities. The physical capability of girls is celebrated in the *Girl's Realm* as it is in the *Girl's Own Paper*, a significant shift beyond the mid-

---

[24] In 1869, Yonge wrote a series of three articles for *Macmillan's Magazine* on "Children's Literature of the Past Century." In the final article in the series, Yonge explains that because "there are so many hours of a girl's life when she must sit still, ... a book is her natural resource, and reading comes to her like breathing" (454).

[25] Tuck co-authored *Wild Nature Wooed and Won* with Oliver Pike in 1909.

A NEW SPORT FOR GIRLS: SKATE SAILING.

This sail is triangular, and is attached to two bamboo poles of extreme lightness. One is upright, the other fastened to it half way down, and extends to the point of the triangle. Equipped with this sail, the skater accomplishes something like *flying, so inconceivably rapid is the speed possible on smooth ice on a windy day. The exertion is not nearly so great as in ordinary skating. All that is necessary is to preserve the equilibrium and let the sail do the rest.*

From an original drawing by B. E. MINNS.

187

Fig. 7.3   A New Sport for Girls: Skate Sailing, *Girl's Realm*, 1902

Victorian difficulty of reconciling the need for healthy, active women to become wives and mothers in a "log cabin or military station" with feminine "weakness" (Bratton "British Imperialism" 197). In the pages of the *Girl's Realm*, girls need to live healthy, active lives.

Reigning in the *Girl's Realm*

Although the magazine was strongly supportive of girls as heroes, the *Girl's Realm* began to retreat from this position in the years leading up to the First World War. Its pictorial covers changed from depicting girls in outdoor activities like golfing, tobogganing, and sailing. The November 1909 cover [Figure 7.4], for example, depicts a girl striding along a narrow path, carrying a set of golf clubs, while the July 1912 cover [Figure 7.5] depicts a classically dressed girl sitting with a flower. Her pretty, demure manner is the focus of the illustration, and she is "framed" by heavy classical columns that contain her image and her spirit. To be fair, the retreat from positioning girls as active and capable was not straightforward or linear. The April 1914 cover [Figure 7.6] presents a girl gazing into her lover's eyes, set against a backdrop of flowering trees while the May 1914 [Figure 7.7] cover shows a girl looking directly at the reader, on board a boat at sea, in keeping with earlier images. Nonetheless, the strongly active girls are increasingly being supplanted by traditionally feminine images.

The fiction was also moving away from the colonial adventure stories of Marchant and her contemporaries. In Elsa Burrows' 1913 "Stone Walls," for example, Diane Vernes feels caged within domestic walls by an impoverished country life. She helps a man whom she believes to be an escaped convict because she cannot stand the idea of him being sent back to prison, and the man realizes that "there were other prison bars—other stone walls, than those literal barriers that can shut a man away from freedom" (375). Unsurprisingly, the man is not a convict, and he returns to Diane's home as a gentleman to free her from her caged life: "The walls had fallen down, the bars were unfastened, and Diane stepped into the open air and sunshine of a new life and a new love, unafraid, with the man who had come to her in so strange a manner, to bear her company on the way" (376). Marriage frees Diane from the drudgery and boredom of her life. Her adventure, saving the "convict," provides her with the opportunity to meet the man she will marry, and her bravery results in marriage.

The feminine ideal of modernity is replaced by a more traditional ideal of marriage in the final years of the magazine's run. The bravery of women's work is refigured in Edna Wallace's 1913 "A Woman's Ruse" to ensure marriage. Hilda Marsden works as a secretary and lives a life of "unvarying monotony, though never quite losing sight of a vague hope hidden away in the secret recesses of her heart that one day 'something would happen'" (451). Her adventure occurs when she goes to the opera and meets a young man who believes that she does not work but instead fills her time with flower arranging and embroidery. He condemns her

Fig. 7.4   Cover of the *Girl's Realm*, November 1909

Fig. 7.5   Cover of the *Girl's Realm*, July 1912

Fig. 7.6   Cover of the *Girl's Realm*, April 1914

April, 1914] LONELY WOMEN: A Modern Problem [Sixpence net

THE
GIRL'S REALM

See the Charming Story by HELEN WALLACE

Fig. 7.7   Cover of the *Girl's Realm*, May 1914

after discovering she is filling a post "which ought by rights to belong to men" because he believes that "woman's right sphere is the home and looking after the comfort of her husband and children" (454). Hilda reveals her loathing both for her job and her limited conditions:

> "And do you think I *like* it?" she asked with a scorn which almost equalled his own. "Do you think we women enjoy spending the best years of our lives 'hammering a typewriter,' or going every day to the hateful stuffy City and working till our eyes and backs ache, very often having to put up with insults which we dare not even show we resent? No, we do it because we *have* to! It is easy enough for you men to sit in judgment upon us, to prate about home being a woman's true sphere; but what do you do to help her towards attaining it? Men can marry when and practically whom they choose—they haven't to sit with folded hands and wait until they're asked, with the humiliating knowledge that unless they're unusually pretty or charming or rich the chances are they'll be passed over altogether!" (455)

When he finally understands that "independent" women are "more to be pitied than blamed," he welcomes the opportunity to help one woman to her "true sphere" (455). As in "Stone Walls," the adventure operates as the vehicle for marriage, and the loneliness and hopelessness of a single woman's life is highlighted. The independence and courage of the modern girl is remodeled in the *Girl's Realm* to support a feminine ideal of marriage and family. Even the working girl resents the circumstances that have led to the necessity of employment and wishes she did not have to face an uncertain and unappealing future as a single woman. Although Hilda has a decent, well-paying position, she can only be content with a husband and the traditional responsibilities of homemaking. This is a far cry from the Suffragette who appears in "A Capable Help" in 1910, and who is thrilled when she is freed from the responsibility of keeping her brother's home when he marries. Although Hilda demonstrates a degree of bravery when she arranges her "ruse" to have the man return her pocketbook, this bravery is intended to produce the desired result of marriage.

The presence of stories like these demonstrates the difficulties of creating female heroes located within England. The challenges of depicting a brave English girl who is nevertheless feminine and attractive prove insurmountable because English girlhood lacks the liberating potential of the colonial adventure stories. There seem to have been few local narratives for girls that were not focused on love and marriage. Although historical figures could easily be heroes, the heroic potential of colonial girlhood cannot be easily located in England. Sally Mitchell explains that "[i]n wilder places, or in wilder times, girls can reveal heroism without qualification—though they may still need gentling at the end" (115). In the *Girl's Realm*, the stories set in exotic locations demonstrate freedoms for female protagonists that are not available to British girls. In foreign settings, girls are free to be as heroic as necessary, but at home, adventurous girls fall prey to traditional ideas of marriage and motherhood because they lack clear alternatives. Their problems are resolved through marriage rather than through any direct action by the girls themselves. Moreover, the adventures of girls within England tend to be tamer and revolve around issues of mistaken identity rather than courage in the face of unsettling or unfamiliar circumstances.

Other critics have drawn similar conclusions. Mary Cadogan and Patricia Craig note that "[b]y 1914, just before its end, the *Girl's Realm* ... had become increasingly conformist, possibly in a desperate endeavour to increase flagging circulation" (79). They scathingly critique the fiction that appears in the later years, claiming the magazine "deserved to fail" (80) because of its poor quality. Yet the return to a more traditional feminine ideal is consistent with other shifts in the girls' periodical press at the time. The troubling fiction set in England would not, in itself, have been problematic for the *Girl's Realm* if it had continued to include stories of colonial adventure. However, the height of the girls' adventure fiction in its pages occurred in 1912, and after that fewer stories depict girls in far-flung locations who face challenging circumstances with courage and capability. At the same time, more stories emphasize a traditional, marriage-based conclusion and reinforce the idea that girls were best kept within the domestic sphere. The adventure and excitement associated with girl heroes gives way to more predictable romances, potentially signalling plans to merge the magazine with a woman's magazine.

Although the girl's adventure fiction in the magazine continues to present heroic girls in foreign locations, the suffrage fiction in local settings presents female heroism within the confines of the traditional ideal of marriage and domesticity. This may be a result of the increasingly violent behaviour of the suffrage campaign, but I would speculate that it reflects a widespread shift in the periodical marketplace. Sally Mitchell has observed that the "apparent diminuendo of girls' culture was not simply a resurgence of conservatism" (176). It was facilitated by the aging and eventual demise of some of the more important women writers of popular literature for girls, like L.T. Meade, Rosa Nouchette Carey, Hesba Stretton, and Alice Corkran. Mitchell also argues that the "free space" occupied by new girls was diminishing as adolescent girls became sexualized and categories of "schoolgirl, teenager, [and] woman" (173) became increasingly differentiated. The concluding years of the *Girl's Realm* contain more stories aimed at younger girls who were less mobile and had less control over their own lives. At the same time, shifts in readership signalled by the name change in 1908 to *Girl's Own Paper and Woman's Magazine* suggest that even long-established girls' periodicals were struggling to attract and retain readers.

When the *Girl's Realm* merged with the adult magazine, *Woman at Home*, in 1915, Leeder claimed it was because of wartime paper shortages and, indeed, he was keen to continue publishing the magazine for as long as he could. Despite increasing paper prices and decreasing advertising revenues owing to war time conditions, Leeder saw it as part of his "national duty" ("Important Notice to Readers" 4) to continue publishing so that men and women would not be thrown out of work. He appealed to his readers to continue purchasing the magazine, claiming, "[t]his is the day of patriotism, loyalty, and sacrifice" (4). Rather cleverly, he positions the purchase of the *Girl's Realm* as the responsibility of every patriotic British girl, taking advantage of the increased patriotism associated with wartime.

In the same "Special Supplement" appearing in 1914, he responds to pleas from his readers about how they can help in the war effort. Having "made inquiries at the proper authorities," he informs his readers that "nurses are still required to supply for those at the front" ("The War" 1) and provides information on where to apply and obtain training. For "every girl or woman with time to spare," he suggests that they begin sewing and provides descriptions and illustrations of the clothes, such as the "Knitted Chest Protector," required by the soldiers. Leeder presents two practical types of assistance that girls might provide, either as nurses or through their sewing. These two options highlight the possible positions for girls. They can be heroes if they choose to nurse, or they can remain in their domestic space and sew. Both types of assistance are necessary and valuable, and both are supported within the pages of the *Girl's Realm*. The negotiation between these two types of femininity is, however, a step back from the modernity it asserted in its earliest days. In the years leading up to World War I, the magazine became increasingly cautious and conservative. It may have been trying to attract an older readership, especially if plans were already in place to merge with a woman's magazine, or it may have concluded that its modern approach was not appealing to its target readership. Without sales figures this is difficult to determine. Nonetheless, at its best, the *Girl's Realm* was a distinctly twentieth-century magazine that broke new ground in portraying girls as both modern and heroic.

Chapter 8
Conclusion

Between 1850 and 1915, many different girls were defined and refined through the periodical press, yet these girls remained inherently "feminine" because of their purity and virtue. The girl of the period was as pure and good as the girl of the past, despite shifting ideas of girlhood and regardless of the multiplicity of voices that came together in print to guide the development of the girl towards behaviours that were considered acceptable. This study highlights the complexities of guiding girls towards acceptable conduct as editors and contributors, and the readers themselves, attempted to manage the tension between a traditional feminine ideal and the shifting expectations of girlhood throughout the second half of the nineteenth century and into the twentieth century. A web of interconnecting discourses regarding education, marriage, religion, health, fashion, heroism, and purity developed during this period. This web was fragile, yet it contained hidden strength that meant an ideal of purity, decorum, modesty, and virtue was not easily set aside in constructions of *fin-de-siècle* girlhood. Instead, these qualities were understood as necessary precursors of femininity, and the shifting expectations about girls' interests and capabilities had to be negotiated within this framework. In girls' periodicals, these tensions often manifest themselves in a reluctance to fully commit to new ideas. The magazines betray unease about how changing expectations of girlhood could be incorporated into existing ideals, and this uneasiness is reflected by an inconsistent approach to girlhood. Even magazines controlled by a strong editorial presence were often unable to overcome these tensions.

This uneasiness is significant because of the great range of influences acting upon and invested in the construction of girlhood during this period, which itself suggests the value assigned to and the anxieties surrounding gender and femininity. I have not tried to develop a narrative of progress. If anything, this study demonstrates how competing discourses operated differently in different periodicals, and even within the same magazine. Nonetheless, feminine agency was clearly developing during this period. Not only were there various ways of being a "girl" at this time, but the girls themselves were becoming increasingly aware of the opportunities available to them and the ramifications of their choices. As consumers, writers, and activists in the periodical press and beyond, they were increasingly involved in the economic, cultural, and political arenas, and their public "work" was commented on, critiqued, and influenced by periodicals targeted at them.

These girls' periodicals reflect significant changes towards girls and their place in society. When the *Monthly Packet* produced its first number, paid employment for middle-class girls and women was extremely uncommon. Female duties were domestic, religious, and charity-driven. Education was largely relegated to the home, guided by a mother or a governess. The Girl of the Period phenomenon provocatively raised the question of women's rights and responsibilities, and the *Miscellany* clearly supports a shift in attitudes and expectations about female behaviour. By the 1890s, *Atalanta* includes a variety of articles encouraging girls to pursue higher education and to develop their intellectual abilities. The *Girl's Own Paper* encourages its readers to stay healthy and fit, in part so that they are able to pursue paid employment. Even the *Young Woman*, which encouraged girls to marry, moved the question of fidelity and the importance of choosing a suitable husband to the forefront of its discussions. The *Girl's Realm* in many ways consolidates the various changes in nineteenth-century girlhood as it encourages girls to believe in, and become, the heroines of their own lives.

The advent of the Great War significantly disrupted the narrative of agency and the development of the modern girl. Publications aimed at girls were curtailed almost immediately because of rising newspaper prices, and the exciting dynamic of modernity that was prevalent in the first decade of the twentieth century was quickly repurposed to support the war effort. The momentum associated with the women's suffrage campaign and the strides accompanying girls' movements into increasingly public spaces through education and employment soon came to an end. However, Sally Mitchell notes that even prior to the beginning of the war, girlhood was increasingly contained within highly sexualized images of femininity. The emergence of the flapper, for example, predates the war. Examples in the *Girl's Realm* in the 1910s emphasize marriage and motherhood at the expense of gains in education and employment. Similarly, the merging of girls' and women's magazines in the early twentieth century suggests that girlhood is no longer viewed as a "separate culture" (Mitchell 3) and is collapsing into a broader category of feminine behaviours emphasizing more traditional ideals.

Moreover, the role of print culture in producing gender is not to be underestimated. The girls of the late nineteenth and early twentieth centuries received, on a weekly or monthly basis, depictions of femininity and girlhood across an array of genres, expressing diverse opinions and discussing current issues, making their magazines an ephemeral yet consistent mode for delivering (and resisting) contemporary gender, social, cultural, and economic ideologies. The girls' periodical press contains depictions of religious girls, fashionable girls, healthy girls, educated girls, marrying girls, and modern girls. Of course, these categories of girlhood are not discrete. Each of these girls overlaps with one or more of the others, and although these girls' magazines encourage a range of behaviours associated with these different girls, no single magazine can successfully embody all of these diverse depictions of girlhood. The wide variety of girls' magazines suggests that there was space for many different kinds of girls to be defined and debated within the periodical press. The heterogeneity of girlhood during this period was, and perhaps is, unprecedented. The instability that Yonge signalled in her first address to the girl readers of the *Monthly Packet* in 1851 is reinforced through the vivacity and variety of publications for girls through to the end of

Queen Victoria's reign and beyond. The varying lengths of the publication runs and the multifaceted girls of the period who appear in these magazines demonstrate that developing a readership based on a particular type of girlhood lasted only as long as that depiction satisfied its consumers. A magazine that was perceived to be out of touch with the girl of the period went out of business and was quickly replaced by a new magazine with newer girls in its pages.

The periodicals in this study reflect the challenges of incorporating new ideas and expectations into the representations of a traditional feminine ideal. Although they attempted to expand existing notions of femininity by favourably comparing the girl of the present with the girl of the past, they often reverted back to the values of the past when they were uncertain about whether, and how, to contain the new girl of the period. In order to maintain their readerships, the editors of these periodicals had to negotiate carefully between shifting feminine ideals. At the same time, their girl readers were rarely shy about inserting themselves into these discussions and asserting their own ideas about how these magazines did, or did not, reflect the realities of their lives.

Works Cited

Primary Texts (Pre-1915)

Advertisement. *The Athenaeum*. 5 June 1869: 775.

Advertisement. *The Athenaeum*. 10 July 1869: 35.

"Aesculapius in Petticoats." *Girl of the Period Miscellany* (1869): 110–11.

Alcott, Louisa May. *Little Women*. Oxford: Oxford UP, 1998.

Alighieri, Dante. *Inferno*. Trans. Michael Palma. Ed. Giuseppe Mazzotta. New York: W.W. Norton, 2008.

Allen, Grant. *Physiological Aesthetics*. New York & London: Garland Publishing, 1977.

———. *The Type-Writer Girl*. Ed. Clarissa Suranyi. Peterborough, ON: Broadview P, 2004.

———. *The Woman Who Did*. Ed. Nicholas Ruddick. Peterborough, ON: Broadview P, 2004.

"Amaryllis." "Answer to Arachne's Question." *Monthly Packet* 9 (Fourth series) (1895): 377–8.

"Answers to Correspondents." *Girl's Own Paper* 1 (1880): 272.

"Answers to Correspondents." *Girl's Own Paper* 2 (1881): 351–2.

"Answers to Correspondents." *Girl's Own Paper* 2 (1881): 366–7.

Arnold, Edwin. "Atalanta." *Atalanta* 1 (1887/8): 3.

Arnold, Mrs. Wallace. "The Physical Education of Girls." *Girl's Own Paper* 5 (1883): 516–17.

"Art and Letters." *Daily News* 17 Nov. 1898: 6.

"*Atalanta*." *The Church Quarterly Review* 27 (1889): 500–501.

Atkins, Frederick A. "The Ideal Husband." *Young Woman* 3 (1894/5): 411.

———. "Sarah Grand On 'The Choice of a Wife.'" *Young Woman* 7 (1898/9): 9.

———. "To Our Readers." *Young Woman* 1 (1892/3): 24.

———. "To Our Readers: The Arrangements For Our New Volume." *Young Woman* 1 (1892/3): 376.

Aubrey, Frank. "Saved by a Cat: A True Story of Adventure." *Girl's Realm* 1 (1899): 90–92.

"Awfully Nice." *Girl of the Period Miscellany* (1869): 31.

Baner, P. "Healthful Exercise." *Girl's Own Paper* 14 (1892/3): 240.

Beale, Dorothea. "Schools in the Past." *Atalanta* 3 (1889/90): 259–61.

———. "Schools of Today." *Atalanta* 3 (1889/90): 311–17.

Bodichon, Barbara Leigh Smith. "Women and Work." *The Exploited: Women and Work*. Ed. Marie Mulvey Roberts and Tamae Mizuta. London: Routledge/Thoemmes P, 1995. 1–55.

Braddon, Mary Elizabeth. "Whose Fault Is It?" *Belgravia* 9 (1869): 214–16.

Bright, Mrs. Jacob. "The Laws Which Affect Women." *Young Woman* 1 (1892/3): 165–8.

Brontë, Charlotte. *Jane Eyre*. London: Penguin, 1996.

Browne, Gordon. "A Girton Girl." *Atalanta* 6 (1892/3): 466.

Browning, Elizabeth Barrett. "The Sweetest Lives." *Young Woman* 1 (1892/3): 14.

Burnett, Frances Hodgson. *A Little Princess: Being the Whole Story of Sara Crewe Now Told for the First Time*. London: Warne, 1905.

Burrows, Elsa. "Stone Walls." *Girl's Realm* 15 (1913): 370–76.

Butler, Josephine. *Social Purity*. London: Morgan & Scott, 1879.

Caird, Mona. "Marriage." *The Fin de Siècle: A Reader in Cultural History C. 1880–1900*. Ed. Sally Ledger and Roger Luckhurst. Oxford: Oxford UP, 2000. 186–201.

Carpenter, Annie Boyd. "At What Age Should a Girl Marry?" *Young Woman* 7 (1898/9): 208.

———. "The Ideal Husband." *Young Woman* 3 (1894/5): 386–8.

Carr, Kent. "Women Students at Oxford." *Atalanta* 10 (1896/7): 43–8.

"Christmas Books." *Times* 2 Nov. 1901: 16.

Church, Alfred J. "The Brown Owl." *Atalanta* 3 (1889/90): 212–14.

Cobbe, Frances Power. "What Shall We Do with Our Old Maids." *Prose by Victorian Women: An Anthology*. Ed. Andrea Broomfield and Sally Mitchell. New York and London: Garland Publishing, 1996. 235–61.

Coleridge, Christabel. *Charlotte Mary Yonge: Her Life and Letters*. London: Macmillan and Co., Limited, 1903.

———. "The China Cupboard." *Monthly Packet* 7 (Fourth series) (1894): 115.

———. "The China Cupboard." *Monthly Packet* 18 (Fourth series) (1899): 705–7.

———. *The Daughters Who Have Not Revolted*. London: Wells Gardner & Co., 1894.

———. "Debatable Ground." *Monthly Packet* 12 (Third series) (1886): 486–92.

———. "The 'New Woman.'" *Monthly Packet* 9 (Fourth series) (1895): 618–19.

———. "We. By Us." *Monthly Packet* 7 (Fourth series) (1894): 453–8.

———. "Work and Workers." *Monthly Packet* 1 (Fourth series) (1891): 66.

———. "Work and Workers: The Lady of All Work." *Monthly Packet* 4 (Fourth series) (1892): 653–8.

Corkran, Alice. "Chat with the Girl of the Period." *Girl's Realm* 1 (1899): 216.

———. "Chat with the Girl of the Period." *Girl's Realm* 1 (1899): 432.

———. "Chat with the Girl of the Period." *Girl's Realm* 1 (1899): 1272.

———. "Chat with the Girl of the Period." *Girl's Realm* 2 (1900): 455–6.

———. "Chat with the Girl of the Period." *Girl's Realm* 2 (1900): 833–4.

———. "Girl Heroines." *Girl's Realm* 1 (1899): 65–9.

———. "My Chat with the Girl of the Period." *Girl's Realm* 4 (1902): 851–2.

———. "My Chat with the Girl of the Period." *Girl's Realm* 6 (1904): 611–12.

———. "My Chat with the Girl of the Period." *Girl's Realm* 6 (1904): 691–2.

———. "My Chat with the Girl of the Period." *Girl's Realm* 10 (1908): 525–6.

———. "My Chat with the Girl of the Period." *Girl's Realm* 10 (1908): 685–6.

———. "My Chat with the Girl of the Period." *Girl's Realm* 11 (1909): 527–8.

———. "Through the Siege of Ladysmith: A Chat with One Who Went through It." *Girl's Realm* 2 (1900): 973–8.

Cowan, Rev. William. "All For Love." *Girl's Own Paper* 11 (1889/90): 456.

Cowell, Sydney. "Healthy Recreation." *Girl's Own Paper* 16 (1894/5): 287.

Crozier, Gladys Beattie. "Caravaning for Girls: A New and Delightful Summer Pastime." *Girl's Realm* 11 (1909): 785+.

Darwin, Charles. *The Descent of Man: And Selection in Relation to Sex.* London: John Murray, 1871.

———. *On the Origin of Species.* Oxford: Oxford UP, 1998.

Davies, Emily. *The Higher Education of Women (1866).* Ed. Janet Howarth. London and Ronceverte: The Hambledon P, 1988.

Davis, Lucien. "The Modern Traveller at Eastertide." *Girl's Own Paper* 29 (1907/8): 385.

Dawson, William James. "The Ideal Woman." *Young Woman* 1 (1892/3): 39–42.

———. "My Study Diary." *Young Woman* 1 (1892/3): 31–3.

———. "Ruskin's Ideal Woman." *Young Woman* 1 (1892/3): 373–6.

"Death of Mr. J. Ashby-Sterry." *Times* 4 June 1917: 5.

Defoe, Daniel. *Robinson Crusoe.* Oxford: Oxford UP, 2007.

Dickens, Charles. *The Posthumous Papers of Pickwick Club.* London: Penguin, 2003.

Dixon, Ella Hepworth. "Why Women Are Ceasing to Marry." *The Fin De Siècle: A Reader in Cultural History C. 1880–1900.* Ed. Sally Ledger and Roger Luckhurst. Oxford: Oxford UP, 2000. 83–8.

D.M. "The Venus of Milo; Or, Girls of Two Different Periods." *Punch's Almanack for 1870.* London: Punch, 1870. np.

"Don't Marry Him!" *Young Woman* 1 (1892/3): 42.

Douglas, R.K. "The Brown Owl: The Forgotten Graces." *Atalanta* 3 (1889/90): 459–62, 642–6.

"Dragon." "Correspondence." *Monthly Packet* 9 (Fourth series) (1895): 252.

Echo, Miss. "The Irony of the Situation." *Girl of the Period Miscellany* (1869): 33–4.

"Edburgha." *Monthly Packet* 1 (1851): 245–6.

"The Education of Women: Science or the Confessional?" *Girl of the Period Miscellany* (1869): 69–70.

Edwarde, Annie. *A Girton Girl.* London: Richard Bentley & Son, 1886.

Elliot, L. "Woman's Suffrage at St. Austin's." *Girl's Realm* 14 (1912): 402–6.

"Emily Davies and Girton." *The Times* 18 Feb. 1927: 10.

Eprutt, Phil. "A Shocked Ancestral Audience." *Girl's Realm* 4 (1902): 584.

Esler, Erminda Rentoul. "Answers to Correspondents." *Young Woman* 7 (1898/9): 78–80.

———. "'Between Ourselves': A Friendly Chat with the Girls—The New Woman." *Young Woman* 3 (1894/5): 106–7.

———. "My Monthly Chat with the Girls." *Young Woman* 1 (1892/3): 62–4.

Everett-Green, Evelyn. "True Stories of Girl Heroines: Catharine the Rose." *Girl's Realm* 1 (1899): 487–91.

"Every Mother Should See the New Number." *Daily News* 15 Nov 1898: 6.

Ewing, Juliana. *Six to Sixteen*. New York: Garland, 1977.

"The Fast Smoking Girl of the Period." *Girl of the Period Miscellany* (1869): 137.

Fenwick Miller, Florence. "The Ideal Husband." *Young Woman* 3 (1894/5): 163–4.

———. "The Twentieth-Century Wife and Mother." *Young Woman* 11 (1902/3): 18–20.

F.H. "Women's Work: Its Value and Possibilities." *Girl's Own Paper* 16 (1893/4): 51–2.

"The First of Its Kind." *Daily News* 6 Oct. 1898: 3.

"The Flirt of the Period." *Girl of the Period Miscellany* (1869): 287–9.

Fraser, C.F. "A Race for a Sweetheart." *Atalanta* 9 (1895/6): 528–30.

Fraser, Mary. "One Woman's Destiny" *Atalanta* 11 (1897/8): 624–6.

Friederichs, Hulda. "The 'Old' Woman and the 'New.'" *Young Woman* 3 (1894/5): 202–4, 273–6.

Garrett Anderson, Elizabeth. "Sex in Mind and Education: A Reply." *Fortnightly Review* 15 (1874): 582–94.

G.C.H. "Hampstead Heath." *Girl's Own Paper* 9 (1887/8): 430.

Giberne, Agnes. "For England's Sake." *Girl's Realm* 2 (1900): 845–51.

———. "The Girl at the Dower House." *Atalanta* 9 (1895/6): 4+.

Gilman, Charlotte Perkins. "The Yellow Wallpaper." *Women Who Did: Stories by Men and Women 1890–1914*. Ed. Angelique Richardson. London: Penguin, 2005. 31–47.

"A Girl's Cricket Club." *Girl's Own Paper* 10 (1888): 33–6.

"Girls Who Play." *Girl of the Period Miscellany* (1869): 16.

"Girls Who Work." *Girl of the Period Miscellany* (1869): 17.

Glott, Polly. "Contributions to a Dictionary of the Future." *Girl of the Period Miscellany* (1869): 67+.

"The Graces of the Period." *Girl of the Period Miscellany* (1869): 20.

Graham, Jean. "The Canadian Girl: Her Home and School Life, Her Sports, Occupations and Amusements." *Girl's Realm* 11 (1909): 654–60.

Grand, Sarah. "At What Age Should a Girl Marry?" *Young Woman* 7 (1898/9): 161–3.

———. *The Heavenly Twins*. Ann Arbor: U of Michigan P, 1992.

———. "The Modern Girl." *North American Review* 158 (1894): 706–14.

———. "On the Choice of a Husband." *Young Woman* 7 (1898/9): 1–3.

———. "On the Choice of a Wife." *Young Man* 12 (1898): 325–7.

———. "The Revolt of the Daughters." *Nineteenth Century* 35 (1894): 23–31.

———. "Should Married Women Follow Professions?" *Young Woman* 7 (1897/8): 257–9.

"Grandmother." "Correspondence: On Dress." *Monthly Packet* 26 (1863): 441–4.

Greg, W.R. "Why are women redundant?" *National Review* 14 (April 1862): 434–60.

"The Gymnasium of the North London Collegiate School for Girls." *Girl's Own Paper* 3 (1882): 494.

Hardy, Rev. Edward John. "On the Choice of a Husband." *Young Woman* 1 (1892/3): 10–11.

Harrison, Irene. "A Capable Help." *Girl's Realm* 12 (1910): 604–6.

Harrison, Ethel. "The Case against Woman Suffrage." *Girl's Realm* 13 (1911): 666–8.

Haweis, Eliza. *The Art of Beauty and the Art of Dress*. New York and London: Garland, 1978.

Haweis, Rev. H.R. "The Engaged Girl." *Young Woman* 5 (1896/7): 256–8.

Henniker, Cicely. "A Dedication to the Readers of '*The Girl's Realm.*'" *Girl's Realm* 1 (1899): 368.

"Henrietta." "Correspondence." *Monthly Packet* 24 (1862): 332–4.

———. "Correspondence " *Monthly Packet* 25 (1863): 109–11.

Hersey, Heloise Edwina. "Cosy Corner Chats: The Manners of the Modern Girl." *Girl's Empire* 1 (1902): 468–9.

———. *To Girls: A Budget of Letters*. Boston: Small, Maynard & Co., 1901.

Henty, G.A. "A Soldier's Daughter." *Girl's Realm* 5 (1903): 553+.

Heron-Allen, Edward. "Suffragettes: 'The Girl of the Period Miscellany.'" *Notes and Queries* s10-X (1908): 467.

Hodgkinson, Mary. "Married Life." *Young Man and Woman* 31 (1915): 23.

Holland, Penelope. "Two Girls of the Period—I. The Upper Side: Our Offence, Our Defence, and Our Petition." *Macmillan's Magazine* 19 (Feb. 1869): 323–31.

Hood, Thomas. "I'm Going to Bombay." *Selected Poems of Thomas Hood, Winthrop Mackworth Praed and Thomas Lovell Beddoes*. Ed. Susan J. Wolfson and Peter J. Manning. Pittsburgh: U of Pittsburgh P, 2000. 58–61.

———. "The Song of the Shirt." *Selected Poems of Thomas Hood, Winthrop Mackworth Praed and Thomas Lovell Beddoes*. Ed. Susan J. Wolfson and Peter J. Manning. Pittsburgh: U of Pittsburgh P, 2000. 141–3.

Hullah, Mary E. "Stand and Wait: An Invalid's Story." *Girl's Own Paper* 13 (1891/2): 621–3.

Ibsen, Henrik. *Hedda Gabler and A Doll's House*. London: Faber and Faber, 1989.

James, Henry. "Modern Woman." *Nation* 22 Oct. 1868 (1868): 332–4.

"Jane." "Correspondence." *Monthly Packet* 24 (1862): 544–6.

Jeune, Lady. "The Ideal Husband." *Young Woman* 3 (1895): 23–4.

Klickmann, Flora. "The Editor's Page." *Girl's Own Paper and Woman's Magazine* 30 (1908): 1.

Knatchbull-Hugessen, Eva. "Oxford and Cambridge College for Women." *Atalanta* 3 (1889/90): 421–3.

"Ladies' Golf." *Girl's Own Paper* 11 (1890): 273–4.

"The Ladies Year." *Punch* 28 June 1890: 309.

"A Lady's Remonstrance." *Girl of the Period Miscellany* (1869): 179.

Lark, Anna Tremayne. "The Governor's Will." *Girl's Realm* 13 (1911): 31–7.

"A Laundress." "My Laundry." *Girl's Own Paper* 23 (1901/2): 42–3.

Layard, George Somes. *Mrs. Lynn Linton: Her Life, Letters, and Opinions*. London: Methuem & Co., 1901.

Leake, Mrs. Percy. "Women Talkers at Leeds." *Monthly Packet* 7 (Fourth series) (1894): 59–63.

Leeder, S.H. "Important Notice to Readers." *Girl's Realm* 16 (1914): 4.

———. "The War: How Girls May Help in Practical Ways." *Girl's Realm* 16 (1914): 1–4.

Leroy, Amélie Claire. (See also Stuart, Esmé.) "Discipline of Reading." *The Woman's Herald* 30 Nov. 1893: 643–4.

"A Letter from Cambridge." *Atalanta* 6 (1892/3): 461–4.

"Letters to a Debutante by a Woman of the World." *Atalanta* 10 (1896/7): 36+.

"Lines To 'A Girl of the Period.'" *Girl of the Period Miscellany* (1869): 303.

Linton, Eliza Lynn. "The Girl of the Period." *Prose by Victorian Women: An Anthology*. Ed. Andrea Broomfield and Sally Mitchell. New York and London: Garland Publishing, 1996. 356–60.

———. "The Ideal Husband." *Young Woman* 3 (1895): 56–7.

"Literary Gossip." *Belfast News-Letter* 7 Sept. 1898: 3.

"Literature." *Derby Mercury* 24 March 1869: 6.

"Literature." *Derby Mercury* 18 Aug. 1869: 6.

"Literature." *Derby Mercury* 20 Oct. 1869: 6.

"Literature." *The Era* 11 July 1869: 6.

"Literature." *The Era* 29 Aug. 1869: 6.

Lonsdale, Sophia. "Work and Workers: Women's Work Amongst the Poor." *Monthly Packet* 2 (Fourth series) (1891): 32–7.

Luard, C.G. "The Brown Owl." *Atalanta* 3 (1889/90): 767–8.

Lynch, Hannah. "A Girl's Ride on an Engine." *Girl's Realm* 2 (1900): 465–9.

Marchant, Bessie. "Bessel's Wedding." *Girl's Realm* 12 (1910): 127–30.

"Mary." "Correspondence: Too Much of Everything." *Monthly Packet* 25 (1863): 555–9.

Maudsley, Henry. "Sex in Mind and Education." *Fortnightly Review* 15 (1874): 466–83.

Mayhew, Henry. *London Labour and the London Poor*. London: G. Woodfall and Son, 1851.

Mayo, Isabella Fyvie. "At What Age Should a Girl Marry?" *Young Woman* 7 (1899): 164.

———. "The Ideal Husband." *Young Woman* 3 (1895): 194–7.

Meade, L.T. "Aunt Cassandra." *Young Woman* 1 (1892/3): 1+

———. Editorial Note. *Atalanta* 3 (1889/90): 461.

———. Editorial Note. *Atalanta* 3 (1889/90): 586.

———. "Girton College." *Atalanta* 7 (1893/4): 325–31.

———. *A World of Girls: The Story of a School*. London: Cassell, 1886.

Menzies, Jane. "Our Monthly Talk: Railway Book-stalls." *A.1.* 2 (1889): 11.

Meyer, Annie Nathan. "Woman's Assumption of Sex Superiority." *North American Review* Jan. 1904: 103–9.

"Middleage." "The Modern Girl." *Monthly Packet* 11 (Third series) (1886): 191–2.

Miles, Afred H., ed. *The Poets and the Poetry of the Century: Humour, Society, Parody and Occasional Verse. Vol. IX.* London: Hutchinson & Co., 1891–97.

Miln, Louise Jordan. "The Fin-De-Siècle Girl." *Monthly Packet* 7 (Fourth series) (1894): 586–90.

Milton, John. "When I consider how my light is spent." *The Riverside Milton.* Ed. Roy Flannagan. Boston: Houghton Mifflin Co., 1998. 256.

Mitchell, Charles. *Newspaper Press Directory and Advertiser's Guide.* Twenty-third edition. London: C. Mitchell, 1869.

Minns, B.E. "A New Sport for Girls: Skate Sailing." *Girl's Realm* 4 (1902): 187.

"Modern Girl." "Two Girls' Views of 'The Girlhood Question.'" *Monthly Packet* 11 (Third series) (1886): 480–2.

Molesworth, Mary. "The Brown Owl." *Atalanta* 3 (1889/90): 520–24.

———. "White Turrets" *Atalanta* 7 (1893/4): 530+.

"Mona." "Correspondence: Too Much of Everything." *Monthly Packet* 26 (1863): 217–20.

"Moonraker." "Two Girls' Views of 'The Girlhood Question.'" *Monthly Packet* 11 (Third series) (1886): 479–80.

Morgan, F. Somerville. "Old Songs." *Atalanta* 1 (1887/8): 1.

Morrison, Henry Steele. "The Conduct of Girls in the War." *Girl's Realm* 2 (1900): 804–6.

Morten, Honnor. "Nursing as a Profession." *Young Woman* 1 (1892/3): 120–21.

"The Mothers of Famous Men." *Young Man and Woman* 31 (1915): 5–7.

"A Muscular Maiden." *Girl of the Period Miscellany* (1869): 78–9.

"My Chignon." *Girl of the Period Miscellany* (1869): 185.

Nesbit, Edith. "The Girton Girl." *Atalanta* 8 (1894/5): 755–9.

Nordau, Max. "Degeneration." *The Fin De Siecle: A Reader in Cultural History C. 1880–1900.* Ed. Sally Ledger and Roger Luckhurst. Oxford: Oxford UP, 2000. 13–17.

"NOT an Indignant One." "The Brown Owl." *Atalanta* 3 (1889/90): 768.

Novra, Lewis. "Contentment." *Girl's Own Paper* 3 (1881/2): 497.

"Nursery Rhymes for the Times." *Punch* 20 Feb. 1875: 68.

"An Old Maid." *My Life and What Shall I Do with It?* London: Longman, Green, and Roberts, 1861.

Pankhurst, Christabel. "What Woman Suffrage Means." *Girl's Realm* 13 (1911): 575–7.

"Paperknife." "Correspondence: English Woman in Office." *Monthly Packet* 9 (Fourth series) (1895): 252–3.

Patmore, Coventry. *The Angel in the House.* London: G. Bell, 1878.

Paton, Sir Noel. "A Girton Girl." *Atalanta* 6 (1892/3): 467.

Pearse, Alfred. "Going Out to Meet the New Century." *Girl's Realm* 3 (1901): 244.

Penny, Mrs. Frank. "Work and Workers: Women's Medical Work in India." *Monthly Packet* 2 (Fourth series) (1891): 260–65.

"The Plain Gold Ring: No. Vi - Domestic Responsibilities." *Girl of the Period Miscellany* (1869): 277–8.

Praed, Rosa Campbell. "A Daughter of Greater Britain: The Australian Girl." *Girl's Realm* 1 (1899): 249–53.

Prescott, E. Livingston. "A Guard's Last Run." *Atalanta* 9 (1895/6): 449–52.

"Prize Chignons from 'The Horticultural.'" *Girl of the Period Miscellany* (1869): 184.

Rawson, Maud. "What Girls Are Doing." *Girl's Realm* 1 (1899): 530.

"The Result of the 'Favourite' Competition Announced in Our October Number." *Girl's Realm* 2 (1900): 293.

Richardson, Sir Benjamin Ward. "On Recreations for Girls." *Girl's Own Paper* 15 (1893/4): 545–7.

Ruskin, John. *Sesame and Lilies*. Ed. Deborah Epstein Nord. New Haven, CT: Yale UP, 2002.

S.L. "Mr. Punch's Designs After Nature." *Punch* 16 Oct. 1869: 145.

Salmon, Edward. *Juvenile Literature as It Is*. London: Henry J. Drane, 1888.

———. "What Girls Read." *Nineteenth Century* 20.116 (1886): 515–29.

Schofield, A.T. "The Cycling Craze." *Girl's Own Paper* 17 (1895/6): 185–6.

Sharp, Evelyn. *Rebel Women*. London: A.C. Fitfield, 1910.

Sidgwick, Eleanor Mildred. *Health Statistics of Women Students of Cambridge and Oxford and of Their Sisters*. Cambridge: Cambridge UP, 1890.

Smith, Laura Alex. "Some Influences of Girlhood." *Atalanta* 7 (1893/4): 351–2.

Spencer, Herbert. *Essays on Education and Kindred Subjects*. London and New York: J.M. Dent & Sons, 1966.

Stables, Gordon. "A Beautiful Skin." *Girl's Own Paper* 5 (1883/4): 643–4.

———. "Beauty Hints." *Girl's Own Paper* 23 (1901/2): 84–5.

———. "Boys' Dogs and All About Them." *Boy's Own Paper* 3 (1879/80): 425+.

———. "The Boy's Own Museum; Or, Birds and Beasts, and How to Stuff Them." *Boy's Own Paper* 3 (1880/81): 21+.

———. "Common Sense About Health and Athletics." *Boy's Own Paper* 10 (1887/8): 491+.

———. "The Cruise of the Snowbird." *Boy's Own Paper* 3 (1880/1): 398.

———. "Cycling: As a Pastime and for Health." *Girl's Own Paper* 17 (1895/6): 722–3.

———. "Exercise, and How to Benefit by It." *Girl's Own Paper* 4 (1882/3): 218–19.

———. "The Girl Crusoes: A Tale of the Indian Ocean." *Girl's Realm* 4 (1902): 188–95.

———. "Health, Strength, and Beauty." *Girl's Own Paper* 11 (1889/90): 758–9.

———. "Healthy Lives for Working Girls." *Girl's Own Paper* 8 (1886/7): 76–9.

———. "I Remember, I Remember." *Girl's Own Paper* 7 (1885/6): 424–6.

———. "Our Bodies Are Our Gardens." *Girl's Own Paper* 5 (1883/4): 218–19.

———. "Remove the Cause." *Girl's Own Paper* 10 (1888/9): 7–8.

———. "Things That Every Girl Should Learn to Do." *Girl's Own Paper* 5 (1883/4): 70–71.

———. "Useful Pastimes for Health and Pleasure." *Girl's Own Paper* 16 (1894/5): 557–8.

————. "Where There's a Will There's a Way." *Girl's Own Paper* 12 (1890/1): 310–11.

————. "Work Versus Idleness." *Girl's Own Paper* 5 (1883/4): 622–3.

Stead, W.T. "Maiden Tribute to Modern Babylon." *Pall Mall Gazette* 6–10 July 1885.

————. "Young Women and Journalism." *Young Woman* 1 (1892/3): 12–14.

Stebbing, Grace. "The New Woman." *Young Woman* 4 (1896): 405–10.

Stuart, Esmé. [Leroy, Amélie Claire.] "Barbara's Book." *Monthly Packet* 20 (1890): 130–38.

"A Sullied Page." *Tomahawk: A Saturday Journal of Satire* 22 Aug. 1868: 71.

Thackeray, Anne. "English Men and Women of Letters of the Nineteenth Century. IV: Jane Austen." *Atalanta* 1 (1888/9): 226–32.

"Theatres and Music." *John Bull and Britannia* 21 Jan. 1860: 43.

"Tourist Girls of the Period. No. 1 – The Climbing Girl." *Girl of the Period Miscellany* (1869): 194-97.

"Transformed." *Girl's Own Paper* 8 (1887): 682+.

Trimmer, Sarah. *Some Account of the Life and Writings of Mrs Trimmer*. London: F.C. and J. Rivington, 1814.

Troubridge, Lady. "None but the Brave." *Girl's Realm* 2 (1900): 793–9.

Tuck, Magdalen F.P. "A Girl Cliff-Climber Down Bempton Cliffs." *Girl's Realm* 11 (1909): 403–6.

Turner, Ethel. *Seven Little Australians*. Montville, Qld: Walter McVitty Books, 1994.

Tuttiett, Mary Gleed. "Sweethearts and Friends." *Atalanta* 10 (1896/7): 435+.

Tynan, Katherine. "At What Age Should a Girl Marry?" *Young Woman* 7 (1899): 165.

Tytler, Sarah. "The Brown Owl." *Atalanta* 3 (1889/90): 113–15.

"Velocipede." "Correspondence: A Few Words from a 'Fast' Young Lady." *Monthly Packet* 27 (1863): 444–7.

"The Victorian Era Exhibition." *Times* 24 May 1897: 5.

Walford, L.B. "The Brown Owl." *Atalanta* 3 (1889/90): 49–51.

Wallace, Edna. "The Cause—and Cupid." *Girl's Realm* 13 (1911): 516–21.

————. "A Twentieth Century Martyr: A 'Votes for Women' Story." *Girl's Realm* 11 (1909): 779–84.

————. "A Woman's Ruse." *Girl's Realm* 15 (1913): 451–5.

Warre-Cornish, Mrs. "Miss Alice Corkran." *Girl's Realm* 15 (1913): 850–51.

Weisskopf, C.M. "Correspondence." *Monthly Packet* 9 (Fourth series) (1895): 376–7.

"What Is the Girl of the Period For?" *Girl of the Period Miscellany* (1869): 5.

Wilde, Oscar. *The Importance of Being Earnest and Other Plays*. New York: Modern Library, 2003.

"William Brunton" *Fun* 3 April 1878: 145.

Wilson, H. Mary, and R. Wilson. "Work and Workers: Hospital Nursing." *Monthly Packet* 3 (Fourth series) (1892): 45–55.

Winter, Jonathan Strange. "The Ideal Husband." *Young Woman* 3 (1895): 119–20.

Wollstonecraft, Mary. *Thoughts on the Education of Daughters, 1787*. Oxford: Woodstock Books, 1994.

———. *Vindication of the Rights of Woman*. Oxford: Oxford UP, 1999.

"Women Students at Oxford." *Atalanta* 10 (1896/7): 43–8.

Wordsworth, William. *William Wordsworth: Selected Poems*. London: Penguin, 1994.

Wynn, Walter. "The Editor's Chat." The *Young Man and Woman* 31 (1915): 1–2.

Yonge, Charlotte M. "Children's Literature of the Past Century." *Macmillan's Magazine* 20 (1869): 229–37, 302–10, 448–56.

———. "The China Cupboard." *Monthly Packet* 9 (Fourth series) (1895): 124–6.

———. "Conversations on the Catechism: Introduction." *Monthly Packet* 1 (1851): 14–17.

———. "The Cumberland Street Children's Hospital." *Monthly Packet* 11 (New Series) (1871): 92–5.

———. "The Daisy Chain: Or, Aspirations, a Family Chronicle." *Monthly Packet* 6 (1853): 26+.

———. "A Few Words on the Choice of Books for Amusement." *Monthly Packet* 2 (1851): 240–43.

———. "Grandmamma: 'My Life, and What Shall I Do With It?'" *Monthly Packet* 21 (1861): 420–26.

———. "Hints on Reading." *Monthly Packet* 2 (1851): 478.

———. "Hints on Reading." *Monthly Packet* 5 (1868): 415.

———. "Hints on Reading." *Monthly Packet* 6 (1853): 160.

———. "Hints on Reading." The *Montly Packet* 7 (1869): 310.

———. "Introductory Letter." *Monthly Packet* 1 (1851): i–iv.

———. Letter to Emily Davies. 22 July 1868. Emily Davies Papers. Girton Archive, Girton College, Cambridge.

———. *The Letters of Charlotte Mary Yonge (1823–1901)*. Ed. Charlotte Mitchell, Ellen Jordan, and Helen Schinske. 2007. 10 June 2008 <http://hdl.handle.net/10065/337>.

———. "New Year's Words." *Monthly Packet* 11 (Third series) (1886): 41–7.

———. "Notice to Correspondent." *Monthly Packet* 1 (1851): 208, 288.

———. "Notice to Correspondents." *Monthly Packet* 8 (1854): 240.

———. "Notice to Correspondents." *Monthly Packet* 16 (1873): 310.

———. "Notice to Correspondents." *Monthly Packet* 17 (1874): 504.

———. "Our Grandmother's Education." *Atalanta* 3 (1889/90): 163–5.

———. *What Books to Lend and What to Give*. London: National Society's Depository, 1887.

———. "Womankind." *Monthly Packet* 17 (New series) (1874): 24+.

———. "Work and Workers: Authorship." *Monthly Packet* 3 (Fourth series) (1892): 296–303.

———. *The Young Step-Mother*. London: Macmillan, 1861.

Yonge, Charlotte M., and Christabel Coleridge. "Editorial Note." *Monthly Packet* 3 (Fourth series) (1892): 47.

"*The Young Woman*." *Myra's Journal* 1 Nov. 1895: 5.

Secondary Texts

Altholz, Josef L. *The Religious Press in Britain, 1760–1900*. Westport, CT: Greenwood P, 1989.

Altick, Richard D. *The English Common Reader: A Society History of the Mass Reading Public, 1800–1900*. 2nd ed. Columbus: Ohio State UP, 1957.

———. *Victorian People and Ideas*. NewYork and London: W.W. Norton & Co., 1973.

Anderson, Benedict. *Imagined Communities: Reflections on the Origin and Spread of Nationalism*. London: Verso, 1991.

Anderson, Nancy Fix. *Woman against Women in Victorian England*. Bloomington and Indianapolis: Indiana UP, 1987.

Ardis, Ann. *New Women, New Novels: Feminism and Early Modernism*. New Brunswick and London: Rutgers UP, 1990.

Attridge, Steve. *Nationalism, Imperialism and Identity in Late Victorian Culture*. Houndsmills, UK: Palgrave Macmillan, 2003.

Beer, Janet. "Charlotte Perkins Gilman and Women's Health: 'The Long Limitation.'" *A Very Different Story: Studies on the Fiction of Charlotte Perkins Gilman*. Ed. Val Gough and Jill Rudd. Liverpool: Liverpool UP, 1998. 54–67.

Beer, Janet and Ann Heilmann. "'If I Were a Man': Charlotte Perkins Gilman, Sarah Grand and the Sexual Education of Girls." *Special Relationships: Anglo-American Affinities and Antagonisms*. Ed. Janet Beer and Bridget Bennett. Manchester: Manchester UP, 2002. 178–99.

Beetham, Margaret. *A Magazine of Her Own? Domesticity and Desire in the Woman's Magazine 1800–1914*. London and New York: Routledge, 1996.

———. "Open and Closed: The Periodical as a Publishing Genre." *Victorian Periodicals Review* 22.3 (1989): 96–100.

Bell, Srilekha. "Mrs. Frank Penny's *A Mixed Marriage*: 'A Tale Worth Reading.'" *English Literature in Transition, 1880–1920* 44:1 (2001): 28–45.

Bemis, Virginia. "Reverent and Reserved: The Sacramental Theology of Charlotte M. Yonge." *Women's Theology in Nineteenth-Century Britain: Transfiguring the Faith of Their Fathers*. Ed. Julie Melnyk. New York and London: Garland, 1998. 123–32.

Bettis, Pamela J. and Natalie G. Adams. "Landscapes of Girlhood." *Geographies of Girlhood: Identities In-Between*. Ed. Pamela Bettis and Natalie Adams. Mahway, NJ and London: Lawrence Erlbaum Assoc., 2005. 1–16.

Bilston, Sarah. *The Awkward Age in Women's Popular Fiction, 1850–1900: Girls and the Transition to Womanhood*. Oxford: Clarendon P, 2004.

Bland, Lucy. *Banishing the Beast: English Feminism and Sexual Morality, 1885–1914*. London: Penguin, 1995.

Bonnefoy, Yves. *Greek and Egyptian Mythologies*. Trans. Wendy Doniger. Chicago and London: U of Chicago P, 1992.

Boufis, Christina. "'Of Home Birth and Breeding': Eliza Lynn Linton and the Girl of the Period." *The Girl's Own: Cultural Histories of the Anglo-American Girl,*

1830–1915. Ed. Claudia Nelson and Lynne Vallone. Athens and London: U of Georgia P, 1994. 98–123.

Bradbrook, M.C. *'That Infidel Place': A Short History of Girton College, 1869–1969*. London: Chatto and Windus, 1969.

Brake, Laurel, and Julie Codell. "Introduction: Encountering the Press." *Encounters in the Victorian Press: Editors, Authors, Readers*. Ed. Laurel Brake and Julie Codell. Houndsmills, UK: Palgrave, 2005. 1–7.

Bratton, J.S. "British Imperialism and the Reproduction of Femininity in Girls' Fiction, 1900–1930." *Imperialism and Juvenile Literature*. Ed. Jeffrey Richards. Manchester and New York: Manchester UP, 1989. 195–215.

———. *The Impact of Victorian Children's Fiction*. London: Croom Helm, 1981.

Briggs, Julia, and Dennis Butts. "The Emergence of Form (1850–90)." *Children's Literature: An Illustrated History*. Ed. Peter Hunt. Oxford: Oxford UP, 1995. 130–65.

Broomfield, Andrea. "Eliza Lynn Linton, Sarah Grand and the Spectacle of the Victorian Woman Question: Catch Phrases, Buzz Words and Sound Bites." *English Literature in Transition* 47.3 (2004): 251–72.

———. "Much More Than an Antifeminist: Eliza Lynn Linton's Contribution to the Rise of Victorian Popular Journalism." *Victorian Literature and Culture* 29.2 (2001): 267–83.

Brown, Penny. *The Captured World: The Child and Childhood in Nineteenth-Century Women's Writing in England*. New York: Harvester Wheatsheaf, 1993.

Burstyn, Joan N. "Education and Sex: The Medical Case against Higher Education for Women in England, 1870–1900." *Proceedings of the American Philosophical Society* 117.2 (1973): 79–89.

———. *Victorian Education and the Ideal of Womanhood*. London: Croom Helm, 1980.

Cadogan, Mary, and Patricia Craig. *You're a Brick, Angela!: A New Look at Girls' Fiction from 1839 to 1975*. London: Victor Gollancz, 1976.

Caine, Barbara. *English Feminism: 1780–1980*. Oxford: Oxford UP, 1997.

Courtney, Julia. "The *Barnacle*: A Manuscript Magazine of the 1860s." *The Girl's Own: Cultural Histories of the Anglo-American Girl, 1830–1915*. Ed. Claudia Nelson and Lynne Vallone. Athens and London: U of Georgia P, 1994. 71–97.

Cox, Jeffrey. *The English Churches in a Secular Society: Lambeth, 1870–1930*. New York and Oxford: Oxford UP, 1982.

Crow, Duncan. *The Edwardian Woman*. London: George Allen & Unwin, 1978.

Cruse, Amy. *The Victorians and Their Books*. London: George Allen & Unwin, 1935.

Cunningham, Hugh. *Grace Darling: Victorian Heroine*. London: Hambledon Continuum, 2007.

Daly, Nicholas. *Literature, Technology, and Modernity, 1860–2000*. Cambridge: Cambridge UP, 2004.

Dixon, Diana. "Children and the Press, 1866–1914." *The Press in English Society from the Seventeenth to Nineteenth Centuries*. Ed. Michael Harris and Alan Lee. London: Associated University Presses, 1986. 133–48.

Doughty, Terry, ed. *Selections from* The Girl's Own Paper, *1880–1907*. Peterborough, ON: Broadview P, 2004.

Driscoll, Catherine. *Girls: Feminine Adolescence in Popular Culture and Cultural Theory*. New York: Columbia UP, 2002.

Drotner, Kirsten. *English Children and Their Magazines, 1751–1945*. New Haven: Yale UP, 1988.

Egoff, Sheila. *Children's Periodicals of the Nineteenth Century: A Survey and Bibliography*. London: The Library Association, 1951.

Elston, M.A. "Anderson, Elizabeth Garrett (1836–1917)." *Oxford Dictionary of National Biography*. Oxford UP, Sept. 2004; online edn, Oct 2005. 1 Dec. 2009 <http://www.oxforddnb.com/view/article/30406>.

Faught, C. Brad. *The Oxford Movement: A Thematic History of the Tractarians and Their Times*. University Park, PA: Pennsylvania State UP, 2003.

Finch, Casey. "'Hooked and Buttoned Together': Victorian Underwear and Representations of the Female Body." *Victorian Studies* 34.3 (Spring 1991): 337–63.

Fletcher, Sheila. *Women First: The Female Tradition in English Physical Education 1880–1980*. London & Dover, NH: Althone P, 1984.

Flint, Kate. *The Woman Reader, 1837–1914*. Oxford: Clarendon P, 1993.

Forrester, Wendy. *Great-Grandmama's Weekly: A Celebration of* The Girl's Own Paper, *1880–1901*. Guildford and London: Lutterworth P, 1980.

Foucault, Michel. *Discipline and Punish: The Birth of the Prison*. New York: Vintage, 1977.

———. *The Will to Knowledge: The History of Sexuality, Volume 1*. London: Penguin, 1990.

Fraser, Hilary, Stephanie Green, and Judith Johnston. *Gender and the Victorian Periodical*. Cambridge: Cambridge UP, 2003.

Fyfe, Aileen. *Science and Salvation: Evangelical Popular Science Publishing in Victorian Britain*. Chicago and London: U of Chicago P, 2004.

Gibson, William. *Church, State and Society, 1760–1850*. New York: St. Martin's P, 1994.

Gorham, Deborah. *The Victorian Girl and the Feminine Ideal*. London and Canberra: Croom Helm, 1982.

Gorsky, Susan Rubinow. *Femininity to Feminism: Women and Literature in the Nineteenth Century*. New York: Twayne Publishers, 1992.

Gray, Donald J. "A List of Comic Periodicals Published in Great Britain, 1800–1900, with a Prefatory Essay." *Victorian Periodicals Newsletter* 5.1 (1972): 2–39.

Habegger, Alfred J. *Henry James and the "Woman Business."* Cambridge: Cambridge UP, 1989.

Hall, Lesley A. "Hauling Down the Double Standard: Feminism, Social Purity and Sexual Science in Late Nineteenth-Century Britain." *Gender and History* 16.1 (2004): 36–56.

———. *Sex, Gender and Social Chance in Britain since 1880*. Houndsmills, UK: Macmillan P, 2000.

————. "Wilson, Helen Mary (1864–1951)." *Oxford Dictionary of National Biography*. Oxford UP, 2004. 17 Sept. 2009 <http://www.oxforddnb.com/view/article/57832>.

Harris, Anita. *Future Girl: Young Women in the Twenty-First Century*. New York and London: Routledge, 2004.

Hayter, Alethea. *Charlotte Yonge*. Plymouth, UK: Northcote House, 1996.

Heilmann, Ann. *New Woman Strategies: Sarah Grand, Olive Schreiner, Mona Caird*. Manchester and New York: Manchester UP, 2004.

Helsinger, Elizabeth K., Robin Lauterbach Sheets, and William Veeder. *The Woman Question: Social Issues, 1837–1883*. Volume II of *The Woman Question: Society and Literature in Britain and America, 1837–1883*. New York & London: Garland Publishing, 1993.

Hunt, Peter, ed. *Children's Literature: An Illustrated History*. Oxford: Oxford UP, 1995.

Jackson, Mary. *Engines of Instruction, Mischief, and Magic: Children's Literature in England from Its Beginnings to 1839*. Lincoln: U of Nebraska P, 1989.

James, Allison, Chris Jenks, and Alan Prout. *Theorizing Childhood*. Cambridge: Polity P, 1998.

Jay, Elizabeth. "Charlotte Mary Yonge and Tractarian Aesthetics." *Victorian Poetics* 44.1 (Spring 2006): 43–59.

Joannou, Maroula. "Suffragette Fiction and the Fictions of Suffrage." *The Women's Suffrage Movement: New Feminist Perspectives*. Ed. Maroula Joannou and June Purvis. Manchester and New York: Manchester UP, 1998. 101–16.

Jones, Susan. "Into the Twentieth Century: Imperial Romance from Haggard to Buchan." *A Companion to Romance: From Classical to Contemporary*. Ed. Corinne Saunders. Malden, MA: Blackwell, 2004. 406–23.

Kearney, Mary Celeste. *Girls Make Media*. New York: Routledge, 2006.

Kemp, Sandra, Charlotte Mitchell, and David Trotter. *Edwardian Fiction: An Oxford Companion*. Oxford and New York: Oxford UP, 1997.

Kent, Susan Kingsley. *Sex and Suffrage in Britain, 1860–1914*. Princeton: Princeton UP, 1987.

King, Jeannette. *The Victorian Woman Question in Contemporary Feminist Fiction*. Houndsmills, UK: Palgrave Macmillan, 2005.

Knight, Mark, and Emma Mason. *Nineteenth-Century Religion and Literature: An Introduction*. Oxford: Oxford UP, 2006.

Krebs, Paula M. *Gender, Race, and the Writing of Empire: Public Discourse and the Boer War*. Cambridge: Cambridge UP, 1999.

Kutzer, M. Daphne. *Empire's Children: Empire and Imperialism in Classic British Children's Books*. New York: Garland, 2000.

Lacey, Candida Ann. "Introduction." *Barbara Leigh Smith Bodichon and the Langham Place Group*. New York and London: Routledge & Kegan Paul, 1986. 1–16.

Lawrence, Jon. "Contesting the Male Polity: The Suffragettes and the Politics of Disruption in Edwardian Britain." *Women, Privilege, and Power: British*

Politics, 1750 to the Present. Ed. Amanda Vickery. Stanford, CA: Stanford UP, 2001. 201–26.

Ledger, Sally. *The New Woman: Fiction and Feminism at the Fin De Siècle.* Manchester: Manchester UP, 1997.

Lewis, Jane. *Women in England 1870–1950: Sexual Divisions and Social Change.* Sussex and Bloomington: Wheatsheaf Books Ltd, 1984.

Liggins, Emma. "'The Life of a Bachelor Girl in the Big City': Selling the Single Lifestyle to Readers of *Woman* and the *Young Woman* in the 1890s." *Victorian Periodicals Review* 40.3 (2007): 216–38.

Lyons, Deborah. *Gender and Immortality: Heroines in Ancient Greek Myth and Cult.* Princeton, NJ: Princeton UP, 1997.

Marcus, Sharon. "Reflections on Victorian Fashion Plates." *Differences: A Journal of Feminist Cultural Studies* 14.3 (2003): 4–33.

Marks, Patricia. *Bicycles, Bangs, and Bloomers: The New Woman in the Popular Press.* Lexington: UP of Kentucky, 1990.

Mays, Kelly J. "The Disease of Reading and Victorian Periodicals." *Literature in the Marketplace: Nineteenth-Century British Publishing and Reading Practices.* Ed. John O. Jordan and Robert L. Patten. Cambridge: Cambridge UP, 1995. 165–94.

McCrone, Kathleen E. *Sport and the Physical Emancipation of English Women, 1870–1914.* London: Routledge, 1988.

Miller, Jane Eldridge. *Rebel Women: Feminism, Modernism and the Edwardian Novel.* London: Virago P, 1994.

Mitchell, Charlotte. "Charlotte M. Yonge's Bank Account: A Rich New Source of Information on Her Work and Her Life." *Women's Writing* 17.2 (Aug. 2010): 380–400.

Mitchell, Sally. *The New Girl: Girls' Culture in England, 1880–1915.* New York: Columbia UP, 1995.

Montague, Ken. "The Aesthetics of Hygiene: Aesthetic Dress, Modernity, and the Body as Sign." *Journal of Design History* 7.2 (1994): 91–112.

Morgan, Sue. "'Wild Oats or Acorns?' Social Purity, Sexual Politics and the Response of the Late-Victorian Church." *Journal of Religious History* 31.2 (June 2007): 151–68.

———. "Women, Religion and Feminism: Past, Present and Future Perspectives." *Women, Religion and Feminism in Britain, 1750–1900.* Ed. Sue Morgan. Houndsmills, UK: Palgrave Macmillan, 2002. 1–19.

Mort, Frank. *Dangerous Sexualities: Medico-Moral Politics in England Since 1830.* London and New York: Routledge & Kegan Paul, 1987.

Morton, Peter. "Grant Allen: A Biographical Essay." *Grant Allen: Literature and Cultural Politics at the Fin De Siècle.* Ed. William Greenslade and Terence Rodgers. Aldershot: Ashgate, 2005. 23–44.

Moruzi, Kristine. "'The freedom suits me': Encouraging Girls to Settle in the Colonies." *Victorian Settler Narratives: Emigrants, Cosmpolitans, and Returnees in Nineteenth-Century Literature.* Ed. Tamara S. Wagner. London: Pickering & Chatto, 2011. 177–91.

Moruzi, Kristine, and Michelle Smith. "'Learning What Real Work … Means': Ambivalent Attitudes Towards Employment in the *Girl's Own Paper.*" *Victorian Periodicals Review* 43.4 (Winter 2010): 429–45.

Nelson, Claudia. *Boys Will Be Girls: The Feminine Ethic and British Children's Fiction, 1857–1917.* New Brunswick: Rutgers UP, 1991.

Nowell-Smith, Simon. *Letters to Macmillan.* London: Macmillan, 1967.

Onslow, Barbara. "Preaching to the Ladies: Florence Fenwick Miller and her Readers in the *Illustrated London News.*" *Encounters in the Victorian Press: Editors, Authors, Readers.* Ed. Laurel Brake and Julie Codell. Houndsmills, UK: Palgrave, 2005. 88–102.

———. *Women of the Press in Nineteenth-Century Britain.* Houndsmills, UK: Palgrave Macmillan, 2000.

Peck, John. *War, the Army and Victorian Literature.* Houndsmills, UK: Macmillan P, 1998.

Pedersen, Joyce Senders. "The Reform of Women's Secondary and Higher Education: Institutional Change and Social Values in Mid and Late Victorian England." *History of Education Quarterly* 19.1 (1979): 61–91.

Phegley, Jennifer. *Educating the Proper Woman Reader: Victorian Family Literary Magazines and the Cultural Health of the Nation.* Columbus, OH: Ohio State UP, 2004.

Poovey, Mary. *Uneven Developments: The Ideological Work of Gender in Mid-Victorian England.* Chicago: U of Chicago P, 1988.

Pykett, Lyn. *The "Improper" Feminine: The Women's Sensation Novel and the New Woman Writing.* London: Routledge, 1992.

———. "Reading the Periodical Press: Text and Context." *Victorian Periodicals Review* 22.3 (1989): 100–108.

Richards, Jeffrey. "Introduction." *Imperialism and Juvenile Literature.* Ed. Jeffrey Richards. Manchester: Manchester UP, 1989. 1–11.

Richardson, Angelique. *Love and Eugenics in the Late Nineteenth Century: Rational Reproduction and the New Woman.* Oxford: Oxford UP, 2003.

Richardson, Angelique, and Chris Willis. "Introduction." *The New Woman in Fiction and in Fact: Fin-De-Siècle Feminisms.* Ed. Anqelique Richardson and Chris Willis. Houndsmills, UK: Palgrave Macmillan, 2002. 1–38.

Rinehart, Nina. "'The Girl of the Period' Controversy." *Victorian Periodicals Review* 13.1/2 (1980): 3–9.

Robson, John M. *Marriage or Celibacy? The* Daily Telegraph *on a Victorian Dilemma.* Toronto: U of Toronto P, 1995.

Rose, Jacqueline. *The Case of Peter Pan or the Impossibility of Children's Fiction.* London: MacMillan P, 1984.

Rover, Constance. *The Punch Book of Women's Rights.* London: Hutchinson & Co, 1967.

Schaffer, Talia. "The Mysterious Magnum Bonum: Fighting to Read Charlotte Yonge." *Nineteenth-Century Literature* 55.2 (2000): 244–75.

————. "'Nothing but Foolscap and Ink': Inventing the New Woman." *The New Woman in Fiction and in Fact: Fin-de-Siècle Feminisms*. Ed. Angelique Richardson and Chris Willis. Houndsmills: Palgrave, 2002. 39–52.

Scraton, Sheila. *Shaping Up to Womanhood: Gender and Girls' Physical Education*. Buckingham and Philadelphia: Open UP, 1992.

Sebag-Montefiore, Mary. "Nice Girls Don't (but Want to): Work Ethic Conflicts and Conundrums in Mrs. Molesworth's Books for Girls." *The Lion and the Unicorn* 26 (2002): 374–94.

Secord, J.A. "Tegetmeier, William Bernhardt (1816–1912)." *Oxford Dictionary of National Biography*. Oxford: Oxford UP, 2004. 12 Nov. 2009 <http://www.oxforddnb.com/view/article/54099>.

Segel, Elizabeth. "As the Twig Is Bent ..." *Crosscurrents of Children's Literature: An Anthology of Texts and Criticism*. Ed. J.D. Stahl, Tina L. Hanlon and Elizabeth Lennox Keyser. New York and Oxford: Oxford UP, 2007. 512–24.

Sharpe, Jenny. *Allegories of Empire: The Figure of Woman in the Colonial Text*. Minneapolis and London: U of Minnesota P, 1993.

Shaw, George Bernard. *Saint Joan: A Chronicle Play in Six Scenes and an Epilogue*. London: Constable & Co., 1924.

Showalter, Elaine. *Sexual Anarchy: Gender and Culture at the Fin De Siècle*. New York: Penguin, 1990.

Skelding, Hilary. "Every Girl's Best Friend?: The *Girl's Own Paper* and Its Readers." *Feminist Readings of Victorian Popular Texts: Divergent Femininities*. Ed. Emma Liggins and Daniel Duffy. Aldershot: Ashgate, 2001. 35–52.

Smith, Michelle J. *Empire in British Girls' Literature and Culture: Imperial Girls, 1880–1915*. Basingstoke, UK: Palgrave Macmillan, 2011.

————. "Nineteenth-Century Female Crusoes: Rewriting the Robinsonade for Girls," *Relocating Victorian Settler Narratives: Emigrants, Exiles, Returnees in Nineteenth-Century Fiction*. Ed. Tamara Wagner. London: Pickering & Chatto, 2011. 165–75.

Spacks, Patricia Meyer. *The Adolescent Idea: Mythos of Youth and Adult Imagination*. New York: Basic Books, Inc., Publishers, 1981.

Spielmann, M.H. *The History of Punch*. London: Cassell & Co, 1969.

Steele, Valerie. *Fashion and Eroticism: Ideals of Feminine Beauty from the Victorian Era to the Jazz Age*. New York and Oxford: Oxford UP, 1985.

Stephens, Barbara. *Emily Davies and Girton College*. Westport, Ct.: Hyperion P, 1927.

Stephens, John. *Language and Ideology in Children's Fiction*. Burnt Mill, UK: Longman Group, 1992.

Sturrock, June. "Establishing Identity: Editorial Correspondence from the Early Years of the *Monthly Packet*." *Victorian Periodicals Review* 39.3 (2006): 266–79.

————. "Women, Work, and the *Monthly Packet*, 1851–73." *Nineteenth-Century Feminisms* 1 (1999): 64–80.

Sullivan, Alvin, ed. *British Literary Magazines: The Victorian and Edwardian Age, 1837–1913*. Westport, CT and London: Greenwood P, 1984.

Swenson, Kristine. *Medical Women and Victorian Fiction*. Columbia and London: U of Missouri P, 2005.

Thompson, Paul. *The Edwardians: The Remaking of British Society*. 2nd ed. London and New York: Routledge, 1992.

Thorne-Murphy, Leslee. "The Charity Bazaar and Women's Professionalization in Charlotte Mary Yonge's *The Daisy Chain*." *Studies in English Literature 1500–1900* 47.4 (2007): 881–99.

Thwaite, Mary. *From Primer to Pleasure in Reading*. 2nd ed. London: Library Assocation, 1972.

Tusan, Michelle. "Inventing the New Woman: Print Culture and Identity Politics During the Fin-de-Siècle." *Victorian Periodicals Review* 31.2 (Summer 1998): 169–82.

Vallone, Lynne. *Disciplines of Virtue: Girls' Culture in the Eighteenth and Nineteenth Centuries*. New Haven: Yale UP, 1995.

Van Arsdel, Rosemary T. *Florence Fenwick Miller: Victorian Feminist, Journalist, and Educator*. Aldershot, England: Ashgate, 2001.

Vertinsky, Patricia. *The Eternally Wounded Woman: Women, Doctors and Exercise in the Late Nineteenth Century*. Manchester and New York: Manchester UP, 1990.

Vicinus, Martha. *Independent Women: Work and Community for Single Women, 1850–1920*. Chicago and London: U of Chicago P, 1985.

Vickery, Margaret Birney. *Buildings for Bluestockings: The Architecture and Social History of Women's Colleges in Late Victorian England*. Newark: U of Delaware P, 1999.

Walkerdine, Valerine. "Girlhood Through the Looking Glass." *Girls, Girlhood and Girls' Studies in Transition*. Ed. Marion de Ras and Mieke Lunenberg. Amsterdam: Het Spinhius, 1993. 9–24.

Wintle, Sarah. "Horses, Bikes and Automobiles: New Woman on the Move." *The New Woman in Fiction and in Fact: Fin-De-Siècle Feminisms*. Ed. Angelique Richardson and Chris Willis. Houndsmills, UK: Palgrave Macmillan, 2002. 66–78.

Woods, G.S. "Stables, William Gordon (1837x40–1910)." Rev. Guy Arnold. *Oxford Dictionary of National Biography*. Oxford UP, 2004. 15 May 2008 <http://www.oxforddnb.com/view/article/36229>.

Worth, George J. *Macmillan's Magazine, 1859–1907: "No Flippancy or Abuse Allowed."* Aldershot and Burlington: Ashgate, 2003.

Zipes, Jack, et al. *The Norton Anthology of Children's Literature: The Traditions in English*. New York: W.W. Norton & Company, 2005.

Index